Yale Historical Publications, Miscellany, 125

Oil, War, and American Security

The Search for a National Policy on Foreign Oil, 1941–1947

Michael B. Stoff

New Haven and London
Yale University Press
1980

Published under the direction of the
Department of History of Yale University
with assistance from the income of the
Frederick John Kingsbury Memorial Fund.

Designed by Sally Harris
and set in Times Roman type.
Printed in the United States of America by
The Vail-Ballou Press, Binghamton, N. Y.

Library of Congress Cataloging in Publication Data

Stoff, Michael B
  Oil, war, and American security.

  (Yale historical publications: Miscellany; 125)
  Bibliography: p.
  Includes index.
  1. Petroleum industry and trade—United States—History.
2. Energy policy—United States—History. 3. United States—
National security—History. I. Title. II. Series.
HD9566.S82   382'.42'2820973   79-24594
ISBN 0-300-02301-4

1   2   3   4   5   6   7   8   9   10

FOR MARY

Contents

Preface

Today oil confounds Americans. Domestic supplies shrink daily. Demand increases in geometric progressions. Almost by the moment, the country grows more and more dependent on oil from abroad. There seems to be no way to retain the independence that has derived from the possession of safe and accessible reserves of petroleum. The crucial link between oil and national security, once solely the concern of military and government officials, has become a matter of public discourse. It is a time of decision, as the American people and their leaders engage in a great debate over national energy policy.

The problem is made more difficult by its apparent novelty. It seems without precedent or parallel. But, in fact, we are dealing with the same questions that have absorbed Americans since the early days of the republic: Where do private interests end and public ones begin? What can public institutions do to protect the interests they were intended to represent?

Those questions have arisen before in the twentieth century, though never with greater urgency than during the Second World War. For a period during the middle of the war, it appeared as if the United States were running out of oil. The alarming consequences of that prospect, considered as they were by men at war, provoked the first serious effort to fashion a coherent national policy for foreign oil. This study records that endeavor, examines its premises and precedents, and explains its demise.

The geographic focus is the Middle East, especially the Persian Gulf basin. The narrowness of that focus reflects the concerns of the men who made policy, though during the war as before and after it other regions attracted their attention as well. In Mexico expropriation of American and other oil investments in the late 1930s led to protracted negotiations that finally reached settlement in the middle of the war. In Venezuela new legislation in 1943 set a precedent for revolutionizing relations between host governments and oil companies by establishing the principle of sharing oil profits equally. In Canada an enormous pipeline, stretching over five hundred miles, was constructed to help meet wartime needs. In one way or another, agencies of the United States government played important roles in each development. Despite those activities the Middle East held primary interest because it represented the future. Although a tiny producer before the war, the region was destined to become, as wartime planners expected, the center of world production.

The substantive focus of this study is the sustained national effort to devise and put into effect a set of principles to guide government policy toward the overseas operations of private oil companies. It may strike informed readers as curious that I chose to investigate an abortive venture. After all, the instruments fashioned by wartime planners to achieve their purposes were quickly cast aside. Even so, I think the effort was important, not for what it accomplished but for what it reveals. I have used the story of this effort to examine the interplay between the public and private sectors as national policy is made. This account has furnished a way of penetrating the complexities of emerging foreign oil policy, which have involved not only relations between governments and oil companies, or among separate oil companies, but also relations within governments themselves and among different ones. Leaders of various segments of the oil industry and leaders of government each had ideas about the directions American oil policy should take overseas. The effort to put those ideas into action brought into sharp relief the differences between the two groups and within them. Furthermore, it confirmed the continuity of those differences during the entire period from the New Deal through the war and uncovered the dynamics of making oil policy. Various tensions within the government, within the industry, and within the Anglo-American alliance also came to light.

The style of the book is narrative—and purposefully so, because only sequential narration conveys a sense of the past as something once alive. For that same reason, character sketches brace the story throughout. Meant to be more than breathing spells for the weary reader, they express my belief that individual personalities matter, that people shape history, and that the decisions they make reflect the world around them.

At the end of a project like this, it is always a pleasant duty to thank those who lent their support. Many people helped in many ways to make this book. John Morton Blum deserves to be mentioned first because I owe a special debt to him. He led me to twentieth-century America, guided my work there, and showed me how history ought to be done. In this project, he read early drafts with promptness and great care. His clarity of expression and conception has proved in this instance, as always, unrivaled and essential.

A number of friends and colleagues read parts or all of the manuscript in its sundry stages. Peter Ripley, Jo Keller, and Jim Davidson forced me to reconsider some early sections and to rewrite others. Gaddis Smith, Firuz Kazemzadeh, and Allan Winkler pointed out problems of both style and substance. Mira Wilkins, generous with her time and her expertise, provided criticism that kept me busy for the better part of three months. Stuart Schoffman attended to my prose with a sharp eye and an even sharper pencil. Mark Lytle deserves a special word of thanks. His work on Iranian-American relations during the Second World War, of considerable intrinsic value, had the added benefit of bringing me to oil. He helped me to define this study and to refine its execution. I am grateful to all these people, though of course none is responsible for the views that follow.

Others helped in different, but no less important, ways. Zeke and Eva Kanter turned my long research trips into working holidays by furnishing bed, board, and warm friendship. So did Leslie Gray and Gary Fay, the latter of whom also took time from his own work to obtain valuable material for me. My typist, Mary Whitney, caught all the errors I threw her way and continually astounded me by making almost none of her own.

A grant from the Yale University Concilium on International and Area Studies provided funds for research in this country and abroad.

Those travels were made easier because of the assistance rendered by several archivists. I am particularly indebted to the staffs of the Sterling Memorial Library, the Franklin D. Roosevelt Library, the National Archives, the Library of Congress, the Public Record Office, and the Beaverbrook Library. Quotations from Crown-copyright records in the Public Record Office appear by permission of the controller of H.M. Stationery Office.

In an earlier version of this book, I acknowledged the contributions, large and small, of Mary Keller. Three anniversaries and two children later, she remains as indispensable as she is incomparable.

Prologue

"Oil," wrote Herbert Feis in 1946, "enough oil, within our certain grasp seemed ardently necessary to greatness and independence in the twentieth century."[1] For Feis, historian and sometime adviser to the State Department, it was that simple. He was describing the motives behind American efforts to fashion foreign oil policy during the Second World War. He knew what he was talking about. During the war, he chaired the Committee on International Petroleum Policy, which carried on the State Department's first serious attempt to define national policy toward foreign oil. He sat with a team of negotiators who tried to buy an oil company for the government in 1943. He pressed vigorously for an oil agreement with Great Britain, which became the focus of foreign oil policy after Feis resigned from government service.

The safety of the nation, Feis was saying from the vantage of the early postwar years, had come to depend on oil. So had the country's ability to pursue its interests in the world. The observation framed the problem easily. Solutions, Feis knew, were harder. Aggressive nationalism might increase the risk of a scramble for oil, but conciliatory internationalism might involve greater costs than benefits. Feis himself favored internationalism, though he felt obliged to minimize its costs, both during and after the war, to the American people. In the end, the success of the endeavor depended less on Feis and his colleagues than on the activities of private oil companies.

This effort to establish a foreign oil policy recalled an earlier one. The First World War had made Americans aware, as never before, of

1. Herbert Feis, *Three International Episodes Seen from E. A.* (1946; reprint ed., New York, 1966), p. 97.

1

the connection between petroleum deposits outside the country and the security of the nation. That awareness came from the trying wartime experience with fuel oil, together with postwar predictions of an impending exhaustion of domestic reserves and a concerted British drive to shut out American capital from promising oil-bearing regions in the Middle East and in the Dutch East Indies.[2]

After the war, as before it, the United States Navy pressed most strenuously for an ambitious American oil policy. In 1904 the Navy Fuel Oil Board had recommended conversion of the fleet from coal to oil. By 1913, as Europe prepared for war, conversion was well under way, and the navy lobbied unsuccessfully for the United States government to enter the oil business. Six years later, the navy was consuming fuel oil at the annual rate of 6 million barrels. Though small compared with the 87 million barrels of gasoline used by all Americans that year, navy consumption suggested the strategic importance of oil.[3]

Aware of that value, the navy urged more aggressive tactics abroad and, at home, advocated closing domestic reserves to exploitation, increasing petroleum imports, and expanding navy storage facilities. The Wilson administration adopted in modified form all shipping recommendations except those that proved politically unfeasible. Meanwhile, in mid-1919, the State Department ordered its diplomatic offi-

2. There are several good studies that include discussions of foreign oil policy during the 1920s. Among them are Gerald D. Nash, *United States Oil Policy, 1890–1964* (Pittsburgh, 1968), pp. 23–98, and Joan Hoff Wilson, *American Business and Foreign Policy, 1920–33* (Lexington, 1971), pp. 184–200. The best regional studies are Joseph Tulchin, *The Aftermath of War: World War I and U. S. Policy toward Latin America* (New York, 1971), pp. 118–54, and John A. DeNovo, *American Interests and Policies in the Middle East* (Minneapolis, 1963), pp. 167–84. For industry developments, see George Sweet Gibb and Evelyn H. Knowlton's book on the Standard Oil Company of New Jersey, *The Resurgent Years, 1911–1927* (New York, 1956) and Harold F. Williamson et al., *The American Petroleum Industry: The Age of Energy, 1899–1959* (Evanston, 1963).

3. For navy efforts before the First World War, see John A. DeNovo, ''Petroleum and the United States Navy before World War I,'' *Mississippi Valley Historical Review* (March 1955), pp. 641–56; Williamson et al., *Age of Energy,* pp. 181–95. The Royal Navy began converting its smaller vessels from coal to oil in 1902. By 1913 the British had made conversion of the entire fleet a priority. On American naval developments, see also Nash, *U. S. Oil Policy,* pp. 9–10, 16–20, 44–45. On Royal Navy conversion, see D. J. Payton-Smith, *Oil: A Study of War-time Policy and Administration* (London, 1971), p. 5, 7.

cers to lend assistance to all legitimate American interests seeking concessions overseas.[4]

Oil men joined the campaign. For more than half a century, the American oil industry had led the world in production, supplying between 60 and 70 percent of global demand. The output came mostly from domestic deposits, although in later years a few oil-hungry firms, led principally by the Standard Oil Company of New Jersey (Jersey Standard), had stepped up activity abroad. Still, those efforts were meager, and American oil men had fallen behind foreigners in cornering new sources of oil outside the United States. They discovered after the war real challenges to their supremacy from the Anglo-Dutch combine, the Royal Dutch/Shell Company (Shell), and the newly formed Anglo-Persian Oil Company, which enjoyed the benefit of partial ownership and full diplomatic support from the British government. Before the war British companies controlled less than 5 percent of world production. By 1919 they had acquired 50 percent of the world's proven oil reserves.[5]

Despite their own laxity, American oil men, led by the brilliant and autocratic Walter Teagle of Jersey Standard, blamed the situation on the United States government. It had failed, in their view, to give diplomatic support as vigorous as their European rivals received. In a way that would become familiar, oil men justified their demands for

4. Tulchin, *Aftermath of War*, pp. 120–21; John A. DeNovo, "The Movement for an Aggressive American Oil Policy Abroad, 1918–1920," *American Historical Review* (July 1956), pp. 854–76. The State Department order cautioned representatives to distinguish between genuine American companies, which deserved diplomatic support, and those masquerading as American companies through incorporation under United States laws but really controlled by foreigners.

5. Leonard M. Fanning, *American Oil Operations Abroad* (New York, 1947), pp. 256–59, 27–28; Gibb and Knowlton, *Resurgent Years*, pp. 391–92; Tulchin, *Aftermath of War*, pp. 134–54; Michael J. Hogan, "Informal Entente: Public Policy and Private Management in Anglo-American Petroleum Affairs, 1918–24," *Business History Review* (Summer 1974), pp. 187–205; E. H. Davenport and Sidney Russell Cooke, *The Oil Trusts and Anglo-American Relations* (London, 1923), pp. 78–79, 84–87; Ralph W. Hidy and Muriel E. Hidy, *Pioneering in Big Business, 1882–1911* (New York, 1955), pp. 259–60, 268, 501–02, 504–05, 566–67, 717; Irvine Anderson, Jr., *The Standard-Vacuum Oil Company and United States East Asian Policy, 1933–1941* (Princeton, 1975), pp. 28–29; DeNovo, "An Aggressive American Oil Policy Abroad," *American Historical Review* (July 1956), pp. 854–76.

greater government support by pointing to a link between the expansion of foreign holdings and the security of the nation, thereby identifying private activity with public welfare. All the same, their interest remained essentially commercial.[6]

Gloomy forecasts of depleting reserves spurred the drive for more forceful government action. Some experts predicted that underground reserves in the United States would last less than ten years. Even the United States Geological Survey was pessimistic. Its director, George Otis Smith, described conditions in 1919 as "precarious." Those predictions made sense to Americans, who knew that their country had literally been the wellhead for the Allied war effort. Great Britain alone had received 80 percent of its petroleum products from American refineries during the first two years of the war. In 1917 the United States had supplied the British with 92 percent of their refined petroleum needs.[7]

Suspicions of British oil tactics accompanied those supplies and continued after the war. Admiral William S. Sims, the navy representative in London during the war, had charged the Admiralty in 1918 with diverting its own tonnage for the benefit of private companies operating in Latin America. During the postwar oil scare, British exclusivity, though practiced for years, nourished American suspicions. Like the Dutch, the British government had banned foreign ownership and operation of oil concessions within its empire, and both governments had prevented the sale of oil property to outsiders, the Dutch in the East Indies and the British in the Middle East.[8]

The boasts of several highly placed Englishmen about their country's success in gaining control of world petroleum deposits did not help matters. Neither did the San Remo Agreement. In repudiation of Wilsonian principles and in violation of the Open Door policy, the

6. DeNovo, "An Aggressive American Oil Policy Abroad," *American Historical Review* (July 1956), pp. 854–76. Oil men also supported government reciprocity tactics to pressure foreign countries.

7. Nash, *U.S. Oil Policy*, pp. 43–48; Feis, *Three International Episodes*, p. 94n; Tulchin, *Aftermath of War*, p. 118.

8. Tulchin, *Aftermath of War*, p. 120. For British exclusive practices, especially in the Middle East, see Payton-Smith, *Oil*, pp. 7–16; for Dutch, see Anderson, *Stanvac and U.S. East Asian Policy*, pp. 28–30.

British had agreed with the French in 1920 to divide the most promising oil regions of the Balkans and Mesopotamia among themselves and had pledged to bar the nationals of other countries from the areas.[9]

The United States refused to recognize the agreement. The State Department registered severe protests, both at the time and later, during the Lausanne Conference in 1923. Congress also retaliated. In May 1920 it passed the Mineral Leasing Act, which provided for reciprocity against foreign exclusivity. According to its provisions, no leases on public lands could be given to nationals of countries that did not grant similar privileges to American interests. That same month, Republican Senator James Phelan of California proposed the formation of a government-owned company, the United States Oil Corporation, to search for oil abroad. The bill was never enacted, largely because of the objections of the State and Commerce departments and the resistance of the oil industry. But Congress kept it ready should other measures fail to open doors overseas.[10]

Government officials who were more conciliatory proposed an international approach. In 1920 Van H. Manning, director of the Bureau of Mines and a hardy advocate of cooperation between government and the industry, called for an international agreement to ensure equitable development of world oil resources. The State Department's petroleum adviser, Arthur C. Millspaugh, took a similar tack. In February 1921 he recommended negotiating a bilateral understanding with the British to defuse Anglo-American rivalry over oil. As Millspaugh envisioned it, the agreement would denounce monopoly

9. See, for example, *Oil and Gas Journal* (5/28/20), p. 73; (6/4/20), p. 2; (7/2/20), p. 3; (8/6/20), p. 2. See also the remarks of Sir Edward Mackay Edgar, which particularly incensed American oil men. Mackay is quoted in *O. and G. Journal* (4/23/20), p. 79; Nash, *U. S. Oil Policy,* p. 52.

10. Nash, *U. S. Oil Policy,* p. 52; Anderson, *Stanvac and U. S. East Asian Policy,* p. 33; Williamson et al., *Age of Energy,* p. 518; DeNovo, "An Aggressive American Oil Policy Abroad," *American Historical Review* (July 1956), pp. 854–76; U. S. Congress, Senate, *Congressional Record,* 66th Cong., 2nd Sess., (Washington, 1920), vol. 59, pt. 7, 7144. Control of the corporation was to have been placed in the hands of nine directors appointed by the president. Private individuals, rather than the government, were to supply the capital. Fanning, *American Oil Abroad,* p. 4; DeNovo, "An Aggressive American Oil Policy Abroad," *American Historical Review* (July 1956), pp. 854–76; Tulchin, *Aftermath of War,* p. 124.

practices in the international industry, affirm the principle of equal opportunity for commercial interests, and offer reciprocity to promote the Open Door.[11]

Before either scheme could gain acceptance, luck and pluck brightened the outlook. Starting in 1924, new discoveries in Texas, Oklahoma, and California erased the threat of depletion. Continued diplomatic pressure by the State Department, along with aggressive private action and the Commerce Department's use of the Mineral Leasing Act against the Dutch, finally broke down barriers to American interests abroad. By 1928 American companies had secured footholds in the Middle East and in the Dutch East Indies. After that, the companies no longer needed government support so desperately, although they continued throughout most of the 1930s to make occasional requests for diplomatic assistance. For its part, the government became less combative in promoting American oil interests abroad. No longer impelled by fears of scarcity, government officials usually responded without vigor to private requests and then acted mainly on the basis of reciprocity and the Open Door. Not until the Second World War did they again turn their attention to developing a comprehensive foreign oil policy.[12]

11. Van H. Manning, "An Oil Entente for All Nations," address delivered to the Kansas-Oklahoma Division of the Mid-Continent Oil and Gas Association, printed in the *O. and G. Journal* (10/22/20), pp. 64, 66–68, 70, 72. For comments see *O. and G. Journal* (11/12/20), p. 2; Tulchin, *Aftermath of War*, p. 127.

12. Nash, *U. S. Oil Policy*, pp. 81–86; Williamson et al., *Age of Energy*, p. 518; Kendall Beaton, *Enterprise in Oil: A History of Shell in the United States* (New York, 1957), pp. 230–34; Hogan, "Informal Entente," *Business History Review* (Summer 1974), pp. 187–205. In an account of oil company problems abroad in the 1930s—and of State Department responses (which sometimes entailed principles other than reciprocity and the Open Door), see Mira Wilkins, *The Maturing of Multinational Enterprise: American Business Abroad from 1914 to 1970* (Cambridge, 1974), pp. 206–41.

1 / Oil at Peace and at War

In the decade before Pearl Harbor the administration of Franklin D. Roosevelt showed no interest in developing a coherent national policy for foreign oil matters. New Dealers in charge of oil concerned themselves with the home front, where economic depression and industrial collapse threatened national survival as much as any war ever had. Only as depression gave way to real war did federal officials turn their attention to foreign oil policy, first as part of the organization for war and much later as part of the preparation for peace.

Still, the New Deal experience mattered. As precedent and portent, it anticipated the course of wartime efforts to frame national policy for foreign oil. New Dealers faced the same divisions within the oil industry that later confounded wartime administrators and planners. Both groups worked along that gray border between the public and private sectors. There they confronted the eternal questions: How much federal interference would industry tolerate? Who would define the terms of that interference—public or private institutions? At length, all of them discovered that oil companies were hospitable only to the species of government meddling that comes at the invitation of business and quickly falls under its control.

Men mattered too, because their personalities helped to shape policy. The New Deal and the war effort both had their share of bureaucratic imperialists. Often those men clashed, sometimes directly, sometimes through surrogates. Usually the squabbles erupted over authority and jurisdiction, because it was Roosevelt's way to conduct government through agencies with overlapping responsibilities. Yet, on occasion, the disagreements involved real differences of opinion over opposing programs. In the early days of the war, when the content of foreign oil policy had yet to be determined, the battle for control was mainly a matter of individual egos. Afterward, with the lines of authority still hazy, conflicts of substance arose.

Depression at Home and Abroad

On the eve of Franklin Roosevelt's election, the American oil industry was in trouble. New discoveries in the Southwest in the late 1920s and early 1930s had created a surplus of oil. Stable demand and growing economic depression caused prices of petroleum and petroleum products to plummet. By 1931 crude oil from Texas, the nation's leading producer, was selling for ten cents a barrel.[1]

Voluntary arrangments to curtail production proved ineffective, and in the absence of federal leadership, oil men turned to local governments for assistance. State legislators responded with compulsory proration laws that placed production quotas on wells that were under their jurisdiction. Though more potent than voluntary action, state laws were unable to control the outpour. Much of the oil that continued to flow from wellheads became "hot oil," lifted by wildcatters in violation of the quotas and shipped across state lines. Even the militia units stationed at fields in Texas and Oklahoma failed to stem the glut. As prices fell further and further below production costs, industry appeals for federal regulation grew more demanding.[2]

American oil companies operating abroad encountered similar difficulties. Overproduction, not only in the United States but all over the world, threatened the international industry too. New fields in Venezuela and Mexico, a flood of cheap oil from Russia, and new production in Iraq had already begun to depress world prices. To make matters worse, in 1927 aggressive Russian sales tactics had ignited a price war over the Indian market between Shell and the American-owned

1. Nash, *U. S. Oil Policy*, pp. 112–27.
2. Ellis W. Hawley, *The New Deal and the Problem of Monopoly* (Princeton, 1966), pp. 212–13. Recent scholarship argues convincingly that oil men sought cooperation with state and federal governments to restrict production not for the sake of efficiency or in the national interest, as so many oil men claimed, but to combat the price-deflating effects of competition. See, for example, Norman E. Nordhauser, "The Quest for Stability: Domestic Oil Policy, 1919–1935" (Ph.D. diss. Stanford University, 1970).

Standard Oil Company of New York (Socony). The intense competition soon developed into a global crisis, which forced some small companies out of business and endangered the profits of large ones.[3]

The internationals fared better than did domestic companies in putting their own households in order. With a handful of giant firms in control of world production and distribution, problems abroad were easier to manage than those at home, where the mammoth integrated companies had to contend with hundreds of other producers, refiners, and distributors, as well as with federal bans on collusive practices. No clear deterrents to collaboration operated overseas. The mistrust of the companies for one another, which was the only factor standing in the way of large-scale cooperation, became eclipsed by fears of surplus and price wars. Accordingly, the three primary contenders— Shell, Anglo-Persian, and Jersey Standard—worked out an agreement late in 1928 to allocate the international market outside the United States in proportion to the shares they held at the time. Though never formally signed, the "Achnacarry Agreement" (named for the Scottish castle in which negotiations took place) furnished the basis for a series of attempted regional understandings to guide international operations. By 1932 all the American companies then operating abroad had approved the agreement, which came to serve as a blueprint throughout the 1930s for the industry's successful effort to maintain prices overseas.[4]

3. Williamson et al., *Age of Energy*, pp. 524–25, 532; Gibb and Knowlton, *Resurgent Years*, pp. 304–05; Williamson et al., *Age of Energy*, pp. 527–30; Henrietta M. Larson, Evelyn H. Knowlton, and Charles S. Popple, *New Horizons 1927–1950* (New York, 1971), pp. 305–06; Anthony Sampson, *The Seven Sisters: The Great Oil Companies and the World They Made* (New York, 1975), pp. 69–71.

4. Hidy and Hidy, *Pioneering in Big Business*, p. 549, 553; Williamson et al., *Age of Energy*, pp. 258–59, 528–30; U. S. Federal Trade Commission, *The International Petroleum Cartel*, FTC Staff Report Submitted to the Subcommittee on Monopoly of the Select Committee on Small Business, U. S. Senate, 82nd Cong., 2nd Sess. (Washington, 1952), hereafter cited as *International Petroleum Cartel*, pp. 199–274. The United States market was specifically left out of the agreement in order to avoid conflict with American antitrust laws, although under existing law combinations of American companies in foreign trade were permitted so long as they did not act in restraint of trade within the United States; John M. Blair, *The Control of Oil* (New York, 1976), p. 60. For a view that minimizes the effectiveness of Achnacarry and subsequent agreements during the 1930s, see Mira Wilkins, "The Oil Companies in Perspective," *Daedalus* (Fall 1975), pp. 159–78.

The New Deal

International collaboration offered scant help to the beleaguered domestic industry. Franklin Roosevelt offered more. He was sensitive to the industry's special problems. Years among the gentry of Dutchess County had reinforced a family passion for preserving natural resources. An apprenticeship as assistant secretary of the navy had taught him the value of oil to the military. And, like his predecessors in office, he recognized the importance of the oil industry to the nation. Stabilization and conservation, the twin problems that had beset earlier administrations, became the heart of New Deal oil policy.[5]

When New Deal planners first turned to the oil industry, they found, as one of them described it, "a discouraged and disorderly mob," unable to agree on a set of regulations to manage operations under the newly formed National Recovery Administration—an experiment in industrial self-government that required each industry to devise a code to govern commercial behavior. In the oil industry, old tensions between majors (the large, integrated companies that controlled every phase of activity from well to service station) and independents (companies that engaged in one or a few phases only) had so far undermined attempts to reach an accord.[6]

Most majors wanted the government to refrain from fixing prices, to regulate fields on a unitized basis (which looked at the productive capacity of each field as a whole), to limit but not to prohibit oil imports, to recognize selected marketing agreements, and to administer the codes under the National Recovery Administration. Independents favored price fixing to bolster sagging incomes and shorter work weeks in order to cut labor costs. They opposed unitization and production controls, which were designed, so they argued, to perpetuate monopoly and to drive them out of business. They advocated excluding

5. For an account of Roosevelt's early years, see Frank Freidel, *Franklin D. Roosevelt: The Apprenticeship* (Boston, 1952); Arthur M. Schlesinger, Jr., *The Crisis of the Old Order* (Boston, 1957), especially pp. 344–46, 348–52, 359–60.

6. Hugh Johnson, quoted in Arthur M. Schlesinger, Jr., *The Coming of the New Deal* (Boston, 1959), p. 116. For a concise and penetrating account of the NRA in theory and in practice, see Hawley, *The Problem of Monopoly*, pp. 19–146.

foreign oil from the domestic market, since they held no overseas concessions. Unwilling to accept marketing agreements on antitrust grounds, they demanded instead that pipelines and refineries be owned by different companies in order to break up the large oil corporations. Finally, they wanted the Department of Commerce to control oil codes because they feared that the NRA would be dominated by the majors.[7]

In mid-1933 oil men came to an agreement under federal guidance. Their code served as the central component in the first stage of the New Deal for oil. From 1933 to 1935 public policy aimed at restricting production and stabilizing prices through the NRA. Like other codes, the Oil Code favored the majors, which had played a key role in drawing it up. The code provided for production restraints, import limitations, and price regulation. It empowered a federal oil administrator to set monthly production quotas on the basis of advice from industry consultants and on the basis of demand forcasts from the Bureau of Mines. State administrators then recommended limits on every field and well through local agencies and industrial groups. Executive orders prohibited interstate shipment of ''hot oil.'' The federal oil administrator was also given the authority to restrict imports, though not to exclude them. In addition, he could issue regulations for marketing refined products.[8]

The second phase of New Deal oil policy came in 1935, when the Supreme Court invalidated the NRA. Voiding the NRA did not terminate government cooperation with the industry, but it did limit the federal role to a supporting one. The demise of the NRA led to piecemeal substitutes, often proposed by oil men themselves, that were intended to maintain commercial practices launched under the Oil Code. Chief among the new regulators was the Interstate Oil Compact Commission. Sponsored by the industry and promoted by governors of oil states, the compact received congressional approval in 1935

7. Harold L. Ickes, *The Secret Diary of Harold L. Ickes, vol. 1: The First Thousand Days, 1933–1936* (New York, 1953), p. 10; Robert Engler, *The Politics of Oil: A Study of Private Power and Democratic Directions* (New York, 1961), p. 139; Nash, *U. S. Oil Policy,* pp. 138–39.
8. Hawley, *The Problem of Monopoly,* pp. 213–14.

as a conservation measure. Member states joined voluntarily and appointed representatives to the commission, which coordinated state proration laws through published reports, recommendations, and discussions with local officials. The commission also provided a forum for consultation and a research center for developing and advertising conservation measures.[9]

For the most part, the federal contribution consisted of enforcing quotas and supplying data. The Connally Act of 1935 replaced the "hot oil" curbs of the NRA with a federal law barring contraband oil from interstate commerce. Along with voluntary agreements among key importers, a tariff was imposed to protect the domestic market from foreign petroleum. The Bureau of Mines continued its statistical service of providing demand projections to guide state agencies in determining monthly production quotas and in allocating oil to different regions. At the same time, a short-lived antitrust program tried to spotlight private abuses. Federal suits ended some collusive practices, but by 1940 political considerations, among them an approaching presidential election, had undercut the program.[10]

As it worked out, responsibility for oil fell to Harold Ickes, the newly appointed secretary of the interior. Until he resigned from office in 1946 he regarded oil as his province, and over the years he continuously attempted to widen the boundaries of his domain. More than any other man, he served during those years as the linchpin that held together disparate efforts to define national oil policy at home and abroad.

Ickes enjoyed the power, for a special kind of ambition drove him. Vanity and arrogance contributed generous shares, but a nobler motive, admirable except for its smugness, lay underneath. Harold Ickes was convinced that, unlike other men, he was incorruptible. That knowledge assured him that the expansion of his authority served the

9. Hawley, *The Problem of Monopoly,* pp. 205–80. The Interstate Oil Compact Code was ratified by Joint Resolution on August 27, 1935, for two-year intervals. In 1943, the intervals were changed to four-year periods. Nash, *U. S. Oil Policy,* pp. 150–51; Williamson et al., *Age of Energy,* pp. 540–66.

10. Nash, *U. S. Oil Policy,* p. 140, 152; Raymond R. Mikesell and Hollis B. Chenery, *Arabian Oil: America's Stake in the Middle East* (Chapel Hill, 1949), pp. 123–24; Hawley, *The Problem of Monopoly,* pp. 217–18, 374; Nash, *U. S. Oil Policy,* p. 152.

nation. He fought for power not as an end in itself but because he believed that he was best able to employ it for the public good. Extending his control became almost a duty, often performed without reference to a rule book. He could bully, cajole, insult, or charm an opponent into submission. Such tactics were permissible when defending the public. To him, all his battles were waged in that defense.

When he took on the additional duties of administering the Oil Code in 1933, Ickes was not quite sixty years old. Although he described himself as a "wobbly Republican," he was, more accurately, a Bull Moose Progressive who, like Theodore Roosevelt, saw the federal government as the steward of the public welfare. Earlier in his career Ickes had been an ardent trustbuster, but the elder Roosevelt's Square Deal won him over in 1904. He believed with Roosevelt that large-scale industrial capitalism was a permanent feature of the twentieth century, and like Roosevelt, he sought to assure an equitable distribution of its benefits. In his view neither the antitrust nor the laissez-faire doctrine was equal to the task. Enforced competition would atomize the economy and destroy the advantages of consolidation, while unrestricted competition would leave the private sector free to engage in unfair practices at public expense. Only a strong and active federal government, Ickes reasoned, could control the excesses of big business and protect the consumer.

A lawyer by training, Ickes was a politician at heart. He wished not to be king but to make kings. He never ran for public office. Instead, he labored in the meeting halls and on the streets of Chicago for those dedicated to honest city government. His candidates rarely won; yet defeat only seemed to buoy his righteousness. Regardless of the outcome, he saw every campaign through the eyes of the Bull Moose: elections were crusades for good or against evil.

And evil, Harold Ickes knew, lurked everywhere. Cautious by nature, he realized that his appointment as secretary of the interior in 1933 would put him in a dangerous position. The Interior Department had been subject to charges of corruption since its creation in 1849. As caretaker of the public domain, the department had often taken better care of special interests than of the national interest. More recent scandals involving the department's alleged misuse of coal fields in Alaska and government oil reserves at Teapot Dome had added to its already unsavory reputation. Ickes would not suffer the persistence of such dishonesty; his character would not allow it.

Meticulous, irascible, suspicious, and incomparably honest, Ickes was the perfect bursar for the nation's natural wealth. He even looked the part. Wary eyes stood watch behind gold-rimmed glasses, while a square, obstinate chin signaled his readiness for a scrap. Stooped shoulders capped a chunky body, which seemed perpetually crouched in a fighter's stance. Conspiracies, he felt, surrounded him, so vigilance became his lifeline. With wiretaps and tails, he spied on subordinates to confirm their fidelity. He encouraged employees to inform on each other. He programmed their days with countless regulations. He would tolerate neither tardiness nor long breaks and once issued an order forbidding his staff from lowering the shades on office-door windows. Privacy, it seemed to Ickes, only hid loafing or scheming. The morale of the department languished during his tenure, but morality thrived.

If Ickes was hard on his personnel, he was merciless on himself. He arrived at the office early and left late. He often closed his wing of the department, and he usually brought work home with him. Since he regarded all the activities of the department as his own responsibility, nothing escaped his supervision. His shirt-sleeves rolled to the elbow, he daily spent hours examining each project in his charge with the care of a nursemaid. He demanded that his staff confer with him on every decision, no matter how trivial, and he still found time to correct any procedure that he disliked. Through scores of letters and memoranda, he ruled his own domain, while he attempted to invade others.

Ickes cultivated the image of himself as a curmudgeon, but the image revealed only part of the man. Beneath the tough exterior lay a tender core, compassionate yet uncertain. Flowers were his passion; he took great pride in possessing the first dahlia patent ever issued. Stamps, too, comforted him in spare moments, and a connoisseur's taste for fine food and wine impaired his reputation for austerity. His deadpan jokes were equally telling and suggested what those close to him knew: for all his bluster, he craved support and affection. Insecure, easily wounded by criticism, Harold Ickes protected himself with a cantankerous face that concealed a warm heart.[11]

Oil men saw little of that warmth. Toward them, Ickes acted with characteristic toughness. As oil administrator, he sought to broaden federal power over the industry. Despite occasional retreats, he pressed for federal authority to fix prices and to set production quotas, and he sponsored legislation in 1934 to centralize his control over production and distribution. After nullification of the Oil Code, he continued to fight for greater authority. In June 1935 he opposed Senator Tom Connally's "hot oil" bill, which earned him the enduring animosity of the Texas Democrat. Ickes opposed the bill because it bolstered state efforts to superintend production. Such regulation, he maintained, could work only under federal supervision, since production and distribution were national, not state, problems. For that reason he worked to block congressional approval of the Interstate Oil Compact and supported legislation to transform the industry into a public utility. The importance of oil to the economy and to national defense, as Ickes saw it, made strict federal control a necessity.[12]

In the end Ickes met with little success. Control of regulation remained firmly in the hands of state legislators and oil men. By vesting authority over production in the states, the Interstate Oil Compact returned power from Washington to local governments, where oil-generated revenues assured the industry of monitors responsive to its needs. Private arrangements fortified those public agencies. The

11. Harold L. Ickes, *The Autobiography of a Curmudgeon* (Chicago, 1969), *passim;* Harold L. Ickes, "My Twelve Years with F. D. R.," *Saturday Evening Post,* June 5, 12, 19, 26, 1948, pp. 15–17, 34–35, 30–31, 36–37, July 3, 10, 17, 24, 1948, pp. 30–31, 32–33, 38, 38; Saul K. Padover, "Ickes: Memoir of a Man Without Fear," *Reporter,* March 4, 1952, pp. 36–38; Walter Lippmann, "Today and Tommorrow," *New York Herald Tribune,* March 7, 1952; Mont J. Harmon, "Some Contributions of Harold L. Ickes," *Western Political Quarterly* (June 1954), pp. 238–52; Eugene Trani, "Conflict and Compromise: Harold L. Ickes and Franklin D. Roosevelt," *No. Dakota Quarterly* (Winter 1968), pp. 20–29; Schlesinger, *Coming of the New Deal,* pp. 282–83, 285–86.

12. Engler, *Politics of Oil,* pp. 273–74; Hawley, *The Problem of Monopoly,* p. 214; John W. Frey and Chandler Ide, *A History of the Petroleum Administration for War, 1941–1945* (Washington, 1946), p. 12; Nash, *U. S. Oil Policy,* pp. 141–45, 151–52.

American Petroleum Institute, the industry's major trade organization, redoubled efforts after 1935 to increase membership and to expand geographically. It also supplemented estimates from the Bureau of Mines with its own surveys and recommendations for adjusting quarterly supply-and-demand schedules. Through intercompany agreements, integrated firms strengthened their hold over marketing, refining, and transportation. All the while their secret buying pools soaked up the excess gasoline of independent jobbers and protected markets from price-depressing surpluses. Stronger than ever, the oil industry could look back on the 1930s as a time of great progress. The New Deal had helped to buttress private controls over production, distribution, and pricing, with which the industry avoided competition and evaded antitrust.[13]

By 1940 the industry had beaten the depression and had repelled the attacks of planners and trustbusters alike. Even Harold Ickes had relaxed his pressure on oil companies. Fear of the industry's impact on the presidential election led him to reject the antitrust program, which had become Washington's primary means of influencing oil companies in the late 1930s. Ickes preferred negotiation to obtain industry compliance with federal policy. He hoped that in exchange for federal repudiation of antitrust the industry would make major reforms. The president, cautious in his bid for a third term, agreed, and before long the Justice Department suspended a suit against some 3,000 oil men.[14]

Although he continued to urge bargaining over litigation after the election, Ickes soon found the issue moot. The outbreak of hostilities in Europe and in the Pacific quickly pushed that and other New Deal debates into the background. By the spring of 1941 the Roosevelt administration had begun in earnest to prepare for war. The president appealed to industry for cooperation above all, and antitrust largely fell victim to mobilization. With a blend of industrialists and civil

13. Hawley, *The Problem of Monopoly*, pp. 217–18; Engler, *Politics of Oil*, p. 275, 141. The Senate Small Business Committee noted in 1949 that the controls formed a "perfect pattern of monopolistic control over oil production, the distribution thereof among refiners and distributors, and ultimately the price paid by the public." Quoted in Hawley, *Problem of Monopoly*, p. 219.

14. Nash, *U. S. Oil Policy*, pp. 152–55; Harold L. Ickes, *The Secret Diary of Harold L. Ickes, vol. 3: The Lowering Clouds, 1939–1941* (New York, 1954), p. 334, 337.

servants, corporate lawyers and public administrators, Roosevelt fashioned a new bureaucracy to organize America for the coming conflict.[15]

Preparing for War

The president expected that mobilizing the oil industry would be easy. At first, he thought that government would simply, as he put it, "manage" oil by controlling transportation. Memories of industry antagonism to federal interference during the New Deal must have dampened the idea, for Roosevelt abandoned it. Like many government officials and oil men, he assumed that the industry, a chronic overproducer since the 1920s, required only modest supervision to meet heavy wartime demands for petroleum. But with the responsibility for administering oil dispersed throughout thirty federal offices, even modest supervision lay beyond government reach. To consolidate the oil program and to avoid rekindling industry enmity required the creation of an overseer with limited powers and unflagging spirit. On May 28, 1941, Roosevelt appointed Ickes Petroleum Coordinator for National Defense.[16]

The president commissioned Ickes by letter, which avoided the formality of more forceful instruments such as statutory authorization or an executive order. He instructed the new "coordinator" (whose very title seemed designed to calm industry anxieties) to establish an office that would serve as the nation's oil broker. The Office of the

15. Ickes, *Secret Diary,* vol. 3, p. 476; Hawley, *The Problem of Monopoly,* p. 442; Richard Polenberg, *War and Society: The United States, 1941-1945* (New York, 1972), pp. 1-36. For notable exceptions to the general thrust of wartime antitrust policy as described here, see Wilkins, *Maturing Multinational,* pp. 263-67.

16. Ickes, *Secret Diary,* vol. 3, p. 476; Frey and Ide, *PAW,* p. 15; Ickes, *Secret Diary,* vol. 3, p. 486. The idea of a petroleum office to coordinate industry activities came from Edwin Pauley, a California oil man and partisan Democrat, who was friendly with many officials in the Roosevelt administration. Pauley, for reasons of his own, thought that the office should be located in the Department of the Interior and placed under Ickes's control, and he lobbied at the White House for those ends. U. S., Congress, Senate, Special Committee Investigating the National Defense Program, *Hearings,* pt. 41, *Petroleum Arrangements with Saudi Arabia,* 80th Cong., 2nd Sess. (Washington, 1948), hereafter cited as *Arabian Oil Hearings,* 25207.

Petroleum Coordinator (OPC) would gather information from public and private sources and make recommendations to government agencies and to the industry to assure maintenance of adequate petroleum stocks. All OPC directives were to be advisory, since Roosevelt had purposely given Ickes no means of enforcing them.[17]

By balancing a weak agency with a knowledgeable and sometimes belligerent head like Ickes, Roosevelt had presented the industry with a peace offering and a caveat. The emphasis on voluntary compliance demonstrated Roosevelt's faith in the productive capacity of the industry and his sensitivity to its fears. Appointing Ickes, long an advocate of federal regulation, warned oil men that the president could act more vigorously if voluntarism proved ineffective.

Ickes's assignment pleased him. He felt that oil belonged under his command. "It will be interesting to see," he had mused before his appointment, "if, even in oil, I am to be deprived of jurisdiction that properly belongs to me. If I am, I am going to be heard from on the subject." His experience as oil administrator during the New Deal made him confident of his ability to handle wartime petroleum problems. In addition, the idea of centralizing responsibility for oil in a single civilian agency under his command appealed to his sense of administrative order as well as his sense of bureaucratic justice.[18]

Continuing duties at Interior and his own broad definition of the new job as getting "oil when and where it was needed" dictated that Ickes select an assistant to manage daily operations. Under the president's authorization, he chose early in June 1941 Ralph K. Davies, a senior executive of the mammoth Standard Oil Company of California (Socal). The forty-five-year-old Davies easily qualified for the position of deputy coordinator. With little more than a high school education, he had worked his way from a junior clerkship in the company's Fresno office to a directorship by 1930. In 1935, after twenty-three years of service, he became senior vice-president, coordinating every phase of Socal's integrated operation. During the 1930s he also

17. Roosevelt to Ickes, May 28, 1941, reprinted in Frey and Ide, *PAW*, pp. 374–75.
18. Ickes, *Secret Diary*, vol. 3, p. 486, 530. Even after the war Ickes pressed for a centralized oil authority under the control of the Department of the Interior. That agency, as Ickes saw it, would administer government oil policy and superintend federal oil reserves. *Arabian Oil Hearings*, 25221.

bridged the gap between the public and private sector as a member of the National Marketing Committee and the Pacific Coast Petroleum Agency of the NRA.[19]

A quiet but firm man, Davies had impressed Ickes early in 1941 with his support for oil conservation in California, even if it meant federal regulation. A few months later, Davies accepted the new government post with the same candor and sensitivity that later came to characterize his entire term as Ickes's aide. He volunteered to sever all connections with Socal, including waiving his pension rights. Ickes refused that offer, but he did accept Davies's pledge to disqualify himself from any question involving Socal. Even the company, Ickes later recalled Davies's promise, "would be surprised at some of the decisions he would make."[20]

At Ickes's request, Davies took charge of OPC and began to assemble a staff. Only the oil industry offered a large pool of trained technicians and administrators capable of mobilizing oil rapidly, so Davies, making sure to balance independents and majors, recruited most of his personnel from oil companies. All worked on a full-time basis with salaries paid jointly by government and industry.[21]

Ickes insisted that no oil company employee be penalized for government work by suffering a reduction in pay or by losing retirement benefits. He gave his staff the maximum his budget would allow, while private employers made up the difference between the new and the old salaries. Davies, for example, earned $10,000 from the government and $47,000 from Socal during each of his five years with the agency. Such an arrangement made for mixed loyalties in some cases, but Davies's devotion to public service, which earned him a discharge from Socal after the war, typified the general demeanor of the staff.[22]

19. Ickes quoted in Engler, *Politics of Oil,* p. 287; Frey and Ide, *PAW,* p. 26; Memorandum entitled "R. K. Davies," n.d., Franklin D. Roosevelt Library, Hyde Park, New York, hereafter cited as FDRL, Robert E. Sherwood Collection, Harry Hopkins Papers, Box 328, Oil Folder.

20. Ickes, *Secret Diary,* vol. 3, p. 456, 533; *Arabian Oil Hearings,* 25235, 25207.

21. Breakdown of Staff of Petroleum Administration for War, April 16, 1943, National Archives, Washington, D.C., hereafter cited as NA, Records of the Office of the Secretary of the Interior, Record Group 48, hereafter cited as RG 48, File 1–188: Petroleum Administration, Folder 2834.

22. *Arabian Oil Hearings,* 25207–209.

The public bureaucracy now organized, Ickes turned to the private sector. The New Deal had taught him that oil men were, in his words, "tough hombres," who "would take the bit in their teeth and run away with it if given any chance." Even the creation of a powerless coordinator had alarmed producers; filling the post with Harold Ickes convinced many that, as one oil man observed, "another drive for Federal control" had begun. Only if oil men participated in determining policy could Ickes secure their full cooperation.[23]

Early in June 1941 Ickes summoned over a thousand representatives of the industry to Washington with a new offer of friendship through cooperation. The familiar link between oil and national defense was the keynote of Deputy Coordinator Davies's welcome, which also contained a warning. "Left to itself," he told the oil men, "there is no way by which the industry can effectively organize its resources and facilities so as to deal quickly and decisively with the extraordinary problems of the day." Davies concluded that the only solution lay in partnership: "Only as a joint endeavor, government and industry cooperating completely, . . . can genuine success attend these efforts."[24]

Their enthusiasm tempered by suspicion, industry leaders responded to Davies's call with a private advisory system that paralleled OPC. Four functional committees in each of five geographic regions advised their OPC counterparts on matters of production, refining, marketing, and transportation. Private committees financed their own staffs, while committee members, chosen by the OPC from industry nominations, worked voluntarily. The chairman of each functional committee served on a district general committee that coordinated lower-level activities and acted as a liaison to the OPC district offices.[25]

Throughout the fall of 1941 problems with the construction of new pipelines, the shortage of tanker cars, and the limited production and supply of petroleum overseas taxed the district system beyond its

23. Harold L. Ickes, *Fightin' Oil* (New York, 1943), p. xiii; William R. Boyd, Jr., quoted in Frey and Ide, *PAW*, p. 12.
24. Frey and Ide, *PAW*, p. 56.
25. Frey and Ide, *PAW*, pp. 56–61; Ickes, *Fightin' Oil*, p. 73.

capacity. Interregional conferences with oil company presidents seemed a cumbersome solution to Ickes. At Davies's suggestion he created two larger forums for discussion. On November 28, 1941, Ickes established the Petroleum Industry Council for National Defense (later renamed the Petroleum Industry War Council) to supplement local committees. In December he formed the Foreign Operations Committee to handle international problems. The council met monthly in Washington to consider any question it believed affected oil on a national level and to recommend action. The Foreign Operations Committee convened once a week in New York and coordinated the work of seven area committees that dealt with overseas matters. For his part, the petroleum coordinator considered suggestions made by both groups, and submitted major policy decisions to the council for review.[26]

The cooperation of the industry, without which speedy mobilization would have been impossible, came at a price. Oil men demanded and received immunity from antitrust laws for their committee system and for their compliance with federal directives. Further, the attorney general promised to review with the petroleum coordinator any negotiations involving litigation against the oil industry.[27]

Under pressure of an impending war and in need of industry assistance, Ickes abdicated his role as reformer with a pledge to leave the competitive positions of oil companies alone. To do otherwise, he believed, would be "an arrogant assumption of power." Although he tried to balance committee and council appointments between large and small companies, he realized that "in a business . . . dominated by big units to the extent that the oil business is, there could not be cooperation, but only a futile attempt at dictation, if the big units were not given the fair and proportionate representation to which they are entitled." When the sixty-six-man Petroleum Industry War Council held its first meeting on December 8, 1941, forty executives of major oil

26. Frey and Ide, *PAW*, pp. 61–62; Ickes, *Secret Diary*, vol. 3, p. 653; Ickes, *Fightin' Oil*, pp. 77–78; Frey and Ide, *PAW*, p. 65.
27. Robert H. Jackson to Ickes, June 3, 1941; Ickes to Jackson, June 16, 1941; Francis Biddle to Ickes, June 18, 1941; Biddle to John Lord O'Brian, April 29, 1941, reprinted in Frey and Ide, *PAW*, pp. 392–94.

companies attended, and at one time in its history, the council contained thirty-nine members who had been or were at that time subject to antitrust actions.[28]

By the end of 1941 the oil industry had made ready for war. In the process, it had also made sure to protect itself from federal meddling. A private advisory system duplicated every branch of the public bureaucracy. No decisions escaped industry scrutiny. Local and national advisory committees gave oil men, who were free from prosecution for many antitrust violations, a dominant voice in formulating and in carrying out policy. As one attorney general later noted, "during the operations of the committee system fundamental questions of basic policy were initially resolved by these committees and . . . resulting government action amounted to no more than giving effect to decisions already made by such committees." Over the next year, some reorganization and a new charter greatly enlarged Ickes's powers, but the committee system remained intact.[29]

Fight over Foreign Oil

With the domestic apparatus functioning, Ickes set to work on foreign oil. Responsibility for overseeing the foreign operations of American oil companies had never been clearly established among the executive departments. After the First World War, when government officials feared a domestic oil shortage, both the Commerce and State departments had encouraged American oil companies to expand overseas operations. During the 1920s and 1930s private initiatives in the Middle East, in the Dutch East Indies, and in Latin America had brought requests from the companies for government support. American oil companies seeking concessions abroad almost always had to deal with

28. Ickes to editors of the *Nation,* October 11, 1941, NA, RG 48, File 1–188: Petroleum Administration, Folder 2825; Engler, *Politics of Oil,* p. 279.

29. Peyton Ford to Oscar Chapman, February 16, 1951, reprinted in U.S., Congress, House, Anti-Trust Subcommittee of the Committee on the Judiciary, *Hearings,* pt. 4, *WOC's and Government Advisory Groups,* 84th Cong., 2nd Sess. (Washington, 1956), 2324–27. For an explanation of Ickes's new powers under the renamed Petroleum Administration for War, see Executive Order no. 9276, Establishing the Petroleum Administration for War and Defining its Functions and Duties, December 2, 1942, reprinted in Frey and Ide, *PAW,* pp. 375–77.

foreign governments, which usually controlled subsoil rights and sometimes owned shares of international oil firms. As the official channel for communication with foreign governments, the State Department was the natural intermediary. Over the years it gradually assumed jurisdiction over foreign oil developments.[30]

Ickes and his new office complicated matters by claiming control over oil and everything related to it. The claim brought him into conflict with the State Department, first with lower-level officials and ultimately with Secretary of State Cordell Hull. This early encounter, although played out partly by subordinates, turned out to be a prelude to later battles between Ickes and Hull for control of foreign oil policy. The struggle continued through most of the war years, and as the first round indicated, it was often a bitter fight.

Ickes and Hull had clashed before. In 1938, when Ickes had cut off shipments of helium to Germany, Hull regarded his action as unwarranted poaching, despite Ickes's claim that the strategic material was being used to prepare Germany for war. The two also had disagreed in 1940 over oil policy toward Japan. Ickes had sided with Treasury Secretary Henry Morgenthau, Jr., who favored embargoing all oil shipments. Hull had opposed an embargo for fear that it would force oil-poor Japan to take bold action in Indochina and in the Dutch East Indies. In the end, Roosevelt chose to follow Ickes's recommendations, though he did so step by small step. Still, Ickes remained impatient with the way the State Department had, as he put it, "piddled around."[31]

That pace, which would never be quick enough to suit Ickes, reflected the temperament of Cordell Hull. Like the department he ran, Hull was slow. He had a mind that approached new ideas as if they were

30. Michael J. Hogan, "Informal Entente: Public Policy and Private Management in Anglo-American Petroleum Affairs, 1918–1924," *Business History Review* (Summer 1974), pp. 187–205; DeNovo, *American Policies in the Middle East,* pp. 167–209; Benjamin Shwadran, *The Middle East, Oil and the Great Powers* (3rd ed. rev., Jerusalem, 1973); Tulchin, *Aftermath of War,* pp. 118–54.

31. Harold L. Ickes, *The Secret Diary of Harold L. Ickes, vol. 2: The Inside Struggle, 1936–1939* (New York, 1954), pp. 391–93, 396–99, 414, 418–420; John M. Blum, *From the Morgenthau Diaries: Years of Urgency, 1938–1941* (Boston, 1965), pp. 348–54; Herbert Feis, *The Road to Pearl Harbor: The Coming of the War between the United States and Japan* (Princeton, 1950).

intruders. He preferred examination to action, skepticism to decision. Proposals for which he assumed responsibility received special scrutiny, and too often he fastened upon problems rather than solutions. Decisions came painfully to him and only after long periods of consideration. Well suited to a scholar, those qualities in a secretary of state upset many around him who mistook his pensiveness for diffidence.[32]

His appearance and manner supported the impression. He could easily have been taken for an antebellum planter, out of place amid irreverent New Dealers. Over sixty when he became secretary of state in 1933, Hull was still a handsome man. He seemed fragile but dignified, with thinning white hair and large features that gave his face a kindly air. His penchant for talking in righteous clichés conspired with his lisping and drawling speech to convince listeners that he was as harmless as he appeared.

Hull had a tougher side. His self-restraint bordered on asceticism. He swore off cigars suddenly after having smoked more than a dozen a day for over thirty years; he kept away from social engagements whenever possible; he drank liquor temperately; and he allowed himself only one regular indulgence: croquet playing with his friend Henry Stimson. Under the courteous demeanor lurked an elephantine stubbornness and a temper that could erupt in a stream of invectives. He was introspective and overly sensitive, and he dwelled too long on what he considered snubs and insults. His brooding produced, in the fashion of his Tennessee kinfolk, long feuds that usually ended with Hull's foot figuratively planted on his opponent's chest. "In no hurry to 'get' his enemy," as one colleague noted, " 'get' him he usually did."[33]

32. Dean Acheson, *Present at the Creation: My Years with the State Department* (New York, 1969), p. 43; Diary of Henry L. Stimson, hereafter cited as Stimson Diary, vol. 44, 101, Sterling Memorial Library, Yale University, New Haven, Conn., Henry L. Stimson Papers; Breckinridge Long, *The War Diary of Breckinridge Long: Selections from the Years 1939-1944,* ed. Fred L. Israel (Lincoln, 1966), p. 210.

33. Acheson, *Present at the Creation,* pp. 30-31, 43n, 44; Cordell Hull, *The Memoirs of Cordell Hull* (New York, 1948), vol. 1, especially pp. 3-4, 24, 37, 48-50, 52, 81, 136-37; Donald F. Drummond, "Cordell Hull," in *An Uncertain Tradition: American Secretaries of State in the Twentieth Century,* ed. Norman A. Graebner (New York, 1961), pp. 184-209; Israel, ed., *Long Diary,* p. 210, 327; Schlesinger, *Coming of the New Deal,* p. 190.

Like a true nineteenth-century liberal, Hull preached the value of eliminating commercial barriers in order to create the economic cooperation necessary for lasting peace. "To me," he wrote at the end of his career, "unhampered trade dovetailed with peace; high tariffs, trade barriers and unfair economic competition, with war." He translated his vision of an open world market into a program of reciprocal trade agreements to curtail restrictions on international commerce. Through the years the program became, in the words of a close associate, "his political raison d'être," and until he died Hull crusaded for world peace through free trade.[34]

Hull, like Ickes, saw in the coming war an opportunity to expand his authority over oil. In July 1941 he brought an oil man into the department to provide technical advice for accumulating strategic reserves of petroleum. Ickes was irate. He believed that his office should handle any oil problem, domestic or foreign. If the State Department needed information, he complained to the president, it could obtain the data from the petroleum coordinator or a member of his staff. After relaying Ickes's complaint to Under Secretary of State Sumner Welles, Roosevelt, preoccupied with events abroad, let the matter drop.[35]

Other executive departments and agencies also laid claims to jurisdiction over foreign oil matters. The War and Navy departments had the clearest stake in the operations of international oil companies. Production overseas would help meet the needs of the military services, while construction of new wells and refineries abroad required military approval for the use of strategic materials and army equipment. The Maritime Commission, in charge of all tankers, was also concerned with oil as part of its overall responsibility for shipping stores from one country to another. Even the Office of Lend-Lease Administration had an interest in foreign oil, since that agency often furnished foreign governments with supplies necessary to increase oil

34. Hull, *Memoirs,* vol. 1, p. 81; Israel, ed., *Long Diary,* p. 242. For the best biography of Hull, see Julius W. Pratt, *Cordell Hull,* vols. 12 and 13 in *The American Secretaries of State and Their Diplomacy,* ed. Robert H. Ferrell and Samuel Flagg Bemis, (New York, 1964). For a revisionist account of the impact of Hull's trade philosophy on New Deal foreign policy during the 1930s, see Lloyd C. Gardner, *Economic Aspects of New Deal Diplomacy* (Boston, 1964), especially pp. 3–174.

35. Ickes, *Secret Diary,* vol. 3, p. 576.

production. By 1941 each department had either established its own oil division or had hired oil men as advisers.[36]

After the Japanese attack on Pearl Harbor, President Roosevelt saw the need for coordinating the activities of these separate offices. He turned to Vice-President Henry A. Wallace, chairman of the newly formed Board of Economic Warfare (BEW). BEW had replaced the prewar Economic Defense Board as the agency to advise the president in a wide range of economic and communication fields, to coordinate the work of different departments in those fields, and to develop plans for the war and postwar periods. As such, BEW seemed the natural home for a foreign oil policy committee. Late in 1941 Roosevelt ordered Wallace to create such a group under BEW auspices.[37]

Wallace called the new group the Foreign Petroleum Policy Committee (FPPC) and at once began to assemble representatives from interested agencies, including the State, War, and Navy departments, the Maritime Commission, the Office of Lend-Lease Administration, and, of course, the Office of the Petroleum Coordinator. All except OPC sent their petroleum experts to sit on the new committee. To assure close cooperation with American and Allied oil companies, the presidents of the major internationals created, at Wallace's request, the Foreign Petroleum Operating Board to act in concert with FPPC. In apparent deference to State Department primacy in foreign policy, Wallace picked Max Thornburg, the department's petroleum adviser, to chair the committee.[38]

36. Frey and Ide, *PAW*, p. 18–21.

37. Acheson, *Present at the Creation*, p. 70. For a fuller discussion of the creation and operation of BEW, see John M. Blum, ed., *The Price of Vision: The Diary of Henry A. Wallace, 1942–1946* (Boston, 1973), especially pp. 22–28, 53–229; Roosevelt to Wallace, December 23, 1941, NA, Records of the Department of State, Record Group 59, hereafter cited as RG 59, 811.6363/399–1/2.

38. The Executive Committee of the Foreign Petroleum Operating Board included John A. Brown, President, Socony-Vacuum Oil Company; Harry D. Collier, President, Standard Oil Company of California; William S. Farish, President, Standard Oil Company of New Jersey; John Drake, President, Gulf Oil Company; William Starling Sullivan Rodgers, President, the Texas Company; Robert Colley, President, Atlantic Refining Oil Company; Basil R. Jackson, representing the Anglo-Iranian and Burmah Oil Company; and Harold Wilkinson, representing the Royal-Dutch Shell Group. Press Release, January 31, 1942, NA, Records of the Foreign Economic Administration, Record Group 169, hereafter cited as RG 169, Box 1612, File OW 113.

The absence of an OPC representative underscored the conflict that Roosevelt's charge created between Ickes and the other agencies, especially the State Department. For months Ickes had been operating on the assumption that he controlled foreign oil. He had already set up a foreign division in OPC to handle transportation and supply problems with the British, Canadians, and Russians. OPC had also established a liaison with both the British Merchant Shipping Mission and the British Petroleum Mission in Washington. In August 1941 OPC had directed American oil companies dealing with Latin American countries to form the Petroleum Supply Committee for Latin America. Later, in mid-December, Ickes's office had helped the industry to organize its foreign operations committee to coordinate the activities of Allied and American oil companies abroad. Not only would Wallace's committee duplicate those efforts, but, still worse, its very existence violated the administrative principle of a centralized oil authority, for which Ickes had fought since the New Deal.[39]

On December 29, 1941, when Ickes learned of Roosevelt's decision to place foreign oil under a separate agency, he wrote the president directly. Ickes based his case for OPC jurisdiction over foreign oil on the fact that he had originally been commissioned petroleum coordinator. Underscoring pertinent clauses, Ickes quoted the president's original letter designating him petroleum coordinator and assigning him the task of ''making petroleum and petroleum products available, adequately and continuously, in the proper forms, *at the proper places, to meet military and civilian needs.''* The letter, Ickes reminded Roosevelt, had also instructed him to ''consult with the petroleum industry and those industries which affect its functioning, to aid them in shaping their policies and operation in the discovery, production, processing, transportation, storage, distribution, marketing, consumption, and *import* and *export* of petroleum and petroleum products.'' Those clauses contained no proscription restricting his duties to the domestic field. In fact, he argued, the passages he had underlined clearly placed foreign oil questions in his hands.[40]

39. Frey and Ide, *PAW*, pp. 250–57.
40. Ickes to Roosevelt, December 29, 1941, FDRL, Franklin D. Roosevelt Papers, hereafter cited as Roosevelt Papers, Official File, hereafter cited as OF (4226).

Ickes knew that quoting Roosevelt's own letters back to him would not, in itself, win disputes over jurisdiction. Any president had the right to modify arrangements that he had previously made, and Roosevelt exercised the prerogative more than most. Ickes, therefore, did not limit his assault on the new committee to reciting the charter of his office. In a characteristic performance, he employed all his wiles to make his case.

At first, with a mixture of indignation and disappointment, he told Roosevelt late in December 1941 that, "at the very least," he had hoped for the chance to show that his record as petroleum coordinator had not been "such a failure as would justify the public rebuke that your delegation of some of my most important functions to the Economic Warfare Board [*sic*] so clearly means." A week later he shifted from lamentation to logic, arguing that domestic and foreign oil operations were virtually inseparable. To ensure that Roosevelt recognized the dangers involved in a fight for control of foreign petroleum policy, he warned the president of "how quick some elements in the oil industry will be to take advantage of division within our official ranks." The tactics proved unavailing. By the next day Ickes was reduced to pleading with Roosevelt for an audience.[41]

While Ickes wrote letters to the president, his assistant, Ralph Davies, was negotiating with FPPC chairman Max Thornburg. Davies and Thornburg were no strangers. Both had worked for the Socal organization before the war—Davies as a senior vice-president of that company and Thornburg as vice-president of two Social subsidiaries, the Bahrein Petroleum Company and the California Texas Oil Company. Now colleagues in Washington, the two men had been getting along well on the basis of their old acquaintanceship. Lately, though, Davies had come to mistrust Thornburg. Thornburg's efforts to build up his own office within the State Department and to extend its jurisdiction beyond that department had disturbed Davies, who suspected that the ambitious Thornburg lay behind the creation of FPPC. He also

41. *Ibid.;* Ickes to Roosevelt, January 5, 1942, FDRL, Roosevelt Papers, OF (4226); Ickes to Roosevelt, January 6, 1942, FDRL, Roosevelt Papers, OF (4226).

doubted Thornburg's scruples and his capacity for loyalty as a public servant, and he communicated these doubts liberally to Ickes. Ickes, in turn, absorbed those misgivings, held fast to them, and looked for confirmation in Thornburg's every move. Thornburg, perhaps sensing Davies's animus, avoided him whenever possible, choosing to deal instead with James Terry Duce, another Socal executive who later served with the Petroleum Administration for War (PAW)— the renamed OPC.[42]

For the moment, Davies and Thornburg were forced to work together. In this instance substantive differences compounded personal difficulties. Like Ickes, Davies believed in the value of centralization and saw the new committee as an attempt to dislodge OPC from the foreign field. Thornburg maintained that the problems of foreign oil supplies for wartime use bore no relationship to the domestic industry. "Most of the problems," he observed, "are entirely foreign— involving companies, oil supplies and governments which are not American but are British, Dutch, Argentinian, Venezuelan, Turkish, Arabian, Iraqian, etc. In time of war each of these sovereign governments exercises plenary powers over its oil operations, guided by political and military understandings between them." The necessity for State Department supremacy in foreign oil matters was a potent argument for denying OPC jurisdiction, since the department had responsibility for dealing with foreign governments in other matters.[43]

Their positions seemingly irreconcilable, neither Davies nor Thornburg held clear advantage. Davies could argue for centraliza-

42. The Diary of Harold Ickes, hereafter cited as Ickes Diaries, vol. 41, 6174, Library of Congress, Washington, D.C., hereafter cited as LC.

43. A brief summary of the negotiations is found in C. V. Barry memorandum for Thornburg, February 25, 1942, NA, RG 169, Box 1612, File OW 113. Reference is made to Davies's position during the negotiations in Davies to Ickes, March 27, 1944, NA, RG 48, File 1-188: Petroleum Administration, Folder 2834. Thornburg memorandum submitted on January 1, 1942, NA, RG 169, Box 1612, File OW 113. According to Thornburg, the function of the petroleum coordinator was to administer oil supplies from the United States and to serve as, in his words, a "clearinghouse" for those countries buying or lend-leasing petroleum products. Thornburg to Milo Perkins, January 7, 1942, NA, RG 169, Box 1612, File OW 113.

tion and might point to the machinery OPC had already developed for handling foreign oil, but he could not get around Roosevelt's predilection for dividing authority. The president liked to retain power by scattering it among competing agencies. Thornburg could assert that most questions involving foreign oil placed the government in contact with foreign powers, but he could not explain away supply programs, such as the production of 100-octane aviation fuel, that required integrating domestic and foreign activities.[44]

Long negotiations drew tempers to a fine edge. Ickes, the veteran of a score of similar battles, later described the episode as "the most savage fight I have ever been through in Washington." "Take my advice and keep out of it," Treasury secretary Morgenthau told an aide, "it is one of the bitterest battles which is going on." President Roosevelt also kept out of it, except for an occasional prod characteristically softened. "It seems to me that this is a matter which can and should be worked out satisfactorily to everybody concerned," he told Ickes early in January 1942. "I do not think there is any desire to push anybody around." Ickes, familiar with the tactic, remained pessimistic, confiding in his diary that the president "is following his terrible old habit of drifting." Should Roosevelt drift too far in Wallace's direction, Ickes was prepared to resign as petroleum coordinator rather than have his authority diluted.[45]

It never came to that. In mid-January Davies and Thornburg finally arrived at a resolution, less a compromise than a working arrangement. The FPPC would act as a coordinating and policymaking board. Its function would be, according to a draft agreement, "to study the problems of oil supply abroad . . . and to formulate—or to learn from other sources of primary authority—the policies, plans and procedures which must be followed in order to bring about the fullest possible

44. Frey and Ide, *PAW*, pp. 194–213. On Roosevelt's peculiar administrative style, see Schlesinger, *Coming of the New Deal*, pp. 533–52, and James MacGregor Burns, *Roosevelt: The Lion and the Fox* (New York, 1956), pp. 372–75.

45. *Arabian Oil Hearings*, 25206; The Diaries of Henry Morgenthau Jr., hereafter cited as Morgenthau Diaries, vol. 482, 44–45, FDRL; Ickes Diaries, vol. 41, 6200, 6217.

utilization of the oil resources of the allied nations in the conduct of war.'' FPPC responsibility for foreign oil ended with statements of policy. For its part, OPC would collaborate in making policy through its representative on the committee and would, ''within its jurisdiction, . . . act as the agency of government which translates such approved programs into effective action on the part of the oil industry.'' That second coordinative function would be carried out through OPC recommendations to industry committees made up of foreign operating companies.[46]

When Ickes initialed the draft agreement on January 19, 1942, he claimed ''complete victory.'' It was something less, though the settlement did secure important advantages for OPC. It made that office the administrative agency for foreign oil policy as it affected the oil industry. It also preserved OPC control over imports and exports of oil. Further, it solidified OPC's role in formulating policy. Even so, OPC had been reduced, in effect, to a liaison in the foreign field whose contribution to policymaking was limited to collaboration.[47]

Eager to cut short his row with Ickes, Wallace signed the agreement on January 20. FPPC had its charter, but problems soon developed as Ickes and Davies became more and more uncooperative. To protest Thornburg's failure to send over a copy of the settlement at once, Ickes ordered Davies to hold back OPC's representative. That reprimand lasted a week. More serious trouble followed, which revealed Ickes's and Davies's intention to short-circuit committee operations and to establish complete control over foreign oil. Davies failed to inform foreign operating companies of the agreement reached between Wallace and Ickes, and he continued to organize and to work through OPC's own foreign division and the OPC-sponsored Foreign Operations Committee. He made his distaste for the new committee known to representatives of the British Petroleum Mission and to the executives of private oil companies. He even refused to allow his tanker

46. Ickes Diaries, vol. 41, 6252–54; Copy of draft agreement, n.d., FDRL, Roosevelt Papers, OF (4226).
47. Copy of draft agreement, n.d., FDRL, Roosevelt Papers, OF (4226). Ickes Diaries, vol. 41, 6288.

expert to discuss with Thornburg's committee recommendations for setting up a tanker coordinating board.[48]

Though FPPC did manage to solve some foreign supply problems, the committee could not overcome the difficulties created by the lack of OPC cooperation. Private companies and foreign governments were reluctant to deal with the new committee for fear of offending Ickes and Davies, upon whom they had come to depend. Other government agencies, aware of the boundary dispute, were unsure about where they should bring their oil problems. The result was confusion, inefficiency, and resentment. "Conditions will not and cannot improve," the committee's executive secretary lamented late in February 1942, "unless and until the jurisdictional questions between the Office of the Petroleum Coordinator and the Policy Committee and the Operating Board are completely clarified." He concluded that, to reach clarification, "accompanied by the sincere will of all concerned to work in harmony and cooperation, there appears to me to be but little if any possibility."[49]

Less than three weeks later Max Thornburg resigned as chairman of the Foreign Petroleum Policy Committee. Earlier he had called the committee an "administrative travesty." It had become an administrative disaster, unable to fulfill its mandate as a policymaking body. Although it did not formally dissolve until December 1942, the committee effectively ended its career with Thornburg's resignation.[50]

The early days of the war left control of foreign oil policy unsettled. Problems involving production and supply at home and abroad fell mostly to Harold Ickes, whose old office was reorganized and renamed late in 1942. The Petroleum Administration for War, as it was now called, was the centralized oil authority that Ickes had wanted since the New Deal. Still, responsibility for federal policy toward the overseas operations of American oil companies remained blurred. Hull and the State Department had an edge, if only because of experi-

---

48. Ickes Diaries, vol. 41, 6253–54; Thornburg to Perkins, February 25, 1942, NA, RG 169, Box 1612, File OW 113.

49. Barry to Thornburg, February 25, 1942, NA, RG 169, Box 1612, File OW 113.

50. Thornburg to Wallace, March 17, 1942, NA, RG 59, 811.6363/399.

ence. But, in the dispute over the Foreign Petroleum Policy Committee, Ickes had revealed his intention to play a leading role. In 1942 responsibility for foreign oil policy was not a matter of moment but of personality. Even then, however, the effects of war on oil companies abroad were beginning to invest the issue with real substance.

2 / The Arabian Connection

In August 1940, as Axis submarines began scuttling Allied ships in the Mediterranean, Fenner and Beane, a prominent New York brokerage house, circulated a confidential memorandum among its clients giving the investment outlook for several American oil companies with concessions abroad. Long experience with petroleum securities gave force to the brokers' observations.

Although they acknowledged the value of the companies' holdings, Fenner and Beane pointed out that the outbreak of war made "definite conclusions" impossible to reach. "The stake of the Standard Oil Company of New Jersey, the Texas Corporation, Socony Vacuum and the Standard Oil Company of California in developments outside the Western Hemisphere is extremely important," the report noted. "In fact," it said, "the questions involved are so important that they concern the foreign policy of the United States as well as the judgement of the individual managements of the different companies." Since the market position of each company's stock would be affected by the course of international affairs, which seemed uncertain at the time, and by the development of American foreign policy, Fenner and Beane could anticipate no more than an average performance from the securities. As a result, they counseled their customers to invest elsewhere.[1]

The forecast must have come as no surprise to the managers of the Standard Oil Company of California and the Texas Company (Texaco). They appreciated the connection between American foreign policy and the value of their concessions, and they recognized the

1. Fenner and Beane, "Confidential Memorandum on the Petroleum Industry," August 16, 1940, NA, RG 59, 811.6363/364.

weak speculative position of their stocks. Until recently, their joint venture in Saudi Arabia had promised huge returns. But the war, along with the local ruler's demands for more money and rumors of British interest in the concession, threatened to destroy the investment. The oil men believed that only the assistance of the United States government could save their property. Under the special circumstances of war, they pressed for financial and political support. Any gains the companies hoped to make would now depend on what the government did.

The Arabian Concession

Socal had negotiated the Arabian concession alone. After spending nearly $50 million in an unsuccessful search for foreign oil in the 1920s, the company had finally acquired prospecting rights in 1930 on the Persian Gulf island of Bahrain through a newly formed subsidiary, the Bahrein Petroleum Company, Ltd. (Bapco). Socal then turned its attention to the mainland, some twenty miles westward, where the kingdom of Saudi Arabia presented attractive prospects. In 1933 the company outbid international competitors for a large concession in the eastern section of the country. To exploit the property, Socal created the California Arabian Standard Oil Company (Casoc). For the first time, a wholly American-owned venture was established in the Middle East.[2]

A relative newcomer overseas, Socal lacked adequate outlets for its recently acquired oil. Bapco had begun shipping crude from Bahrain,

2. After negotiations, the myth arose that Ibn Saud had granted the concession to Casoc because he admired American policy and ideology, and because he feared the spread of British influence in his country. Indeed, according to the story, the absence of any pressure from the American government was instrumental in the king's decision. Recent scholarship argues convincingly that the only consideration involved was money. Hull, *Memoirs,* vol. 2, p. 1511; *New York Times,* July 15, 1933; Charles Rayner to Edward Stettinius, March 1, 1944, NA, RG 59, 890F.6363/131; Shwadran, *MEOGP,* p. 310n; Wilkins, *Maturing Multinational,* p. 120, pp. 214–16. When the United States government recognized Saudi Arabia in 1931, the country was called the "Kingdom of the Hedjaz and Nejd and Its Dependencies." The name was changed to the "Kingdom of Saudi Arabia" in 1932. For the sake of clarity, I have used Saudi Arabia throughout.

and although oil had yet to be discovered in commercial quantities on the mainland, field explorations seemed promising enough to persuade Texaco to invest in Socal's operation. With a vast marketing organization in Europe, China, Australasia, Africa, and the Far East, Texaco was interested in gaining sources of supply nearer to the Far East than the United States, which had furnished the company's requirements. In 1936 Texaco received half of Bapco in exchange for turning over its marketing facilities east of Suez to the California Texas Oil Company, Ltd. (Caltex), a Bapco subsidiary. Socal continued to provide staff for Bapco and Caltex, even though both companies were now owned jointly. Later that year Texaco obtained a half-interest in Casoc and the Arabian concession and agreed to pay as consideration $3 million in cash, plus an additional $18 million in deferred payments from future production in Arabia. Now Socal had its marketing outlets as well as a partner to share the risks of exploration and development, while Texaco had its stake in Eastern Hemisphere production. All this had been accomplished without upsetting existing marketing positions and triggering an international price war.[3]

Then as now, the men involved in the international oil business were realists with an uncanny ability to prosper even in the most luckless circumstances. They had a talent for making useful connections and a knack for developing strategies that maximized options as well as profits. The twists and turns of events rarely surprised them; their livelihood depended on anticipating the inconstant. Their capacity for improvising was limitless, their practice of diplomacy masterful.

3. H. St. J. B. Philby, *Arabian Jubilee* (London, 1952), pp. 176–79; Karl S. Twitchell, *Saudi Arabia* (Princeton, 1947), pp. 147–51; Stephen H. Longrigg, *Oil in the Middle East: Its Discovery and Development* (London, 1954), p. 107; Roy Lebkicher, *Aramco and World Oil* (New York, 1952), pp. 25–28; Shwadran, *MEOGP*, p. 307; *International Petroleum Cartel*, pp. 72–75, 114–16; *Arabian Oil Hearings*, 24708–709, 24803, 24836–37, 24902–905, 25016, 25029. As part of the Casoc transaction, Texaco also received a half-interest in N. V. Nederlandsche Pacific Petroleum Maatschappij, which owned concessions in Sumatra and Java. For the exact terms of the deal and of the original Casoc concession, see Wilkins, *Maturing Multinational*, pp. 214–16.

Whatever their nationality, they were conspicuous in their patriotism; yet they owed their primary allegiance to "the company."

Casoc managers and engineers conformed squarely to that profile. This was fortunate, for Saudi Arabia, inhospitable and nearly impenetrable, strained even their considerable talents. One-quarter the size of the United States, it lies below the fertile crescent of the Tigris and Euphrates—a great expanse of desert dotted with a few oases and rimmed by fringes of green. Its interior was largely inaccessible, except by camel. In the eastern province, where the oil lay, withering heat and hostile tribesmen made drilling expensive and dangerous. So did the fine-grained sand. In the fierce windstorms that beset the desert, breathing was difficult, travel impossible. Even on windless days company vehicles were in danger of getting stuck in the sand, until the oil men finally developed special tires that distributed weight more evenly.

Religious fundamentalism further hampered operations. The near literal adherence of the ruling Moslem sect to the Koran produced objections to all sorts of modern appliances from phonographs to cameras. The Americans had to permit their Arab employees five worship periods daily and had to make allowances for Ramadan, a daytime fasting period that lasted nearly a month. The oil men also had to train those employees, most of whom had been illiterate nomads before the company arrived. Many could not read Arabic when they learned to read English, and most had to be taught even the fundamentals of industrial technology—they had never heard of the nut and bolt. The success of the oil men in adapting to the unfriendly environment and the relative speed with which they made their operation a going concern testified to their ingenuity.[4]

Diplomatic Representation

Although the company had obtained the Arabian concession without the aid of the United States government, Casoc officers soon felt the

4. Wilkins, *Maturing Multinational*, pp. 220–21.

need for diplomatic representation in the country. In a region dominated by Great Britain, the company looked to Washington for support
and protection, but officials there proved unhelpful. The United States
had never taken much of an interest in the Middle East, let alone in
Saudi Arabia. Before the First World War, government authorities
had looked upon the Arabian peninsula as falling within Britain's
sphere of influence. The United States maintained only one consulate
in the area, at Aden on the southern tip of the peninsula. American
contact with local sheikhdoms, protectorates, and other political en-
tities was limited to the forays of a few missionaries and adventurers.
After the war ancient squabbles among Arab sheikhs erupted into
full-scale war, and Abd al Aziz Ibn Saud, sultan of Nejd and religious
leader of the puritanical Wahhabi-Ikhwan sect of Islam, emerged the
victor in 1926. The United States recognized his newly constituted
kingdom of Saudi Arabia in 1931. In 1933 the two governments
signed a treaty of commerce and navigation, which also provided for
an exchange of diplomatic officers.[5]

Without great investment in the country, the United States saw no
need to carry out the arrangement. Managers of the oil company
thought differently. Immediately after negotiating the concession,
Casoc agents began lobbying at the State Department for official
American representation at Jidda, the Saudi capital. For the next six
years company men besought the government to establish a diplomatic
post there. Each time they came to Washington, Casoc representatives
found State Department officials sympathetic but uncooperative.
Those officers understood the company's arguments but worried
about sending a representative "just to please Socal." In their view
the level of American political and economic involvement did not warrant such a move.[6]

Casoc's prospects for obtaining the post brightened by 1939. For

5. Charles Hamilton, *Americans and Oil in the Middle East* (Houston, 1962), pp.
132–41; for correspondence relating to United States recognition of and treaties with
Saudi Arabia, see U. S. Department of State, *Foreign Relations of the United States*
(Washington, 1852–), hereafter cited as *FRUS* (year), (1931), vol. 2, pp. 547–54;
FRUS (1933), vol. 2, pp. 986–1001.

6. Joseph William Walt, "Saudi Arabia and the Americans, 1923–1951" (Ph.D.
diss., Northwestern University, 1960), pp. 186–93.

one thing, the company had discovered its first commercial well in 1938. For another, Casoc had increased its staff in Saudi Arabia to include over 300 Americans. More important, the company had recently negotiated, in competition with German, Japanese, Italian, and British nationals, a supplemental agreement that extended its lease for sixty years and enlarged the original concession area by some 80,000 square miles. The new concession, together with the interest in Arabian oil shown by foreign powers, gave the company more leverage at the State Department, where it could now claim that increased American interests in Saudi Arabia more than ever required protection from envious foreigners.[7]

In the spring of 1939 Casoc's supplications began to make sense to State Department officials, who were already concerned about belligerent European and Asian powers. Casoc played on those fears. While the company was still negotiating the supplemental agreement of 1939, Casoc lobbyists warned the department of scheming German, Japanese, and British concession hunters "supported actively by their governments," which were "in all cases represented by Ministers accredited to the King of Arabia." After the agreement had been signed, the company told the department confidentially that, in spite of larger offers from the Japanese and the British, Ibn Saud had granted the new concession to the Americans because of his "faith in

---

7. Shwadran, *MEOGP*, p. 307. In 1936 Secretary of State Cordell Hull authorized Leland Morris, American Consul General at Alexandria, to visit Saudi Arabia and to report on the prospects for establishing diplomatic relations. On March 23, 1937, Morris submitted a long report that concluded "that the development of American interests does not warrant the establishment of any sort of official representation at Jidda at this time." Among his reasons for rejecting such representation was that Casoc's operations, in Morris's view, had not progressed sufficiently to ensure its permanence in Saudi Arabia. G. S. Messersmith to Bert Fish, May 24, 1939, *FRUS*, (1939), vol. 4, pp. 324–25; Morris's report is quoted in Walt, "Saudi Arabia," pp. 189–90, 190–91n. Fish to Hull, June 21, 1939, *FRUS* (1939), vol. 4, pp. 826–27. Estimates of the total size of the concession vary according to the source. According to a company memorandum written for Harold Ickes and dated February 8, 1943, the area of the entire concession was 250,000 square miles, *Arabian Oil Hearings,* 25385. James Terry Duce, an executive with Socal, placed the area at 440,000 square miles, James Terry Duce, *Middle East Oil Developments* (New York, 1952), p. 13. Shwadran accepts Duce's figures and estimates the size of the supplemental concession at 80,000 square miles, Shwadran, *MEOGP,* p. 307.

the United States,'' his fear of British influence, and his satisfaction with Casoc operations.[8]

After some corroboration from its men in the field, the State Department accepted the company's version of events in Saudi Arabia. The department officials did not realize, however, that the company had obscured what really happened. Both the Germans and the Japanese had indeed sent diplomatic representatives to the Saudi court during negctiations for the concession, but that hardly gave them, as the company contended, ''frequent access to high Arabian officials.'' In fact, neither country maintained a diplomatic establishment in Saudi Arabia. The German minister resident at Baghdad had only recently been accredited to the court, and the Japanese had no formal relations at all with the Saudis. Casoc's explanation of the king's motive for granting the concession was equally suspect. According to the terms of the original concession agreement, the company had preferential rights to the adjoining territory on the condition that it meet the offers others might make. Ibn Saud probably gave the lease to the Americans because they again outbid the competition. By making it appear as though its concession depended solely on the goodwill of the king, the company increased its pressure on the State Department, which was also aware of Ibn Saud's desire for an exchange of diplomatic representatives to bolster the standing of his country.[9]

In June 1939 the department yielded. After checking with the American legations in Egypt and Iraq, Secretary of State Hull recommended accrediting the American minister resident at Cairo to the court of Ibn Saud. Hull believed the United States government could, in that way, ''make representations on any matters affecting American interests which might urgently arise'' without incurring the expense of establishing a separate diplomatic post. The presence of Germans and

8. Francis Loomis to Hull, April 25, 1939, quoted in Walt, ''Saudi Arabia,'' pp. 192–93; Fish to Hull, June 21, 1939, *FRUS* (1939), vol. 4, pp. 826–27.

9. Fish to Hull, June 21, 1939, *FRUS* (1939), vol. 4, pp. 826–27. Loomis to Hull, April 25, 1939, quoted in Walt, ''Saudi Arabia,'' pp. 192–93; Hull to Roosevelt, June 30, 1939, *FRUS* (1939), vol. 4, pp. 827–28. Shwadran argues persuasively that, as in 1933, money was once again the primary consideration, Shwadran, *MEOGP*, pp. 313–14n.

Japanese plotting at Jidda, Hull told the president, might well give the United States cause to make those representations. "Excellent idea," Roosevelt responded, and on July 12, 1939, he appointed Minister Bert Fish the American envoy to Saudi Arabia.[10]

Loans and Subsidies to Arabia

Two months later war broke out in Europe; its effects reached Arabia within the year. During the first two months of 1940 Casoc's enterprise was flourishing. The company had been shipping oil out of its new refinery site at Ras Tanura for almost a year. By February, the same month in which Minister Fish presented his credentials to Ibn Saud, the company's field crew had grown to 371 Americans and over 3,000 non-Americans. Daily production had jumped to an average of 30,000 barrels, up nearly 20,000 barrels from 1939. But in June, Italy's entry into the war disrupted the burgeoning oil industry. Increased Axis patrols on the Mediterranean led to the immediate suspension of operations at the Ras Tanura refinery. In October the Italians bombed oil installations on the island of Bahrain and at Dhahran, a drilling site on the mainland. Astonishingly, they missed their defenseless targets, but by the end of 1940 the war had forced Casoc to close Ras Tanura and to trim its American staff to 226.[11]

The Saudi Arabian government fared even worse than did the oil company. Its economy, always fragile, threatened to shatter under wartime stress. The country had almost no industry, except for the manufacture of ornamental swords and knives, rudimentary leather making, and some rug weaving. Its population of desert nomads lived on the edge of starvation. The government depended for financial survival on income from the Moslem pilgrims who came annually to retrace the flight of the Prophet Muhammad from Mecca to Medina. With the money they spent, as well as the revenue collected from cus-

10. Hull to Roosevelt, June 30, 1939, *FRUS* (1939), vol. 4, pp. 827–39, 828n.
11. Richard R. Sanger, *The Arabian Peninsula* (Ithaca, 1954), p. 104; Shwadran, *MEOGP,* p. 308; Walt, "Saudi Arabia," pp. 144–45; *Middle East Oil Developments* (New York, 1948), p. 24.

toms duties and from oil and mineral concessions, Ibn Saud financed his government and subsidized local tribes to retain their allegiance and so keep peace. The outbreak of war in 1939 drastically reduced the number of pilgrims and all but eliminated customs duties. When Casoc began curtailing its operations a year later, the government found itself deprived of royalty payments. Without normal revenues, the Saudi economy faced collapse under the weight of wartime inflation, recent crop failures, and the fixed costs of government.[12]

Despite his predicament, King Abd al Aziz Ibn Saud had assets whose value the war could not deflate. He was a shrewd man with an instinctive grasp of politics and a genius for desert warfare. His conquest of Arabia had made him a legend throughout the Arab world, as had his ability to preserve Saudi independence against ambitious Europeans and ancestral rivals. He governed his feudal kingdom according to the harsh law of the Koran, which prescribed severe penalties for even the smallest crimes. Although such a fundamentalist regime retarded his efforts to modernize the country, Ibn Saud was bound, as head of the Wahhabi dynasty, to follow the code of the Koran strictly. By applying it equitably and publicly he brought order to a country that had known only lawlessness, and he enhanced his prestige among Arabs and Westerners alike.

Life as a warrior had left his body lame and scarred. He claimed ignorance of his age, but most observers placed him in his mid-sixties during the war. Time and illness had stooped his frame, and, like many other Arabs, he was afflicted with cataracts, which impaired the vision of one eye. As if to stay the years, he had dyed his pointed beard

12. In addition to the oil concession, Ibn Saud had also granted a mining concession in 1934 to another American firm, the Saudi Arabian Mining Syndicate, Ltd. The mining operation was small, yielding the Saudi Arabian government about $50,000 annually, and never became an important source of revenue. Twitchell, *Saudi Arabia*, p. 200; *Arabian Oil Hearings*, 25382. Beyond exportation of oil and gold, the country remained almost completely unproductive and relied upon imports to supply most of its foodstuffs and manufactured goods. Roy Lebkicher memorandum, "The Situation in Saudi Arabia—February 1942," February 26, 1942, NA, RG 59, 890F.6363 Standard Oil Company/138. W. S. S. Rodgers memorandum, "Memorandum . . . by Mr. W. S. S. Rodgers, Chairman of the Board, The Texas Company," April 27, 1944, reprinted in *Arabian Oil Hearings*, 25380–87.

black, but the difficulty with which he moved quickly betrayed him. In spite of all his infirmities, he remained an imposing figure. He was a massive man, six feet six inches tall and well over 200 pounds. His bearing, solemn and dignified, gave his gentle voice a commanding aspect. His fondness for parables revealed that his mind retained the agility his body had lost. Experienced statesmen found him a sagacious negotiator with unfaltering resolve and a keen sense of political realities, though he had never ventured beyond the borders of his country. As wily a politician as Franklin Roosevelt confessed that, of all the men with whom he had ever bargained, he received the "least satisfaction" from the intractable Ibn Saud.[13]

Ibn Saud had other, more tangible resources upon which to draw. His country's untapped oil reserves, which promised to be of enormous value, offered some relief from his immediate problems. For years Casoc had been advancing him money against government royalties on future production. Company managers recognized that the goodwill of the king, who could cancel the concession at any moment, and the stability of his government were necessary for the success of their venture. From 1933 to 1939 they loaned the Saudi government over two and a half million dollars above the rent, royalties, and other fees charged for the lease. Though his deficits had grown larger since the war began, the king could expect the company to continue those loans and even increase them, should he exert the pressure.[14]

Advances from the oil company were not the only sources of revenue available to Ibn Saud. His country lay astride the land, sea, and air routes from the United Kingdom to India and the Pacific dominions.

13. "The Position of Saudi Arabia in the Arab World," February 4, 1944, NA, RG 59, Research and Analysis Report no. 1652; "King Ibn Saud: Summary," n.d., FDRL, Franklin D. Roosevelt Papers, Map Room File, Box 165, Folder 4, A-16; Blum, ed., *Wallace Diary*, p. 255; C. L. Sulzberger, *A Long Row of Candles: Memoirs and Diaries, 1939–1954* (Toronto, 1969), pp. 325–31; Robert Sherwood, *Roosevelt and Hopkins* (New York, 1950), p. 872; William D. Leahy, *I Was There* (New York, 1950), p. 326; Roy Lebkicher, George Rentz, Max Stiencke, *The Arabia of Ibn Saud* (New York, 1952), pp. 44–71; Elliot Roosevelt, *As He Saw It* (New York, 1946), p. 245.

14. Rodgers memorandum, April 27, 1944, reprinted in *Arabian Oil Hearings*, 25380–87.

As such it occupied a position of strategic value to the British Empire. Indeed, the whole Middle East was virtually a landbridge that traversed imperial lines of supply and communication. Keeping those lines open was important in time of peace; during war, it was essential. British oil concessions in Iran, Iraq, and Kuwait added to the value of the region. So did the large refinery at Abadan, which provided the United Kingdom with vital petroleum products.[15]

For generations Great Britain had maintained friendly relations with local rulers in an effort to strengthen its influence over the area. It courted Arab sheikhdoms and states with subsidies and treaties that guaranteed their independence and territorial integrity but often reduced them to protectorates of the British Empire. Ibn Saud had preserved his tiny sheikhdom of Nejd through such an arrangement in the years before he conquered Arabia. Although the British had discontinued their cash grants to the king after the First World War, the new war made his friendship a commodity again worth paying for. More than merely strategic considerations entered into British thinking. The king's position as guardian of the Holy Land made his friendship even more valuable to the British Empire, which had large Moslem populations in India and in the Middle East.[16]

Late in 1940 Ibn Saud began exploring the possibilities open to him. During the year the British, in recognition of the importance of a stable Saudi Arabia to the war effort, reintroduced subsidy payments, which

15. Memorandum by Anthony Eden, Secretary of State for Foreign Affairs, "British Policy in the Middle East," July 12, 1943, Public Record Office, London, hereafter cited as PRO, CAB 66, War Cabinet Memoranda WP and CP Series, hereafter cited as CAB 66, WP(43)301. For general studies of British interests in the Middle East during the war see George Kirk, *The Middle East in the War* (London, 1952); J. P. Hurewitz, ed., *Diplomacy in the Near and Middle East: A Documentary Record: 1914–1956* (Princeton, 1956); D. J. Payton-Smith, *Oil: A Study of Wartime Policy and Administration* (London, 1971).

16. Payton-Smith, *Oil*. The British first signed a treaty with Ibn Saud in 1915 that established a protectorate relationship between the British government and the Sultanate of Nejd. In addition, the British undertook to pay Ibn Saud a subsidy of £5,000 a month if he refrained from attacking his ancestral rival, Hussein, Sherif of Mecca. The British were backing Hussein in an effort to reduce the Turkish hold on the Middle East by building an Arab empire based on Hussein's Sherifian family. When that empire failed to materialize, the British cut off subsidies to Ibn Saud, which left him free to make war on Hussein.

totaled nearly £400,000. Casoc also contributed, with a loan of almost $3 million. Still, the king could not hope to meet his budget of $10 million for 1941 without more substantial advances from his benefactors. He pressed the company for more and more money throughout 1940. Company managers were determined to hold down payments, and as 1940 drew to a close, Frederick A. Davies, president of Casoc, and Lloyd Hamilton, a senior executive of the company, traveled to Arabia to discuss the financial arrangements. Both men had been with the company for years; each had a personal interest in keeping the concession solid. Davies, a former football player from Pennsylvania, was one of the early promoters of the Arabian venture, and Hamilton had negotiated the original concession himself.[17]

When they arrived in Arabia Davies and Hamilton found a resolute Ibn Saud demanding $6 million from the company to keep his government solvent during 1941. The king consoled the shaken executives with assurances that he expected the rest of his budget to be financed by the British. That consolation offered little relief to the oil men, who found the king's request unacceptable. With production already curtailed, the company could not afford to underwrite the Saudi government for yet another year. Further, company managers feared that increasing their advances might set a dangerous precedent that would make them liable for supporting the king indefinitely and at spiraling rates.[18]

Davies and Hamilton refused to pay but were willing to talk. By early January 1941 they had succeeded in placating the king with a shrewd compromise. According to the understanding, the company contracted to lend the government $3 million outright for the coming

17. Baxter minutes regarding Anglo-American Oil Agreement Discussions, March 16, 1944, PRO, British Foreign Office Political Correspondence, Class F. O. 371, hereafter cited as FO 371, registry number E1775/128/25. Baxter lists the 1940 subsidy paid by the British government to Ibn Saud as exactly £396,582. Oil company executives claimed the figure was £100,000, Rodgers memorandum, April 27, 1944, reprinted in *Arabian Oil Hearings,* 25380–87. See also *Arabian Oil Hearings,* 25051–57; Leonard Mosley, *Power Play: Oil in the Middle East* (New York, 1971), p. 68; Shwadran, *MEOGP,* pp. 307–308.

18. J. T. Duce to F. A. Davies, January 7, 1941, no. 178, reprinted in *Arabian Oil Hearings,* 25389.

year. Davies pledged to do all he could to raise that loan to $6 million when he returned home. He also agreed that the company would "continue to assist the Government as much as it can," if the crisis extended beyond 1941. For its part, the Saudi government would undertake to repay the loan at an undetermined date and to extend the term of the concession for another two years. As proof of its trust in the company, the government allowed Casoc to deduct ten cents from royalty payments on each ton of crude produced and also granted the company's request for permission to cut back its operation during the war without suffering any penalty. So great was Saudi faith in the agreement, as one high official told Davies, that "we are figuring out our budget for this year on six million dollars."[19]

Davies had made his promises even though Socal executives had informed him ten days earlier that they would not grant a loan exceeding $3 million and that he should refrain from leading the king to expect additional advances during the emergency. Although Davies's pledges appeared to violate those directives, he had committed himself only to lobby for an increase in the loan. He had legally obligated his company to do nothing more than consider Saudi requests for further assistance. He had qualified both promises sufficiently to make them worthless should the government attempt to hold him to the letter of the agreement; yet he gave the appearance of acceding to the king's demands with enough sincerity to convince the Saudis that more money would be forthcoming.[20]

The Moffett Mission

By April 1941 Casoc had failed to meet the Saudis' expectations. It even seemed unwilling to come up with the $3 million it had agreed to pay. Ibn Saud had received only $1 million, and his patience was running as low as his treasury. The passage of the Lend-Lease Act in March 1941 suggested to the company a way out of its predicament: if Casoc could persuade President Roosevelt that Saudi Arabia was elig-

19. Abdulla Es Sulaiman to F. A. Davies, January 18, 1941, F. A. Davies to Abdulla Sulaiman, January 19, 1941, reprinted in *Arabian Oil Hearings*, 25409-11.
20. *Arabian Oil Hearings*, 25409-11.

ible for some form of assistance, the United States government might render part or even all of the financial aid required by the king.[21]

Company officers had hit upon an ingenious plan that held several advantages. Financial support for the king from the United States government would fulfill all the obligations that they had undertaken without costing them anything and would also reduce the influence of Great Britain. Company officials were worried that renewed subsidies from Great Britain would give British agents Ibn Saud's ear and possibly his oil. The commitment of official American funds would, above all, place Arabia—and Casoc's concession—under the protection of the United States government. Although the company never admitted it in public, that protection had been its aim since 1933.[22]

Early in April the company made ready for an expedition to Washington. Davies and Hamilton, recently returned from Arabia, met with James A. Moffett, a sometime New Dealer and a Caltex executive well acquainted with the domestic and international oil industry. They explained to him that the king had now boosted his request to $6 million a year for the next five years. The company, they said, could not possibly meet that demand when annual royalties were amounting to barely $1.5 million. Their only hope lay in approaching the United States government. Moffett agreed and offered to present their case to the president.[23]

No better champion for the company's cause could have existed than James Andrew Moffett. Known in some Washington circles as a playboy who was, according to one administration official, "difficult to take seriously," Moffett was a serious oil man with years of experience in business and government. He graduated from Princeton in 1906 and went directly to work for Jersey Standard, searching for oil in the Dutch East Indies. During the First World War he had supervised petroleum purchases for the Allies through the United States

21. F. A. Davies to W. J. Lenahan, April 11, 1941, no. 269, W. J. Lenahan to F. A. Davies, April 21, 1941, no. 270, Rodgers memorandum, April 27, 1944, reprinted in *Arabian Oil Hearings,* 25392, 25394, 25380–87.

22. F. A. Davies to W. J. Lenahan, April 11, 1941, no. 269, Rodgers memorandum, April 27, 1944, reprinted in *Arabian Oil Hearings,* 25392, 25380–87.

23. Shwadran, *MEOGP,* pp. 316–17; Rodgers memorandum, April 27, 1944, reprinted in *Arabian Oil Hearings,* 25380–87.

Fuel Administration. When the war ended he returned to Jersey Standard, where he was promoted after 1924 to senior vice-president in charge of all foreign and domestic sales. In 1933 Moffett resigned after a spat with company president Walter Teagle. Socal employed him immediately as a consultant, and he soon went to work full time for Socal subsidiaries.

In 1933 Moffett also helped to draft the Oil Code under the NRA and sat on its planning and coordinating committee. In 1934 Roosevelt named him Federal Housing Administrator, although his qualifications for the job eluded most observers. He stayed only a year, but in that time he managed to provoke Harold Ickes, with whom he clashed over the new public housing program. Moffett won that encounter when the president scrapped Ickes's scheme for low-cost housing under federal control in favor of Moffett's plan for middle-income housing to be constructed by private companies. Two years later, in 1936, his earlier work for Socal paid off when he was named chairman of the board of the Bahrein Petroleum Company, which he had organized to handle Socal's Bahrain concession. Subsequently he took up the same position with Caltex.

Moffett owed his success in the oil business to talent and ambition, but his career as a Washington bureaucrat was the result of his friendship with the president. He met Roosevelt during the First World War, when he and the then assistant secretary of the navy worked together on Allied oil problems. The two maintained contact after the war, and over the years Moffett became Roosevelt's unofficial adviser on oil matters. Moffett also served as a trustee of the Warm Springs Foundation, an organization set up by Roosevelt to transform the rickety health resort at Warm Springs, Georgia, into a treatment center for polio victims. Because Roosevelt, crippled by the disease himself, spent much time there swimming in the therapeutic waters, Moffett had easy and regular access to the president.[24]

On April 9, 1941, Moffett met with Roosevelt in Washington and

24. *Arabian Oil Hearings,* 24707–709; Ickes, *Secret Diary,* vol. 3, p. 62; *NYT,* March 3, 1944; *Oil and Gas Journal,* February 24, 1949; William E. Leuchtenburg, *F. D. R. and the New Deal* (New York, 1963), p. 135; Schlesinger, *Crisis of the Old Order,* p. 373; *Arabian Oil Hearings,* 24711.

explained in detail the conditions in Saudi Arabia. Stressing the loyalty of the king to the Allied cause, Moffett emphasized the prestige Ibn Saud commanded in the Arab world and among Moslems everywhere. The king was desperate now, Moffett said, and the oil company could no longer "continue the growing burden and responsibility of financing an independent country, particularly under the present abnormal conditions." Unless Saudi Arabia received the necessary financial assistance, Ibn Saud had, as Moffett put it, "grave fears for the stability of his country."[25]

Although the situation looked grim, Moffett had a solution. He proposed that the United States government loan "five or six million dollars annually" to the king for the next five years. Casoc would then waive title to an unspecified amount of oil in the ground, which would serve as collateral for the loan. If the Saudis defaulted, the company would produce and ship the oil to the United States at a charge to be mutually agreed upon. To supplement the loan, Moffett suggested that the State Department ask the British to increase their annual subsidies. He warned the president, however, that "any British advances should be on a political and military basis and should not involve their getting any oil from this concession." In fact, he maintained, "the . . . Government should procure a commitment from the British that neither the Government nor any company of British nationality, nor a British National will during the life of the present concession, either directly or indirectly, attempt to acquire any interest therein, or take any other action in derogation of such concession." Having laid bare the company's distrust of the British, Moffett made two final recommendations, which revealed Casoc's desire for more active American involvement in Saudi Arabia: the appointment of a "combination Minister and Consul" residing permanently at Jidda and the selection of an American-approved financial adviser to the king.[26]

25. *Arabian Oil Hearings,* 25379.

26. *Arabian Oil Hearings,* 25379–80, 24838–39. Moffett stipulated that, to avoid competition with Casoc and its subsidiaries, the United States government would have to move the crude oil and its products "outside an area approximately as follows: Egypt, the east coast of Africa, South Africa, Australasia, India, the Straits Settlement, China, Japan, and possibly the Philippines."

The president, though interested, had misgivings about the plan. Since the country was not yet at war, Roosevelt had to move cautiously if he wanted to continue aiding the Allies without aggravating congressional criticism. He knew of no legislation that would permit him to lend $6 million to a neutral regime that was under the mantle of the British Empire. He told Moffett that, under the circumstances, the government could not buy "oil in the ground." He would be willing, though, to consider purchasing finished petroleum products from the Saudi government to build up supplies at new American naval bases. Since tankers were scarce and transporting the products would be a problem, Roosevelt also offered to place four Danish vessels recently acquired by the government at the disposal of the company.[27]

The president's sympathetic response left Moffett encouraged. Within a few days of the meeting he received a telegram from the White House asking for a copy of the proposal. After conferring with Davies and Hamilton, Moffett on April 16 sent a memorandum that confirmed his interview with the president and incorporated Roosevelt's suggestions into a new plan for rescuing the king. Instead of using Arabian oil reserves as collateral for an American loan, the company now proposed that the United States government buy annually from the Saudis $6 million worth of oil products at a reduced rate for the next five years. Casoc would contract with the king to produce and to load those products at a Persian Gulf port, while the king would agree to waive royalties on an amount of crude equivalent to $6 million at current royalty rates. Moffett again asked for an increase in British advances and repeated his warning that the British should not receive repayment in oil for that increase. In case anyone failed to recognize the importance of the proposal, Moffett concluded that, "unless this is done, and soon, this independent kingdom, and perhaps the entire Arab world, will be thrown into chaos."[28]

Though no one seriously believed that the Middle East would col-

27. Moffett to Roosevelt, April 16, 1941, NA, Records of the Reconstruction Finance Corporation, Record Group 234, hereafter cited as RG 234, Petroleum Reserves Corporation–War Assets Corporation File, Folder 1; Murray to Hull, May 10, 1941, *FRUS* (1941), vol. 3, pp. 632–33.

28. *Arabian Oil Hearings,* 25383; Shwadran, *MEOGP,* p. 317; Moffett to Roosevelt, April 16, 1941, NA, RG 234, Petroleum Reserves Corporation–War Assets Corporation File, Folder 1.

lapse if the Saudi government declared bankruptcy, Wallace Murray, chief of the State Department's Near East Division, did believe that the United States could not allow Ibn Saud's regime to falter. Murray regarded the Middle East as his province, a province he had come to know intimately since his tour of duty at the American embassy in Iran during the 1920s. Secretary Hull relied on Murray for advice about the region. Murray, in turn, offered ready counsel, sprinkled generously with his own biases. Among them were a deep distrust of the British and the Russians and a fear of the effects of untutored public opinion. In this instance Murray believed that, because Ibn Saud was "unquestionably the outstanding figure in the Arab world, a good case can be made out in favor of granting him financial support." Although Murray was willing to ask the British to increase their aid, he insisted that an American grant should also be made. Toward that end he formulated an alternative plan that avoided what he saw as the pitfalls of Moffett's scheme.

Murray feared that if the navy were unable to use the entire $6 million worth of petroleum products the government would be forced to sell the remainder in competition with private oil companies. Because Moffett had stipulated that the government must sell any unused products outside of his company's Pacific market, Murray argued that the administration might be open to charges that "the commercial part of Mr. Moffett's proposal was of direct benefit to the California Arabian Standard Oil Company and that the proposal was designed to relieve the company of the difficult situation in which it had been placed." Murray planned instead to combine direct purchases of petroleum with the extension of Lend-Lease assistance. That way the government would buy only as much petroleum as it needed, while still furnishing the Saudis with money and supplies. "Such help," he noted late in April 1941, "might be extended in return for satisfactory political assurances and commitments by Ibn Saud." Doubtless those commitments involved aiding the Allies and keeping the American oil concession secure.[29]

29. Murray to Hull, April 21, 1941, *FRUS* (1941), vol. 3, pp. 633–34. On Wallace Murray, see Ickes Diaries, vol. 52, 8570–71, 8576; Mark H. Lytle, "Oil and Conflict: The United States, Iran and the Cold War," chap. 2, p. 12 (manuscript in author's possession).

While State Department officials urged Murray's scheme on the president, Harry Hopkins, Roosevelt's close friend and adviser, came up with a similar solution. "It occurred to me," Hopkins wrote the influential Secretary of Commerce Jesse Jones in June 1941, "that some of it [assistance to Arabia] might be done in the shipment of food under the Lend-Lease Bill, although just how we could call that outfit a 'democracy' I don't know." Hopkins was referring to the type of Lend-Lease aid that Congress had agreed to supply to the "democratic allies" of the United States. Because he realized that Jones, a towering Texan who was head of the federal lending agencies, would have much to say about any financial arrangements with Saudi Arabia, he asked him to look into the matter. "The RFC [Reconstruction Finance Corporation]," Hopkins concluded hopefully, "has done some funny things since that man from Houston [referring to Jones] took charge of it."[30]

The oil company also knew who would determine the fate of its proposal. During the spring of 1941 its representatives became fixtures at the State Department, where Murray and Secretary Hull encouraged their overtures. Moffett called on navy secretary Frank Knox in May, and later that month he accompanied Texaco board chairman W. S. S. Rodgers on one of his many visits to Jones's office. Both Knox and Jones gave the company a chilly reception. Knox, formerly publisher of the Chicago *Daily News* and a voice for moderate internationalism in Republican circles, regarded the loan as a political matter, the outcome of which did not interest the navy. After conducting an investigation, he reported to the president that, although he would like the United States to secure the military support of Ibn Saud, he found the sulfur content of the king's oil too high for navy use.[31]

30. Paul Alling memorandum, May 13, 1941, *FRUS* (1941), vol. 3, pp. 633–34; Hopkins to Jesse Jones, June 14, 1941, reprinted in *Arabian Oil Hearings*, 25415; Alling memorandum, June 18, 1941, *FRUS* (1941), vol. 3, p. 638. Whether Hopkins came up independently with the idea of using Lend-Lease remains unclear. Hopkins had discussed the question of extending financial assistance to Saudi Arabia with the president before he wrote Jones, and the president had already conferred with State Department officials.

31. Alling memorandum, April 29, 1941, Murray to Hull, May 10, 1941, Alling memorandum, May 15, 1941, John D. Jernegan memorandum, August 7, 1941, *FRUS*

Jones was no more reassuring. Without him the oil company stood little chance of success, not only because of his control over federal lending but also because of his ties to powerful southerners on the Hill. Jones wanted to oblige the oil company, but he could see no way of accommodating Moffett's plan under existing legislation. When he later suggested creating the necessary capital through a purely commercial arrangement between Casco and the United States government, Moffett rejected the idea, claiming that such help would have a less "salutary effect" on the king and on the Arab world; only direct aid from the United States to Saudi Arabia would do.[32]

As they searched for an acceptable way to render assistance to the Saudis, American officials also appealed to the British to step up their advances. In mid-May the president decided to defer any decision on Moffett's proposals until he could discover what the British were prepared to contribute. Through the spring and summer Hull and his staff discussed the matter with members of the British embassy in Washington.[33]

The British were anxious to comply. They thought that a program of Anglo-American aid to Saudi Arabia might quell anti-British feeling among Arab nationalists, who resented British influence over the Middle East. Collaboration with the Americans would appear to check British power in the area by linking Great Britain to a country with professed anticolonial sentiments. By the end of May 1941 the British had deposited an additional £200,000 into Ibn Saud's coffers, and in

(1941), vol. 3, pp. 629–32, 632–33, 634–35, 643–45; Thornburg to Stoner, September 29, 1941, Lloyd Hamilton notes, May 13–15, 1941, reprinted in *Arabian Oil Hearings,* 25480–82; Alling memorandum, May 10, 1941, Frank Knox to Roosevelt, May 20, 1941, *FRUS* (1941), vol. 3, pp. 633–36.

32. *Arabian Oil Hearings,* 25383–84; Jones to Hopkins, July 22, 1941, NA, RG 234, Petroleum Reserves Corporation–War Assets Corporation File, Folder 1. To meet Jones's objections, Rodgers even had his legal counsel draw up memoranda explaining precisely how the loan could be made under existing legislation, *Arabian Oil Hearings,* 25436–38; Moffett to Jones, July 22, 1941, NA, RG 234, Petroleum Reserves Corporation–War Assets Corporation File, Folder 1.

33. Alling memorandum, May 13, 1941, *FRUS* (1941), vol. 3, pp. 633–34; Hull memorandum, May 7, 1941, Murray memorandum, May 29, 1941, Alling memorandum, July 2, 1941, *FRUS* (1941), vol. 3, p. 632, 636–37, 639–40; Thornburg notes, May 8, 1941, reprinted in *Arabian Oil Hearings,* 25478–79.

July they gave the king free of charge nearly $2 million in newly minted Saudi coins. The British hoped, Minister-Consul Neville Butler told Wallace Murray, that now "the United States Government could see its way clear to offer financial assistance to Saudi Arabia."[34]

To the dismay of the British and of oil company managers, Roosevelt could find no way of supplying direct aid for the king. Lend-Lease, still a new device for supporting the Allies, had already provoked criticism. With the United States not yet at war, the president was unwilling to risk confrontation with congressional isolationists over assistance to neutral Saudi Arabia. Despite a formal plea from the king, Roosevelt, on Jones's advice, decided in July 1941 that the British should handle the finances. "Will you tell the British," he wrote Jesse Jones in mid-July, "I hope they can take care of the King of Saudi Arabia. This is a little far afield for us!"[35]

When Jones met with British treasury officials in August to discuss closing a $425 million loan from the United States, he showed them Roosevelt's note and requested that they supply the king with the necessary funds from the American loan. Two months later he informed Moffett that, although he could find no method of advancing money himself to the Saudis, he had asked the British ambassador, at the insistence of the president and of the secretary of state, to furnish Ibn Saud with his requirements. Jones added, "The oil companies interested might, if they wanted to do so, work out some arrangement between the British Government and the King."[36]

The oil men were prepared to deal with Great Britain, though they remained suspicious of British designs on Arabia. Those fears, however, were subordinate to their desire to relieve the company of the financial burden imposed by the king's demands, even if it meant shifting the entire load to Britain. Company managers had already

34. *Arabian Oil Hearings,* 25478–79.

35. *Arabian Oil Hearings,* 25445; Jones to Hull, August 6, 1941, *FRUS* (1941), vol. 3, pp. 642–43. Jones apparently wrote the note, which Roosevelt then signed. Jesse Jones, *Fifty Billion Dollars* (New York, 1951), pp. 241–42.

36. Jones, *Fifty Billion Dollars,* pp. 241–42; Jones to Moffett, October 9, 1951, reprinted in *Arabian Oil Hearings,* 25384.

begun laying the groundwork for increased British payments when it appeared as though more assistance from London might facilitate an American loan. The oil men had carried information between the two governments and had cultivated old acquaintances at the British embassy in Washington, where they suggested that cooperating with the Americans might buoy declining British prestige among Arabs. And, while keeping the British ambassador at Jidda informed of their own progress in the United States, they had coaxed him to persuade his government that additional aid from Great Britain was essential.[37]

In September 1941, when Casoc officers learned that no American financial assistance would be forthcoming, they became anxious over the possibility, as they described it, of "being placed in a three cornered squeeze play," with both the British and the Saudis pressing them for more and more money. They dealt firmly with the king: $3 million, they told him, was the "absolute maximum" he would receive from the company during 1941 and again in 1942. At the same time they supported the Saudis in their effort to have the British make up the balance of the king's deficit. "Getting British to accept responsibility most logical constructive solution of immediate problems," Casoc representative Roy Lebkicher wired from Jidda in October 1941, "and also offers permanent solution which United States Government loan does not." With the concurrence of the home office, Lebkicher passed his opinion on to the Saudi director of mines and to

37. For example, before his appointment as Petroleum Adviser to the State Department and while he was still within the Socal organization, Max Thornburg had a number of meetings in May 1941 with his friend Sir Vivian Gabriel, a British official of long service in the Middle East but at the time attached to the British Air Mission in Washington. Gabriel and Minister-Counsel Neville Butler were concerned over the spread of anti-British sentiment among Arabs. Thornburg suggested that Anglo-American collaboration in assisting Ibn Saud might assuage those sentiments. The idea excited Gabriel, who became an active promoter of the scheme. Thornburg notes, May 9, 1941, Gabriel to Thornburg, May 12, 1941, Gabriel to Thornburg, May 23, 1941, Hamilton notes, May 13-15, 1941, W. J. Lenahan to F. A. Davies, May 26, 1941, no. 281, Davies to Lenahan, June 2, 1941, no. 290, Lenahan to Davies, June 2, 1941, no. 283, Davies to Lenahan, June 9, 1941, no. 294, reprinted in *Arabian Oil Hearings*, 25478-83, 25421-22; Alling memoranda, May 13, 1941, May 15, 1941, *FRUS* (1941), vol. 3, pp. 633-35.

the British minister. A month later, under pressure from the Roosevelt administration, the Saudi government, and the oil company, the British agreed to continue and to increase their payments to the king.[38]

Company executives never abandoned efforts, in their words, to "educate Washington" about the king's needs, but they did alter their techniques. During 1942 they kept the State Department apprised of their own and of British advances to Ibn Saud. They made no mention of the alarm they might have felt over British encroachment. On the contrary, their dispatches described the British as disinterested collaborators who had, according to one company cable, not "the slightest inclination to gain political advantages . . . or to infringe upon the country's sovereignty." No longer was the assistance of the United States government essential; now it was merely "a pity that America is not contributing and collaborating." Like Great Britain, the United States too could reap rewards from assisting Ibn Saud, whose goodwill would be valuable to the war effort.[39]

Official government interest in Saudi Arabia grew after American entry into the war. American supply routes across the Middle East to Russia and the Allied campaign in North Africa, launched in the spring of 1942, required, as Secretary Hull later recalled, "stability in the Near East, toward which end stability in Saudi Arabia was essential." Military operations also required, Hull added, transit rights over

38. Davies to Lenahan, September 4, 1941, no. 311, F. W. Ohliger to Davies, September 17, 1941, no. 766, reprinted in *Arabian Oil Hearings,* 25426; Davies to Roy Lebkicher, October 13, 1941, no. 316, Lebkicher to Davies, October 16, 1941, no. 308, Lebkicher and Ohliger to Davies, November 17, 1941, no. 318, Rodgers memorandum, April 27, 1944, reprinted in *Arabian Oil Hearings,* 25428–29, 25432, 25380–87; Lebkicher to Davies, October 16, 1941, no. 308, reprinted in *Arabian Oil Hearings,* 25428–29; Davies to Lebkicher, October 28, 1941, no. 321, reprinted in *Arabian Oil Hearings,* 25430; Lebkicher to Davies, November 3, 1941, no. 313, Davies to Lebkicher, November 3, 1941, no. 322, Lebkicher to Davies, November 7, 1941, no. 316, Lebkicher and Ohliger to Davies, November 17, 1941, no. 318, reprinted in *Arabian Oil Hearings,* 25431–33; Alling memorandum, November 4, 1941, *FRUS* (1941), vol. 3, p. 651.

39. Davies to Lebkicher, October 9, 1941, no. 314, reprinted in *Arabian Oil Hearings,* 25427; Roy Lebkicher memorandum, "The Situation in Saudi Arabia—February 1942," February 26, 1942, Lebkicher, "Notes on British Aid to Saudi Arabia," May 22, 1942, NA, RG 59, 890F.6363 Standard Oil Company/138, 143.

and airfields on Arabian soil. Toward those ends, and with an eye on relieving the king's disappointment, President Roosevelt approved in January 1942 Ibn Saud's request for an agricultural mission, and in May he ordered the opening of an American legation at Jidda.[40]

Meanwhile, Casoc managers were growing dissatisfied with the settlement they had helped to arrange. British gold, although easing the financial drain on the company, increased its fears about British sway over the king. The company felt that the British government was receiving credit that really belonged to the United States, since British advances were possible only because of American aid. Rising British influence in Arabia had frightening corollaries for the oil men. "We felt," chairman W. S. S. Rodgers of Texaco later said, "that if it were left to Britain to make all the necessary advances to the king, Britain would be able to do this because of the aid she would be receiving from the United States through lend-lease; but if this happened Britain's prestige and influence in Saudi Arabia would be so enhanced that ultimately that country might be drawn into the so-called sterling area and we might not be able to maintain the American character of our enterprise."[41]

Company executives became convinced that the British were devising all sorts of schemes to deprive them of their concession. When the British suggested reforming the Saudi Arabian currency system to stabilize the Saudi economy and to control their own cash payments to the king, Casoc president Fred A. Davies described it as "one of the most obvious steps that . . . we had been afraid of all the time out there, the encroachment of the British into the oil picture." A team of British experts ostensibly sent to Arabia to combat locusts was in fact, according to the company, a secret mission for surveying potential concession sites. The company even refused reimbursement from the British

40. Hull, *Memoirs,* vol. 2, p. 1512; Alling to Sumner Welles, September 27, 1941, Hull to Alexander Kirk, September 26, 1941, *FRUS* (1941), vol. 3, pp. 650–51, 658–59; Hull to Kirk, February 6, 1942, Welles to Roosevelt, February 12, 1942, Berle to Twitchell, March 19, 1942, Welles to Murray, February 12, 1942, Welles to Murray, May 1, 1942, *FRUS* (1942), vol. 4, p. 559, 561–62, 565.

41. *Arabian Oil Hearings,* 25091, 24805.

for installing apparatus that would prevent the enemy from using local oil wells, if the country were overrun.[42]

For its part, the British government was not interested in divesting the oil company of its concession. Since oil holdings in Iran and in other Middle Eastern countries were sufficient to satisfy empire needs from the area, Great Britain had no desire to provoke its creditor—the United States government—over Arabian oil. Rather, the British wished only to remain in the good graces of the king, whose political support was, as one Foreign Office official later observed, "too important to us, in view of the large Moslem populations with which we have to deal and the most delicate Arab questions which are pending (especially Palestine), for us to be able to afford to offend him." Their primary concern was to hold subsidies from their war-drained treasury to a minimum. Restructuring the Saudi economy and advising the king on fiscal matters were part of Britain's solution to that problem, not the perfidious plan oil men had suspected. In fact, responsible financial administration was a goal of the company as well and had been one of the reasons for Moffett's earlier recommendation that a financial adviser be appointed to the king's court.[43]

Lend-Lease to Saudi Arabia

By 1943 the oil men could no longer contain their fears. Afraid of losing, if not their entire concession, then at least "a portion of our control," as Rodgers put it, and unwilling to make any more advances

42. *Ibid.*, 25094–95; 24830; U. S., Congress, Senate, Foreign Relations Committee, *Hearings, Petroleum Agreement with Great Britain and Northern Ireland,* 80th Cong., 1st Sess. (Washington, 1947), hereafter cited as *AAOA Hearings,* 114; Hull to Cairo Legation, August 26, 1942, NA, RG 59, 890F.6363/40.

43. Llewellyn Woodward, *British Foreign Policy in the Second World War* (London, 1962), p. 399; Payton-Smith, *Oil,* p. 16, 24–25; Feis, *Three International Episodes,* p. 111; Baxter memorandum, "Anglo-American Discussions: Saudi Arabia," March 16, 1944, PRO, FO 371, E1775/128/25. For further examples of continuing British desire to retain the goodwill of Ibn Saud and to cooperate with the United States in aiding the Saudi government, see Jordan to Anthony Eden, September 6, 1944, no. 88, PRO, FO 371, E5672/128/25; Moyne to Eden, September 29, 1944, PRO, FO 371, E6177/128/25; *Arabian Oil Hearings,* 25379–80.

to the king, Rodgers and Socal president Harry D. Collier again solicited the aid of the United States government. During the first two weeks of February Collier and Rodgers repeatedly impressed upon several high-level officials the importance of the Arabian concession, now in their view endangered by the possibility of cancellation and renegotiation with the British. They suggested extending Lend-Lease assistance to Arabia as a way of offsetting British influence and of maintaining the American character of the enterprise.[44]

After meeting with the oil men early in February, Harold Ickes, concerned as petroleum administrator over wartime depletion of domestic reserves, offered to put the company's case before the president. A conference with Roosevelt helped to produce the desired effect. On February 16, 1943, Roosevelt informed Lend-Lease administrator Edward R. Stettinius, Jr., that "the defense of Saudi Arabia is vital to the defense of the United States" and ordered the extension of Lend-Lease aid. In July 1943 the State Department raised its chargé d' affaires at Jidda to the rank of Minister Resident.[45]

44. During their visit to Washington, Collier and Rodgers saw Ickes, Murray, and Paul Alling of the Near East Division of the State Department, Secretary of War Stimson, Navy Secretary Knox, Under Secretary of the Navy James Forrestal, and Under Secretary of State Sumner Welles. Max Thornburg, at the time Petroleum Adviser to the State Department, acted as go-between for the oil men at the State Department and made appointments for them to see department officials. Thornburg to Welles, Murray, Alling, February 3, 1943, NA, RG 59, 800.6363/1105; Ickes Diaries, vol. 46, 7425–26; U.S., Congress, Senate, *Congressional Record,* 80th Cong., 2nd Sess. (Washington, 1948), vol. 94, pt. 4, 4947.

45. *Congressional Record,* 80th Cong., 2nd Sess., vol. 94, pt. 4, 4948. Ickes later disclaimed any responsibility for having convinced the president to extend Lend-Lease assistance to Saudi Arabia. "I do not think," he said in 1947, "that I ever recommended to the President that he cut Saudi Arabia in on lend-lease." Ickes did, however, seem interested enough in the oil men's suggestion to request a memorandum from them at the time. If Ickes did object to making Saudi Arabia eligible for Lend-Lease, the president did not take his advice. *Arabian Oil Hearings,* 25233, 25236; Roosevelt to Stettinius, February 18, 1943, *FRUS* (1943), vol. 4, p. 859; Hull, *Memoirs,* vol. 2, p. 1512. The decision of the State Department to raise the status of the American representative at Jidda from chargé d'affaires to minister resident was based on similar considerations as the decision to extend Lend-Lease assistance. Alling to Erhardt and Shaw, March 10, 1943, NA, RG 59, 124.90F/31a. In addition, Hull included the interest of the War and Navy departments in obtaining oil reserves in Saudi Arabia as one of his reasons for making the recommendation. Hull to Roosevelt, March 30, 1943, *FRUS* (1943), vol. 4, p. 830.

The intercession of Rodgers and Collier was probably unnecessary, although their presence in Washington likely added weight to their case and may even have converted some doubting officials. A month before the oil men arrived in Washington, the State Department had recommended that Saudi Arabia be declared eligible for Lend-Lease assistance. Dean Acheson, then assistant secretary of state and always an impeccable internationalist, justified the move on several grounds. Saudi Arabia, he argued, lay along vital Allied supply routes; yet it was the only major Middle Eastern country so far deemed unworthy of aid. The king, with enormous prestige and influence in the Arab world, had already been "highly sympathetic" to the Allied cause and now needed help. Without it, he might be unwilling to grant privileges in addition to the flyover rights he had recently allowed. "Lend-Lease assistance," Acheson concluded, "would constitute recognition of his loyal and courageous attitude and facilitate the prosecution of the war.'"[46]

Although he made no mention of it, Acheson also may have seen the aid as a way of helping the British. The assistant secretary, a staunch anglophile always concerned about the shaky condition of British finances, was pressing to elevate their gold and dollar balances. American assistance to Ibn Saud was congruent with that view, since it would relieve the British of financial pressure from the king. Even without that additional justification, Lend-Lease administrator Stettinius had approved, and on January 12, 1943, well in advance of the oil men's arrival, he had sent his recommendation to the White House.[47]

Missing from Acheson's endorsement was any reference to oil. He was doubtless aware of its importance, because the Near East Division's proposal for extending Lend-Lease had specifically noted it. That recommendation, sent to Acheson in December 1942, had pointed to the Arabian oil fields as among the most promising in the world and had warned that British penetration might threaten American ownership of the concession. Perhaps Acheson had failed to refer

46. Acheson to Stettinius, January 9, 1943, *FRUS* (1943), vol. 4, p. 854.
47. Stettinius to Acheson, January 12, 1943, *FRUS* (1943), vol. 4, p. 855.

to oil in order to avoid a divisive issue. All the same, whether Acheson acknowledged it or not, oil had played a role in the department's decision to recommend Lend-Lease assistance.[48]

In 1943, when the United States extended Lend-Lease to Saudi Arabia and raised the level of diplomatic representation there, Casoc managers saw important company goals realized. The presence of official political and economic support ensured that they would no longer have to sustain the Saudi government alone; that their standing with the king would be enhanced; and that their concession would be protected from foreign, particularly British, incursion. Only the military exigencies of war now threatened their enterprise. The oil men could be sure that the United States and its allies were doing everything in their power to end that threat too.

The United States government had become incrementally involved in Saudi Arabia. For ten years oil men had worked to keep official attention on the country, but oil alone had not been enough to warrant official action. In the end, war necessitated involvement. Only after oil joined with pressing strategic incentives did the government act conclusively. Even so, oil had been among the considerations, and the whole episode underscored the absence of a coherent approach to the operations of American oil companies in the Middle East. As relations with Saudi Arabia indicated, Washington no longer looked on the Middle East as a British preserve, too remote for American attention. More and more the region assumed importance because of its oil. As it did, the need for developing a foreign oil policy became more compelling.

48. Alling memorandum to Acheson, Berle, December 20, 1942, NA, RG 59, 890F.24/20.

3 / The Genesis of Foreign Oil Policy

When Casoc managers first approached the president in 1941, he had already directed his staff to begin drafting plans for the postwar world. He could not forget the bitter defeats suffered by Woodrow Wilson after the last war. Wilson's portrait hung in the cabinet room, almost a reminder of those trying days. As assistant secretary of the navy, Roosevelt had been captivated by Wilson's vision, if not his conduct. Now, as president, Roosevelt was loath to allow the country to be as ill prepared for shaping the peace as Wilson had left it after the First World War.

The task that Roosevelt assigned his staff did not require the definition of principles to guide the nation, since they had emerged with clarity and force over the past two centuries. What was needed was the application of those doctrines to circumstances that could be but dimly foreseen in the early years of the war. Although the efforts of some planners had no impact until the war ended, the schemes of those responsible for foreign oil, their eyes drawn to the Middle East by appeals from Casoc, became vital components of wartime policy.

Early Efforts

The search for a long-range policy for foreign oil began in 1941. Until then, foreign oil policy, as a discretely defined set of precepts, remained indistinct from the general commercial policy of the United States government. That meant official insistence on (though not always official application of) the principle of nondiscrimination in foreign trade, investment, and commerce, long since enshrined in the phrase Open Door. It also meant making the State Department's "good offices"—the use of department personnel to facilitate communication between disputing parties—available to oil men. In special circumstances it even meant the use of force to protect American property. Such intervention had become increasingly rare after the First World War. Roosevelt's administration had abandoned the use of force altogether as a way of keeping American enterprises safe in time of peace. As a result, formal government policy with respect to American oil companies in foreign lands had, for the most part, left it to oil men to conduct their own diplomacy.[1]

Still, oil continually remained a special case, considered on an ad hoc basis. In the wake of the First World War, when anxiety over the possible exhaustion of American oil intensified Anglo-Ameican competition for new reserves, government officials had become active promoters of an acquisitive policy abroad. They had used promises of reciprocity and threats of exclusion to pressure Europeans into giving American companies access to the oil-rich lands of the Middle East and the Dutch East Indies.[2]

More recently, when the Bolivian government had confiscated American oil property in 1937 and the Mexican government had followed suit in 1938, the response of the United States had come in measured tones, which reflected a new caution in its official support of the oil companies. Roosevelt's desire for friendly relations with his southern neighbors and the need for hemispheric solidarity in the face of war constituted national interests superior to the commercial concerns of the companies. Although the disputes remained unsettled in 1941, the State Department had already begun pressing the oil men to accept Latin American demands for diplomatic negotiations, despite company insistence on juridical arbitration.[3]

Predictably, an oil man brought to Washington as part of the prewar

1. For a succinct description of the principles governing American commercial policy, see Thomas G. Paterson, *Soviet-American Confrontation: Postwar Reconstruction and the Origins of the Cold War* (Baltimore, 1973), pp. 1–29. On oil, see Nash, *U. S. Oil Policy,* pp. 1–156; Blair, *Control of Oil,* pp. 25–183.

2. John A. DeNovo, "The Movement for an Agressive Oil Policy Abroad, 1918–1920," *American Historical Review* (July, 1956), pp. 854–76.

3. Bryce Wood, *The Making of the Good Neighbor Policy* (New York, 1961), pp. 159–282. See also, Herbert S. Klein, "American Oil Companies in Latin America: The

mobilization of business talent first urged the need for refining policy toward American oil companies abroad. Max Thornburg came to the State Department as its petroleum adviser in July 1941 from the Bahrein Petroleum Company, a Middle Eastern subsidiary of Socal and Texaco. His title—special assistant to the under secretary of state—was less a description of function than, as one member of the department described it, a question of "convenience and negotiation." Thornburg's official job was to assist the department's economic advisor, Herbert Feis, in the accumulation of strategic war materials and to advise the department on petroleum matters.[4]

No one in the State Department seems to have questioned Thornburg's connection to the large oil companies that, at the time of his appointment as petroleum advisor, were lobbying for a substantial loan to Saudi Arabia. Officials were no doubt aware of the tie, because Thornburg had already visited the department several times on the companies' behalf. If anything, department officers saw Thornburg's experience with the Bahrein Petroleum Company as an asset. Feis, who recruited Thornburg, later recalled that "even then the importance of middle eastern oil was apparent, and so an individual possessing specialized knowledge . . . promised to be most useful." Those who, like Feis, had participated in the appointment assumed that Thornburg had severed all but "remnant connections" with his private employers. "Remnant connections," Feis explained, might include such things as pension rights, but they would be attachments "of no present significance and not of great amount."[5]

Such was not the case. While serving in the department, Thornburg continued to receive $29,000 annually from the oil companies in addition to his $8,000 government salary. That practice was not unusual. Many business executives brought into government during the war

---

Bolivian Experience,'' *Inter-American Economic Affairs* (Autumn 1964), pp. 47–72. For other examples of the complexities of diplomatic involvement by the United States government, see Mira Wilkins, "Multinational Oil Companies in South America in the 1920s: Argentina, Bolivia, Brazil, Chile, Ecuador, and Peru," *Business History Review* (Autumn 1974), pp. 414–46.

4. Feis, *Three International Episodes,* p. 120; *Arabian Oil Hearings,* 25272.
5. On Thornburg, see chap. 2. *Arabian Oil Hearings,* 25272, 25273, 24857, 25213.

were permitted to make up the difference between their new and old salaries by accepting compensation from former employers. What was unusual in Thornburg's case was that no one appears to have been aware of the arrangement. When Thornburg's connections to the oil companies came to the attention of government authorities in December 1943, Secretary Hull asked for his resignation. Thornburg of course complied, but the whole episode cast a harsh light on his tenure, which might have been diffused by the termination or early disclosure of his company salary.[6]

While in the department, Thornburg continued to see himself and to act not merely as an oil man but as a company man. Correspondence exchanged between Thornburg and Socal vice-president R. C. Stoner in September 1941 illustrates his attitude. Describing his objections to a proposal for sending a government-sponsored agricultural mission to Arabia, Thornburg explained that, although he thought the mission's head, Karl Twitchell, well meaning, "I don't see any good coming out of getting another man into our part of the picture. And, of course, his interests are not ours." By "ours" Thornburg meant the interests of the oil companies.[7]

While other oil men in government, such as Ralph Davies, withdrew their counsel from decisions involving their companies, Thornburg continued to work for Socal interests. He lobbied in Washington for the Moffett plan before his appointment and, after becoming petroleum adviser, continued to press for government involvement in Arabia. He kept the home office of Socal apprised of oil policy developments through letters detailing his conversations with other members of the department. He also advised the company on the

6. The full extent of Thornburg's connections with the oil companies was not revealed until after the war during the Senate investigation of American petroleum arrangements with Saudi Arabia. Secretary of State Cordell Hull informed two members of Congress a few months after asking for Thornburg's resignation that he had asked Thornburg to leave the State Department after he "learned of his [Thornburg's] former affiliations with the Standard Oil Company of California." Memorandum of Hull conversation with Maloney and Smith, May 10, 1944, NA, RG 59, 800.6363/1736; Hull, *Memoirs,* vol. 2, p. 1517.

7. Thornburg to Reginald Stoner, September 29, 1941, reprinted in *Arabian Oil Hearings,* 25444–45.

most effective tactics to employ with its own and with foreign governments.[8]

Thornburg did not seek or receive from any oil company orders directing his actions. He would have acted no differently had he received no salary at all from Socal. Thornburg was a businessman with a lifetime of associations in the oil industry and with an outlook guided by business concerns. As a private citizen or as a public servant, he advanced projects and policies designed to support the oil industry abroad because he genuinely believed in the coincidence of national and commercial interests. All the same, by directing at least some of his attention toward the welfare of his own company, he tainted his activities with the suspicion that whatever he did as petroleum adviser was expressly for the benefit of Socal.[9]

Shortly after coming to the State Department, Thornburg broke away from Feis's staff and began, in Feis's words, "operating as a semi-independent branch of the department." None of Thornburg's superiors objected. The duties of a special assistant were vague enough to give any incumbent latitude in defining his responsibilities. Thornburg's expertise in oil made establishing his own office especially easy. He alone possessed specialized knowledge of a commodity vital to the war effort. With that knowledge, he was able to work on his own and to capitalize on competition from other agencies for control of foreign oil matters. In the State Department, already sensitive to its declining role in making foreign policy, that tactic enhanced Thornburg's position.[10]

8. *Arabian Oil Hearings,* 25444–45. Though only one letter has become public, it seems reasonable to assume from the contents of the correspondence that there were other such letters. Harold Ickes, for example, claimed after the war that he had thought all along that Thornburg's, as Ickes put it, "principal interest . . . in Government, was to protect the interests of the big integrated companies." *Arabian Oil Hearings,* 25212.

9.A perusal of some of Thornburg's early projects, like his proposed study of American foreign oil policy or his recommendation for the covert reentry of American oil companies into Mexico, indicates that at least some of his aims were to ensure government support for the operations of American oil companies abroad. See, for example, Thornburg memorandum, "Foreign Oil Policy of the United States," October 20, 1941, NA, RG 48, File 1–188: Petroleum Administration, Folder 2827; Thornburg to Welles, February 8, 1943, FDRL, Roosevelt Papers, President's Secretary's File, hereafter cited as PSF, (88); Thornburg to Messersmith, March 10, 1943, NA, RG 48, File 1–188: Petroleum Administration, Folder 2828.

10. *Arabian Oil Hearings,* 25272.

In October 1941 Thornburg, now working out of his own office, commissioned a study of national policy for foreign oil under the direction of Walton C. Ferris, a member of his staff. While at Socal Thornburg had begun a similar project whose purpose was twofold: to unify the overseas policies of major American oil companies and to bring them into harmony with government policy. Before he could finish he was called to government service.[11]

In November Ferris sent Thornburg a detailed prospectus, "Project for Study of United States Foreign Oil Policy." As Thornburg had directed, Ferris focused on the long-term aspects of foreign oil policy. Although the available information could not describe all the problems with which oil policy would have to contend, the data did indicate two of the most pressing ones: how to use foreign oil to conserve domestic reserves, and how to deal with a probable clash after the war between the United States and Great Britain for reserves abroad. Ferris offered no clear-cut solutions, but he did suggest that increasing oil imports would forestall dependence on foreign petroleum by reducing the drain on domestic reserves. He also predicted that diminishing domestic oil resources would force the United States, regardless of imports, to pursue a "more and more aggressive foreign oil policy aimed at assuring access to petroleum overseas."[12]

During the next year Thornburg promoted the project. He circulated Ferris's prospectus among the divisional and regional offices of the State Department, and he continually urged his superiors to lend their assistance to developing a national policy for foreign oil. "The fact is," he wrote Under Secretary of State Sumner Welles in March 1942, "that hardly a week passes without some step being taken which will be significant in fixing some dimension of our post-war oil economy.... No time could be too soon to perceive the general pattern toward which we must be working." Although Welles had approved the project earlier, Thornburg was having trouble obtaining responses from other sections of the department, because their staffs were preoc-

11. Thornburg memo, "Foreign Oil Policy of the United States," October 20, 1941, NA, RG 48, File 1-188: Petroleum Administration, Folder 2827; Thornburg to Welles, January 12, 1943, NA, RG 59, 811.6363/525.
12. Walton Ferris to Thornburg, "Project for Study of U. S. Foreign Oil Policy," November 24, 1941, NA, RG 59, 811.6363/1-2142.

cupied with other wartime problems. Without their involvement and approval, he knew his project might never get under way.[13]

Thornburg did receive a few responses, notable more for the conflicting approaches to postwar problems they revealed than for the criticisms they contained. On one side stood Leroy Stinebower, a tough-minded economist who worked for the adviser on international economic affairs. He had no quarrel with Ferris's analysis. He accepted the assumptions that the postwar period would be characterized by a struggle over the world's resources and by the need to conserve oil reserves at home. Since such circumstances would require each nation to look after its own interests, Stinebower proposed that any petroleum products lend-leased to Great Britain should be repaid in kind after the war. If American oil companies objected to placing such large amounts of petroleum in government hands, Stinebower suggested that "the British turn over certain of their foreign petroleum properties, especially in this hemisphere, rather than deliver the petroleum products themselves."[14]

Nothing came of Stinebower's scheme because, after Pearl Harbor, Roosevelt had come to see the Lend-Lease program as a partnership for pooling common resources in a common effort. Also, reverse Lend-Lease repaid some American oil used by Great Britain during the war. Stinebower's suggestion that the British relinquish some of their holdings in Latin America was too farfetched to merit consideration. The fact that similar proposals reappeared from time to time became one measure of the concern American officials felt over oil reserves and the suspicions they harbored about Anglo-American collaboration after the war.[15]

Members of the department's Division of Commercial Treaties and

13. Thornburg to Welles, January 12, 1943, NA, RG 59, 811.6363/525; Thornburg to Emilio Collado, December 2, 1941, NA, RG 59, 800.6363/1-2142; Thornburg to Wallace Murray, January 5, 1942, NA, RG 59, 800.6363/501-1/2; Thornburg to Welles, March 23, 1942, NA, RG 59, 800.6363/579-1/2; Thornburg to Murray, January 5, 1942, NA, RG 59, 800.6363/501-1/2.

14. Leroy Stinebower to Feis, "Petroleum Policy in the Post-War Era," December 26, 1941, NA, RG 59, 811.6363/12-2641.

15. William Hardy McNeill, *America, Britain and Russia: Their Cooperation and Conflict, 1941-1946* (New York, 1956), p. 772. For an example of another proposal that suggested compensation in the form of British oil property, see James F. Byrnes to Roosevelt, October 15, 1943, reprinted in *Arabian Oil Hearings*, 25430.

Agreements also agreed about the need for developing a national policy for foreign oil, but they found Ferris's approach too pessimistic. His description of a fiercely competitive postwar world contradicted their understanding of the goals of the war and their vision of the peace to follow. To them, reflecting as they did the view that dominated State Department thinking, the war was a fight for international principles. Those principles, best articulated in the Atlantic Charter, would redress the kind of economic imbalances that had led to war and would ensure peace based on unrestricted trade and collective security. Particularly important for any consideration of oil policy were those clauses of the charter that pledged the signatories to seek no territorial aggrandizement and to guarantee all countries equal access to world trade and to raw materials. Ferris, division officials argued, had ignored those principles. He should instead, they believed, stress ways of harmonizing oil policy with the Atlantic Charter. "It is to be hoped," division chief Harry Hawkins wrote, "that the post war world will not be one in which such a cut-throat oil policy would be necessary, and it is suggested that we should formulate and advocate policies now which are designed to bring about and maintain a better world order than the one which set the stage for the present war."[16]

In spite of those views, Thornburg had made some headway by the end of 1942. The department had begun collecting information about petroleum laws abroad, another of Ferris's recommendations. Under Secretary Welles, in addition to endorsing the study, had approved Thornburg's suggestion of attaching petroleum experts to diplomatic missions in key petroleum-producing countries. Pressing on, Thornburg had Ferris draw up an addendum to his prospectus that answered the criticisms and incorporated the advice so far received.[17]

16. Harry Hawkins to Acheson, January 9, 1942, NA, RG 59, 800.6363/514–1/2; for a summary of conversations between T. A. officials and Ferris, see Ferris to Thornburg, January 15, 1942, NA, RG 59, 800.6363/1–2142. The Division of Near Eastern Affairs also responded to Thornburg's proposal. Assistant chief Paul Alling agreed that some type of international petroleum organization would be needed after the war, but he warned that basing such an organization on the model of the multinational Iraq Petroleum Company might produce undesired results. Paul Alling memorandum, May 12, 1942, NA, RG 59, 800.6363/382–1/2.

17. Duggan to Welles, February 10, 1942, NA, RG 59, 800.6363/541–1/2. The petroleum attaché program was originally begun by the Office of the Petroleum Coor-

Late in November 1942 Thornburg presented his case to Dean Acheson. The prospect of the United States becoming an oil importer, he told the under secretary, coupled with deteriorating relations between American oil companies and several Latin American producers, raised an overriding question: "Is our foreign oil policy aimed at maintaining a strong American influence in the distribution of oil throughout the world, thereby both serving our own national interests and keeping us in position to serve weaker nations according to our ideals—or to allow our present and historical strength in this field to pass into other hands?" Simply choosing between those alternatives, Thornburg warned, did not mean that a policy had been formulated. Not until officials had devised ways of carrying out their program would their task be completed.[18]

The Petroleum Reserves Corporation

In answer to the need for developing a foreign oil policy, Secretary Hull created in January 1943 the Committee on International Petroleum Policy, to forecast and to study postwar petroleum problems abroad. Feis chaired the group, which included representatives from each of the department's geographic offices as well as petroleum adviser Thornburg. During the next eight months the committee met sporadically to consider questions ranging from the aims and interests of the United States government in foreign petroleum to the immediate and prospective petroleum problems of key regions. More and more, Feis and his colleagues devoted their attention to an issue causing considerable anxiety in public and private circles—the uncertain future of American oil reserves.[19]

---

dinator in 1941. Frey and Ide, *PAW,* p. 22. For an example of the type of reports the department received from its representatives in oil-producing countries, see Moose to Hull, Enclosure no. 1, July 2, 1943, NA, RG 59, 890F.6363/55. Thornburg to Welles, "Post-War Arrangements Concerning Oil and the United Nations," March 23, 1942, NA, RG 59, 800.6363/579-1/2. See also, Thornburg to Acheson, May 18, 1942, NA, RG 59, 800.6363/690-1/2; Thornburg memorandum, "Extract from AP Study on a Foreign Oil Policy for Administration," Folder 2827.

18. Thornburg memorandum for discussion at Acheson meeting, November 11, 1942, NA, RG 48, File 1-188: Petroleum Administration, Folder 2827.

19. Feis memorandum, "Meeting Petroleum Policy Study Group," January 11, 1943, NA, RG 59, 800.6363/1091; "Minutes of Committee on International Petroleum

Concern over the exhaustion of domestic reserves reached a new peak during the Second World War. As early as 1941, experts had begun predicting that at current rates of consumption domestic reserves would last no more than fourteen years without new discoveries.[20] Few authorities shared that view, but in 1942 two studies, one conducted by the Petroleum Administration for War and the other by the Petroleum Industry War Council, demonstrated that since the outbreak of war, production had exceeded new discoveries. Furthermore, new discoveries had decreased just when wartime needs were increasing the demand for petroleum and petroleum products. Other figures indicated that although revised estimates of the contents of known fields from 1938 to 1942 had made aggregate proven reserves greater in each successive year, the annual increments to those reserves were diminishing. If those trends continued (and many experts believed they would), the United States was destined to lose self-sufficiency in oil.

There were sound explanations for the slack in new discoveries. Material and manpower, made scarce by the war, were being channeled into other sectors of the economy. The resources that the industry did receive were being used to meet the most pressing deficiencies—shortages of transportation and refining facilities. Calmer souls generally believed that once the war ended, expanded exploration and drilling programs would find new oil to replenish depleted reserves. Even if those measures turned out unsuccessful, the United States still possessed the technology to manufacture all the

---

Policy,'' March 15, 1943, NA, RG 48, File 1-188: Petroleum Administration, Folder 2828; Hull, *Memoirs,* vol. 2, p. 1517.

20. Ferris to Thornburg, Enclosure no. 1, November 24, 1941, NA, RG 59, 800.6363/1-2142; Ickes to Roosevelt, July 7, 1941, FDRL, Roosevelt Papers, PSF (73); Feis to Ralph J. Watkins, September 27, 1941, NA, RG 59, 800.6363/466A; Ralph Davies to Roosevelt, October 15, 1941, FDRL, Roosevelt Papers, PSF (10); Frey and Ide, *PAW,* p. 174; Max W. Ball, ''Report on Oil Situation,'' February 15, 1948, NA, RG 48, File 1-322: Administration, Folder 3178; Reginald Stoner to H. A. Stuart, ''The Importance of Foreign Oil Reserves to the United States,'' December 29, 1942, NA, Records of Interservice Agencies, Record Group 334, hereafter cited as RG 334, ANPB: Petroleum Division, Subject Numeric File, 1942-46, Folder EF-4; U. S., Congress, Senate, Special Committee Investigating Petroleum Resources, *Hearings, American Petroleum Interests in Foreign Countries,* 79th Cong., 1st Sess. (Washington, 1946), 1-2; Herbert Feis, *Petroleum and American Foreign Policy* (Stanford, 1944), pp. 14-15.

petroleum necessary from its huge deposits of natural gas, shale, and coal, though the price of such fuels would be high.[21]

Nineteen forty-three was not a time for calm consideration of the reserve problem. Wartime stresses made reasonable assessments difficult. The invasion of North Africa had driven Allied demands for American petroleum sharply upward in 1942. By 1943 two out of every three tons of cargo shipped to American forces were petroleum or petroleum products. At the same time, the Germans had captured the oil of Rumania and two of the most important Russian fields. It seemed likely that the reserves of the Middle East were their next target. With German submarines disrupting shipping from the Caribbean to the United States and with Pacific oil in the hands of the Japanese, the possibility existed that all the Allied nations might become completely dependent on the United States for oil.[22]

On the home front, chronic transportation problems, the use of petroleum-coke in war industries, and the diversion of oil for diesel-fuel and synthetic-rubber production had brought on gasoline and fuel oil shortages in 1942 and again in 1943. By the end of the year total proven reserves showed a decline for the first time since 1932. The United States indeed seemed to be running out of oil. "During the past year," Commodore Andrew F. Carter, executive officer of the Army-Navy Petroleum Board, wrote early in 1944, "it has become more and more apparent that known petroleum reserves within the continental limits of the United States are inadequate to meet over a period of years either the wartime needs of the United States or the needs of the civilian economy once normal conditions are established."[23]

Not all government and military men shared Carter's pessimism about inadequate petroleum supplies during the war, but they did share

21. Frey and Ide, *PAW,* p. 174; "Oil From Coal," *Collier's,* December 4, 1943, pp. 18-19, 28; Michael Brooks, *Oil and Foreign Policy* (London, 1949), p. 22. Brooks points out that in 1942 and 1943, there was a 40 percent decrease in the number of wells drilled in the United States.

22. Ickes, *Fightin' Oil,* p. 9; Feis, *Three International Episodes,* pp. 96-97.

23. Richard R. Lingeman, *Don't You Know There's a War On?* (New York, 1971), pp. 286-87, 295, 307; Andrew F. Carter to Frank Knox, January 17, 1944, NA, RG 334, File ANPB: 14/1-Foreign Petroleum Policy, Misc. Folder.

his concern for the future. The war had underscored the importance of oil to national security. By 1939 almost all navy vessels and 85 percent of the world's merchant ships used petroleum-based fuels. A typical armored battalion required 17,000 gallons of gasoline to move but 100 miles. In less than two months the United States Fifth Fleet burned 630 million gallons of fuel oil. At the peak of fighting on the western front, the United States Army Air Force by itself consumed fourteen times the total amount of gasoline shipped to Europe for all purposes between 1914 and 1918. With the armed forces using oil at that rate, petroleum administrator Ickes wondered whether the United States could "oil another war." Becoming dependent on other countries for petroleum would endanger that capability. In that event, as Herbert Feis pointed out, "American security, power and freedom would be in peril."[24]

What began as a committee to study international postwar petroleum problems had become by the spring of 1943 a group primarily concerned with safeguarding the reserve position of the United States. In March Feis and his committee, proceeding from the premise that dwindling domestic reserves would compromise the safety of the nation, recommended creating a Petroleum Reserves Corporation to acquire oil overseas. Like the abortive United States Oil Corporation of the early 1920s and like many New Deal agencies, the PRC would be government owned. Its board of directors would be composed of representatives from the State, Navy, War, and Interior departments. To emphasize the primacy of the State Department, its representative would serve as chairman, and the secretary of state would have final approval of all actions. As its first project the committee recommended that the PRC purchase options on Arabian oil.

The committee also suggested studying the feasibility of an international petroleum agreement. Committee members rejected pursuing the agreement until the pattern of the peace settlement became more apparent. In addition, as they observed in their report, "no international agreement could assure one of the underlying aims of the Com-

24. Lon Tinkle, *Mr. De: A Biography of Everett Lee DeGolyer* (New York, 1970), p. 267; Williamson et al., *Age of Energy,* p. 748; Feis, *Three International Episodes,* p. 95, 99.

mittee's proposals—that is, the current protection against impairment of the present overseas oil position of the United States in order to safeguard the interests of the United States in the event that postwar international economic or security arrangements are inadequate.'"[25]

By recommending the postponement of an international agreement, the committee indicated its willingness to proceed unilaterally when national security was involved. Several factors accounted for that departure from multilateralism: the condition of domestic reserves made prompt action imperative; option contracts would place large stockpiles of oil at the government's disposal right away; it might take years to conclude an international agreement, and even then there was no guarantee that the accord would give the United States quick access to foreign reserves. Further, some American oil companies, faced with nationalization of their property in Latin America and with signs of British intrusion in Saudi Arabia, had recently sought assistance from the government. An official claim by the United States to oil in foreign territories might provide those companies with the protection they needed.[26]

The possibility that unilateral action would jeopardize a collective approach to postwar problems appeared a danger to only a few members of the committee. Most agreed that in the end option contracts would not militate against an international pact or against general economic collaboration. As Max Thornburg explained, the contracts could actually be used to promote international cooperation and security. By writing certain conditions into contracts, the United States could exert some control over private activity. "Contracts with oil companies might stipulate," Thornburg said, "that the company must not refuse to sell available oil to any buyer within whatever international security plan is currently in effect." Option contracts would

25. Feis to Hull, "Report of the Committee on International Petroleum Policy," March 22, 1943, NA, RG 59, 800.6363/3–2243. Earlier the committee had recommended that the United States government arrange, as part of the Lend-Lease agreement with Saudi Arabia, for the Saudi government to waive royalties on a specified amount of oil "which this Government may contract for from the California-Arabian Standard Oil Company for reserve purposes." Feis to Acheson, March 3, 1943, NA, RG 59, 811.6363/520–1/2.

26. Feis to Acheson, March 3, 1943, NA, RG 59, 811.6363/520–1/2.

thus be, in his expansive view, a "realistic start" toward putting the Atlantic Charter into effect and promoting international postwar security. "Some of us merely recognize," Thornburg told critics who accused the scheme of subverting the ideals of the charter, "that it isn't the man on the soap box that endows a hospital." He failed to mention that any company could undermine the plan by refusing a contract whose provisions it found too restrictive.[27]

Harold Ickes had been thinking along similar lines for almost two years. He had foreseen the possibility of postwar oil shortages as early as 1941. Since then he had been urging the president to purchase the recently expropriated oil properties in Mexico to meet future requirements. Roosevelt, unwilling to embroil the United States government further in the nationalization controversy, rejected the plan. Early in 1943, when Casoc executives asked Ickes to plead their case, he saw the chance to acquire the needed reserves. He became an advocate of American development of Arabian oil, not by private firms but by the government.[28]

After hearing State Department proposals for option contracts to

27. Representatives from the department's Division of Commercial Treaties and Agreements argued that such unilateral action as the committee recommended indicated a lack of trust on the part of the United States government in a multilateral peace settlement. They believed option contracts would confirm the British in their policy of maintaining tight control of oil resources within their spheres of influence and would hamper the president in proposing international solutions regarding oil problems. Instead, they urged that the United States government first pursue an international agreement, which, if successful, would not prevent the country from taking unilateral action. "Minutes of the Committee on International Petroleum Policy," March 15, 1943, NA, RG 48, File 1-188: Petroleum Administration, Folder 2828. Thornburg to Hull, March 27, 1943, NA, RG 48, File 1-188: Petroleum Administration, Folder 2828; Thornburg to Ickes, March 27, 1943, NA, RG 48, File 1-188: Petroleum Administration, Folder 2828.

28. Ickes to Roosevelt, July 1, 1941, FDRL, Roosevelt Papers, PSF (73); Ickes to Roosevelt, February 20, 1942, NA, RG 48, File 1-188: Petroleum Administration, Folder 2828. Ickes later sent to Roosevelt what Ickes called an "indiscreet memo" written by Max Thornburg. In it Thornburg outlined a plan for having American oil companies return to Mexico in forms other than, as Thornburg put it, "popularly recognizable" ones. Thornburg made no concrete recommendation except that the memorandum be kept confidential, but he continued to press for government support for American oil companies interested in returning to Mexico. Thornburg to Welles, February 8, 1943, FDRL, Roosevelt Papers, PSF (88); Ickes to Roosevelt, March 15, 1943, NA, RG 48, File 1-188: Petroleum Administration, Folder 2828; Bonsal memorandum, May 1, 1943, *FRUS* (1943), vol. 5, p. 461.

obtain Saudi reserves, Ickes sent President Roosevelt in June 1943 a proposal of his own to establish the direct federal control over petroleum that he had sought since the early days of the New Deal. He explained that impending oil shortages would threaten the armed forces and essential civilian industries as early as 1944. He too advised creating a government agency to get hold of oil abroad, but his Petroleum Reserves Corporation, as he also called it, would actually "acquire a proprietary and managerial interest in foreign petroleum reserves." He outlined the functions and membership of the proposed corporation, though he made no mention of State Department participation. The omission reflected Ickes's dislike for Hull as well as his dim view of the department. He suggested that, as its first undertaking, the PRC buy a controlling interest in Casoc. That way, Ickes noted, the United States would get its oil and the concession its protection.[29]

Ickes's colleagues at the Navy Department also elected unilateral action. Like him, they favored exploiting Arabian oil through government purchases of company stock. Navy secretary Frank Knox, always a vigorous crusader, drummed up support for the plan among other members of the cabinet, while Under Secretary William C. Bullitt characteristically went straight to Roosevelt. Ambitious, incisive, and a malicious gossip, Bullitt from time to time enjoyed the confidence of the president. On this occasion he used his access to plead the need for acquiring the Arabian concession. Diminishing reserves and current domestic shortages, he told Roosevelt in June 1943, necessitated obtaining alternate sources of oil "in all quarters of the earth." Saudi Arabia, where he saw British intrigue threatening the

29. Ickes believed that the State Department should take the lead in efforts to secure foreign reserves. He suggested to Thornburg in February 1943 that the department urge the president to appoint a committee of cabinet rank to recommend appropriate action. Ickes to Thornburg, January 29, 1943, LC, Harold Ickes Papers, hereafter cited as Ickes Papers, Secretary of Interior File, Box 220, Oil (25) Folder; Thornburg to Welles, February 18, 1943, NA, RG 59, 800.6363/1101-1/2. For transmission of the report of the Committee on International Petroleum Policy to other cabinet officers, see Hull to Ickes, Stimson, Knox, March 31, 1943, NA, RG 59, 811.6363/524A. Ickes to Roosevelt, June 10, 1943, NA, Records of the Petroleum Administration for War, Record Group 253, hereafter cited as RG 253, Grey Box 2, R. K. Davies File; Ickes Diaries, vol. 47, 7672, 7751.

American-owned concession, could help to meet that necessity. Using the Anglo-Iranian Oil Company—a majority share of which was owned by the British government—as a model, Bullitt urged similar American involvement in Saudi Arabia through the Petroleum Reserves Corporation. Such a corporation should "drive as hard a bargain as possible," acquire no less than 60 percent of Casoc, and finance construction of a refinery on the Persian Gulf. Arabian oil, in short, should not be left to oil men.[30]

The Joint Chiefs of Staff agreed on ends but offered slightly altered means. In a report to the president on June 8, 1943, they too recommended creating a federal corporation to acquire oil abroad, specifically in Saudi Arabia. They added a new twist by suggesting that the corporation first attempt to negotiate a fresh concession with Ibn Saud. "No one doubts about the need of getting the reserves of oil," Secretary of War Henry Stimson observed later that month, "but the question was what method and means to be used in securing them."[31]

The schemes all had drawbacks. Each one increased the risk of touching off an international scramble for oil among the major powers. All ran the danger of intensifying trends toward nationalization in oil-producing countries, which feared the influence of foreign governments even more than that of foreign capital. And none could guarantee the availability of Middle Eastern oil to the United States during war. Wartime access depended less on ownership than on actual physical control of the property.

Of the three plans, the proposal of the Joint Chiefs of Staff offered the least chance of success, since the richest oil-bearing land already

30. Carter to Knox, April 9, 1943, NA, RG 334, File ANPB: 14/1–Foreign Petroleum Policy, Misc. Folder; Carter to Gingrich, April 23, 1943, NA, RG 334, File ANPB: 21/2–Petroleum Reserves—Foreign; Stimson Diary, vol. 43, 94, 99, 104; Feis to Hull, June 10, 1943, NA, RG 59, 890F.6363/80; Feis to Hull, June 11, 1943, NA, RG 59, 890F.6363/79; William Bullitt to the President, June 1943, reprinted in *A Documentary History of the Petroleum Reserves Corporation, 1943–1944* (Washington, 1974), pp. 3–6. Bullitt even went so far as to suggest to Harold Ickes that, as Ickes recalled it, "he wouldn't put it past the British to have King Ibn Saud assassinated, if necessary, and set up a puppet who would see the oil situation through their eyes." Ickes Diaries, vol. 48, 7804.

31. Joint Chiefs of Staff to Roosevelt, June 8, 1943, *FRUS* (1943), vol. 4, pp. 921–22; Stimson Diary, vol. 43, 107.

belonged to Casoc. The stock-acquisition method held greater promise. Purchasing a company would give the government complete control over reserves of proven worth, while it would clearly separate the interests of the government from those of the oil companies. By selling oil produced from the concession or by granting managerial rights to private companies making competitive bids, the government could also create substantial revenue for itself. In addition, the use of military action in defense of the fields, whether because of confiscation or invasion, could be more easily justified to the public if the government actually owned the property. The disadvantage lay in potential resistance, especially in Congress, to having the government enter the oil business—a step, in the view of conservatives, that would undermine free enterprise.

Option contracts could achieve comparable results without the same risks. They too would give the United States access to oil. Because contracts would not directly involve the government in the oil business, they would protect Washington from charges of competing with the private sector. They would also be less likely to bring on nationalization, since relationships between oil companies and local governments would be left untouched.

Option contracts did have liabilities. No matter how carefully they were negotiated, they would still leave the government vulnerable to accusations of using its prestige and resources to benefit specific private interests. Indeed, some officials believed that the government might find itself a junior partner in the very cartel arrangements it condemned. Further, since no one could accurately determine the amount of oil in the ground, private companies could exhaust reserves before the government received its share.

Though they disagreed over details, officials had no trouble reaching a consensus about broad outlines. On June 12, 1943, James F. Byrnes, a kind of assistant president for domestic affairs then serving as director of the Office of War Mobilization, presided over a White House meeting attended by Ickes, Knox, Stimson, Feis, and General Boykin Wright of the War Department. These officials agreed that the government must itself secure new reserves of oil abroad. Toward that end they prescribed the creation of a new government corporation prior to July 1, 1943, to develop oil in Saudi Arabia. A series of inter-departmental meetings held over the next two weeks tackled specifics and produced a proposal for quick purchase of the company.[32]

On June 26, 1943, Hull, Stimson, Ickes, and Acting Navy Secretary James Forrestal endorsed the recommendations of the inter-departmental committee. Roosevelt also approved the findings, and on June 30 the Reconstruction Finance Corporation chartered the PRC. In July the president designated as members of its board of directors the secretaries of state, navy, war, and the interior as well as the director of the Foreign Economic Administration. He selected Ickes as chairman and ordered the board to negotiate with Casoc to purchase all of its stock.[33]

Under Ickes's guidance, the new corporation began planning for, as a disgruntled Hull described it, "the injection of the Government into

32. Hull, *Memoirs,* vol. 2, p. 1518; "Recommendations as to Petroleum Reserves," June 25, 1943, *FRUS* (1943), vol. 4, pp. 925-30. After Byrnes's group reached its decision to recommend creation of the PRC, Hull had Feis draw up a memorandum for the president in which Feis made clear Hull's reluctance to become involved in a controversy over the means for obtaining foreign reserves. After recommending that the government finance a refinery in Saudi Arabia and make agreements with the interested companies for "setting aside such reserves as the Army and Navy deem necessary for their requirements," Hull urged the president to decide the matter. Hull to Roosevelt, "Memorandum for the President," June 14, 1943, NA, RG 59, 800.6363/1243A; Ickes Diaries, vol. 48, 7898-99; Hull, Stimson, Forrestal, Ickes to Roosevelt, June 26, 1943, Enclosure, "Recommendations as to Petroleum Reserves," June 25, 1943, *FRUS* (1943), vol. 4, pp. 924-30. Members of the committee included Herbert Feis of the State Department; Assistant Secretary of War Robert P. Patterson, General Boykin Wright and Colonel William Covell of the War Department; William Bullitt and Captain Andrew F. Carter of the Navy Department; and Abe Fortas of the Interior Department.

33. Hull, Stimson, Forrestal, Ickes to Roosevelt, June 26, 1943, Enclosure, "Recommendations as to Petroleum Reserves," June 25, 1943, *FRUS* (1943), vol. 4, pp. 924-30. *Federal Register,* 8, July 2, 1943, 9044. Some confusion developed as to which method for acquiring reserves Roosevelt had actually chosen. When Feis and Wallace Murray went to the White House to clarify the issue, Roosevelt also told them that he would like the PRC to offer Ibn Saud the right to establish an oil reserve for Saudi use. "It was evident," Feis noted, "that he thought some such gesture on our part would predispose Ibn Saud to the sale of the concession and also have an extremely healthy influence throughout the Arab world." Feis to Hull, July 3, 1943, Hull to Roosevelt, July 6, 1943, NA, RG 59, 890F.6363/52. Ickes had hoped that the PRC would come under control of the Interior Department, but Roosevelt rejected the idea. Ickes to Roosevelt, July 26, 1943, Ickes to Roosevelt, July 27, 1943, Roosevelt to Ickes, July 30, 1943, FDRL, Roosevelt Papers, OF (4435).

oil fields not only in Saudi Arabia but in other areas as well.'' The projects, centered in the Middle East, included expanding operations of the British-owned Anglo-Iranian Oil Company, building a new pipeline from the British-controlled fields in Iraq to the Mediterranean, and constructing new refineries in British India and in Saudi Arabia. All were anathema to Hull, who objected to such heavy-handed use of federal power. Also, he feared that British oil men might derive competitive advantage after the war from wartime expansion of their facilities.[34]

Buying an Oil Company

Negotiations between PRC representatives and the managers of Casoc's parent companies began on August 2, 1943. Ickes attended the first few sessions, as did Rodgers of Texaco and Collier of Socal. When it became evident that discussions would continue for some time, Ickes left things to subordinates. Before leaving, he secured at the request of the president a pledge from the oil men to conduct the meetings in secret to avoid rattling nerves in Arabia or in Congress.[35]

The executives reacted with astonishment and indignation to Ickes's proposal that the PRC buy out their interest in Casoc. "I had literally taken their breath away,'' Ickes confided in his diary. Though pleased with the attention the government had so far shown in Saudi Arabia, they were unprepared to part with their concession. They now felt their venture secure, and they looked on the Arabian fields, whose value they claimed defied measurement, as a reward for years of exploration and investment. According to their plans Arabian oil would supply company refining and marketing facilities throughout the Middle East. They also expected to exchange Arabian crude with other Middle Eastern distributors for oil produced in the Western Hemisphere, where their subsidiaries needed supplies. Selling the conces-

34. Hull, *Memoirs,* vol. 2, pp. 1520–21.

35. Feis to Hull, August 8, 1943, NA, RG 59, 890F.6363/9–943. Negotiations were carried on primarily by government representatives Alvin J. Wirtz, Mortimer Kline, and Herbert Feis. Harry D. Collier, W. S. S. Rodgers, C. E. Olmstead, and Harry Klein represented the companies. Ickes Diaries, vol. 49, 7989, 8050–51.

sion would ruin those plans, even though Ickes promised to supply the companies with enough Arabian oil to maintain business. Further, the companies feared that the stock sale would disturb Ibn Saud, with whom they were enjoying happy relations. He might see the transaction as a threat to his independence. Worse still, the purchase might stimulate British and Russian activity in the area or make other oil-producing countries reluctant to deal with Americans for fear of government intervention. In any case, the companies argued, it would be unwise for the United States to seek security in oil through the control of underground reserves in Arabia. Military exigencies could easily make them unavailable when they were needed the most. Instead, the companies counseled, the government should promote private exploitation in order to conserve more accessible sources in the Western Hemisphere. In that event the companies would be happy to draw up long-term sales contracts to meet government requirements.[36]

Negotiations continued for the next three months. With the companies disinclined to relinquish ownership, Ickes made more modest proposals, first for a controlling interest, then for a full partnership, and finally for a third of the companies' stock. He also began exploring alternatives to Saudi Arabia for government oil operations. Through such means he could at the same time pressure the parent companies and increase his own options.[37]

Ickes's first move was to inform Socal and Texaco that the Petroleum Reserves Corporation was suspending consideration of a government-financed refinery in Arabia until after the conclusion of stock purchase discussions. Casoc had been planning the construction of a new refinery to supplement inadequate facilities at Ras Tanura but required financial assistance from the government. The refinery project had been approved by the Joint Chiefs of Staff in August 1943 ostensibly to meet military needs in the Far East and to draw more

36. Ickes Diaries, vol. 49, 7989, 8050–51. "Minutes of the Petroleum Reserves Corporation," August 9, 1943, NA, Records of the Office of War Mobilization and Reconversion, Record Group 250, hereafter cited as RG 250; Feis to Hull, September 9, 1943, NA, RG 59, 890F.6363/66; "Minutes of the Petroleum Reserves Corporation," September 9, 1943, NA, RG 250.

37. *Arabian Oil Hearings,* 25240; Ickes Diaries, vol. 50, 8135–36, 8170, 8223.

heavily on Persian Gulf sources. At the time Ickes thought that government financing of the refinery gave him leverage to pry the Arabian concession from its owners. But when the companies agreed to construct the facility under PRC auspices, he found them less, not more pliant, since they felt that government financing indicated greater official support for their operation. By suspending government aid for the refinery Ickes now hoped to shake company confidence and regain the upper hand.[38]

Ickes also started investigating other prospects. Certain of receiving government approval for an alternative site, he approached the hardbitten J. F. Drake, president of the Gulf Oil Corporation. Drake's company held half-interest in a promising concession in Kuwait, and he had come to Washington in September 1943 to request assistance from the State Department in abrogating restrictive marketing and producing agreements with his partner, Anglo-Iranian. During this visit Ickes asked Drake whether Gulf would be willing to erect a refinery in Kuwait, and he also mentioned that the government might be interested in becoming an owner of the Kuwait Oil Company, the joint subsidiary that held title to the concession. The idea must have revolted Drake, a resolute defender of free enterprise. However, aware that the diplomatic support he wanted might turn on his reply to Ickes,

38. Feis to Hull, September 15, 1943, NA, RG 59, 890F.6363/65. Ickes had already sent, on September 4, 1943, a letter of intent to Fred A. Davies, president of Casoc, which authorized the company to begin construction of the refinery. "Minutes of the Petroleum Reserves Corporation," September 1, 1943, NA, RG 250. For a review of all pertinent correspondence between the PRC and Casoc, see Harper to Ickes, October 26, 1944, NA, RG 48, File 1–188: Petroleum Reserves Corporation, Folder 2845. On company plans for refinery, see Ickes Diaries, vol. 49, 8121. Joint Chiefs of Staff Memorandum, JCS 218.2, July 30, 1943, August 3, 1943, NA, Records of the United States Joint Chiefs of Staff, Record Group 218, hereafter cited as RG 218, CCS 463.7/4–9–43, Sec. 2. The company had originally contemplated building a refinery with a capacity of approximately 40,000 barrels/day, but the Joint Chiefs thought a larger facility was necessary and proposed a 100,000–150,000 barrel refinery at a cost of $105,503,000. Feis to Hull, July 26, 1943, NA, RG 59, 890F.6363/57. Feis and Carter both expressed their doubts about the effect of the refinery on stock purchase negotiations. They both believed that committing the government to the project would weaken the position of the PRC in upcoming negotiations. Feis to Hull, September 9, 1943, NA, RG 59, 890F.6363/66; "Minutes of the Petroleum Reserves Corporation," September 13, 1943, NA, RG 250; Feis to Hull, September 16, 1943, NA, RG 59, 890F.6363/69.

he promised to consider the offer. He had never been one, he told Ickes, "to stick his head in the sand and say 'no' when some new proposition came along."[39]

Nothing came of either venture, probably because Ickes had proposed them not as serious projects but as catalysts for the Arabian deal. No doubt, he would have been pleased had he been able to obtain the oil of Kuwait without difficulty, but an untroubled transaction was unlikely. Drake, crafty and seemingly cooperative, demonstrated his unwillingness to sell Gulf's share by offering it at a price so high that Ickes had to refuse. Ickes not only rejected the offer but dropped serious efforts to purchase an interest in the company. Even if an acceptable price had been reached, the British probably would have repudiated the agreement, since they had long resisted penetration by American oil capital in the Middle East. Government intrusion in the form of a federal oil company would not find a warmer reception.[40]

The refinery project was more improbable still. When the British army shut in Kuwait's nine active wells in 1942, the country had yet to produce oil in commercial quantities. In large part the sluggishness stemmed from British attempts to hold down production, since their fields in Kuwait competed with Anglo-Iranian's fields in Iran. With operations already suspended and with the British reluctant to increase development, Kuwait could not possibly support the refinery. Although it might draw oil from other sources, a refinery in Kuwait, at the northern end of the Persian Gulf, would still be more remote from producing fields than one located on Arabian shores.[41]

39. Feis to Hull, September 16, 1943, NA, RG 59, 890F.6363/69; Alling to Gray, September 13, 1943, NA, RG 59, 890F.6363/68; Feis to Hull, September 16, 1943, NA, RG 59, 890G.6363/418. Ickes did, in fact, receive permission from the Joint Chiefs of staff to choose another site. "To expedite the project," their covering letter read, "and to permit greater flexibility in its negotiations the Army-Navy Petroleum Board requested that the Petroleum Reserves Corporation be allowed greater flexibility in the selection of the site." General Thomas H. Handy to Chief, Logistics Group, September 24, 1943, NA, Records of the War Department General and Special Staff, Record Group 165, hereafter cited as RG 165, 600.12ME, case 10. Ickes Diaries, vol. 50, 8175, 8188.

40. "Minutes of the Petroleum Reserves Corporation," September 28, 1943, NA, RG 250; Ickes Diaries, vol. 50, 8216, vol. 51, 8331, 8405–406, 8422.

41. Shwadran, *MEOGP,* p. 388; Mosley, *Power Play,* pp. 79–80.

However unfeasible, Ickes's overtures did seem to make Socal and Texaco more amenable to his proposals. By the end of September the negotiators had reached a tentative agreement for the PRC to purchase one-third of the parent companies' interest in Casoc. As part of the deal, the government would receive preemptive rights to buy all the company's production during national emergencies and a bit over half at all other times. The government could also prohibit any foreign sales it deemed a threat to national security and could control the rate of production should reserves become dangerously depleted. As compensation, the PRC agreed to pay each parent company $20 million and to finance the construction of the refinery.[42]

The arrangements seemed to benefit all concerned. The government received its oil, the Joint Chiefs of Staff their refinery, and the companies the support they sought. All the same, early in October W. S. S. Rodgers repudiated the agreement on the grounds that the government's offer failed to include an additional $40 million, which his company was demanding to cover "extra war costs" involved in constructing the refinery. Such an inflated price, Ickes observed, "would make our stock purchase anything but the good thing it had appeared." Despite reports that further talks could produce a settlement, Ickes had had enough. He thought Rodgers's new demands were unreasonable—more a device for, as Ickes described it, "stringing along" the government than a serious proposal for selling a share in the company. "Apparently," he told Rodgers, "the Texas Company was prepared to pull a different card from a different deck every time that it appeared that we were about to get together." Later that day Ickes terminated negotiations. Two weeks thereafter, on November 4, 1943, he canceled the refinery project.[43]

42. Feis to Hull, September 25, 1943, NA, RG 59, 890F.6363/70; "Minutes of the Petroleum Reserves Corporation," September 28, 1943, NA, RG 250. The government was even willing to give up equal representation on the Board of Directors of the new company by allowing the companies to appoint four of the seven directors. Ickes Diaries, vol. 50, 8279.

43. Ickes Diaries, vol. 50, 8284–84; "Minutes of the Petroleum Reserves Corporation," October 14, 1943, November 3, 1943, NA, RG 250; *Arabian Oil Hearings,* 25241–43; Ickes to Hull, November 22, 1943, NA, RG 48, File 1–188: Petroleum Reserves Corporation, Folder 2845; L. P. Padgett to Knox, November 25, 1943, NA,

Ickes attributed the breakdown in discussions to military circumstances. He later maintained that the companies refused to sell right after Allied forces had removed Axis armies from North Africa and cleared Middle Eastern supply routes. James Byrnes believed that the companies' attempt to "drive a hard bargain" prevented Ickes from obtaining the stock at a fair price. Rodgers claimed that, for reasons he could not determine, Ickes abruptly decided to break off negotiations at the moment when "we were just about at a meeting of the minds."[44]

None of those explanations was adequate. By 1943 the companies were more concerned about losing their concession to British competitors than to Axis troops. Axis forces in North Africa had surrendered on May 13, 1943, three months before negotiations began. Perhaps, as Byrnes suggested, company avarice drove the price beyond the reach of the government. But if Rodgers, veteran negotiator that he was, really wanted money, he would have asked for a higher bid in the first place. Yet he did just the opposite. Such a move could only provoke Ickes, who, after three months of discussions, was in no mood for haggling.[45]

More likely, the companies entered into negotiations to fortify their position in Saudi Arabia, not to surrender their concession or any part of it. Although the extension of Lend-Lease had already demonstrated official interest in Saudi Arabia, it left unspecified the reasons for that interest. Discussing the sale of the Arabian concession with the Petroleum Reserves Corporation would signal foreign powers as well as the Saudi government that access to Arabian oil was imperative to the United States. A government-financed refinery would transmit even stronger signals. Since Ickes refused to discuss the facility apart from

RG 334, ANPB: Carter File; Harper to Ickes, October 26, 1944, NA, RG 48, File 1–188: Petroleum Reserves Corporation, Folder 2845. Ultimately the oil companies built their own 50,000-barrel refinery at a cost of between $60 million and $70 million. They completed the plant in September 1945. *Arabian Oil Hearings,* 24866–67.

44. *Arabian Oil Hearings,* 25241, 25387, 24868; Byrnes to Roosevelt, January 25, 1944, FDRL, Roosevelt Papers, OF (56). Carter thought that the companies were "unpatriotic" and vowed that he would oppose oil facilities for Saudi Arabia, should he ever be asked. Sappington memorandum, November 11, 1943, NA, RG 59, 800.6363/1375.

45. Richard W. Leopold, *The Growth of American Foreign Policy* (New York, 1952), p. 600.

the stock purchase, the companies had to continue discussing the sale in order to obtain the refinery. Continuing negotiations also afforded the companies an opportunity to peddle their oil. By convincing federal officials that options on Arabian reserves would ensure the safety of the nation, the companies would gain a guaranteed market for their products. Such sales would have provided their concession with a measure of security as well, because government options would mark the fields as an official American preserve. To relinquish ownership or even a fraction of control was unnecessary once the United States had indicated its interest in the oil.

Whatever the motives of Casoc's parent companies, Ickes realized that more was at stake than the sale of an oil company. "As we discussed foreign oil operations," Ickes mused early in the negotiations, "more and more interesting vistas opened up. If we can really get away with it, the Petroleum Reserves Corporation can be a big factor in world oil affairs and have a strong influence on foreign relations generally." Placing the government in the oil business would establish a precedent for federal regulation of international operations. In possession of large foreign reserves and production facilities, the government could use its oil as a yardstick for influencing prices and for combating restrictive practices in the international marketplace.[46]

During the war the prospect of regulating the industry, though of great value, remained a secondary consideration. What Ickes really sought was, in his words, "access to oil for National defense and the power to prevent the company from making any International agreements or come to any understanding even with foreign corporations without the consent of the government." He hoped someday to have oil reserves in strategic parts of the world "in such quantities that there would be no question [of] maintaining ourselves in the event another global war."[47]

He saw the Arabian concession in just those terms. "This was more than a business enterprise," he said later, "this involved the defense and safety of the nation." To guarantee that safety Ickes sweetened the

46. Ickes Diaries, vol. 49, 8126.
47. *Ibid.*, vol. 50, 8279, vol. 51, 8417.

deal by forswearing government interference with the management of daily operations even though he had planned initially to have federal directors play a large role in commercial activities. He was even willing to enter into a contract for the life of the concession that would provide for continued exploration, production, and marketing. What he asked in return was "the right to insist upon clauses that would protect the National interest." In short, he demanded broad control of company policy to make certain that the company kept enough oil in the ground to meet national requirements in wartime and refrained from doing business that ran against what he saw as national welfare. With that control and with the stock interest he hoped to obtain, he could ensure the access he sought on the terms he felt necessary. He, in turn, could then offer the companies the full diplomatic and military support they sought—support, as Ickes understood it, that would be acceptable to the American people only if their government participated in the venture itself.[48] To effect those goals, he and his colleagues embarked on a unilateral course of action that threatened to put security, at least in terms of oil, on a competitive basis.

The link between oil and national security, forged during the First World War and tempered in the Second World War, seemed to make government ownership of the Arabian concession a natural consequence of company requests for official support and protection. In no other way could the United States make certain that the conduct of American oil companies abroad would be in harmony with government policy. The companies, however, resisted authorities in that endeavor. Federal ownership threatened to alter in fundamental ways the relationship between government and the industry. Once involved in the international petroleum business, the government would no longer be limited to a supportive role. Government corporations would carry out their own policies, affecting every phase of foreign oil operations.

48. *Arabian Oil Hearings,* 25240–41; Ickes Diaries, vol. 50, 8184, vol. 51, 8417–18, 8429–30. Ickes's growing disenchantment with public management of day-to-day commercial operations seems also to have been prompted by Bernard Baruch, the wealthy financier, counselor to presidents, and sometime public servant. See Ickes Diaries, vol. 49, 8094–95.

The reluctance of Socal and Texaco to give up possession of their property was but a small measure of the industry's unwillingness to give up the initiative in framing national policy for foreign oil. Ickes's doggedness reflected his intention to see that initiative placed in public hands.

4 / Public Cooperation / Private Salvation

Early in December 1943 Secretary of State Cordell Hull asked Lord Halifax, the British ambassador in Washington, to relay a message to Whitehall. "In view of the great and world-wide importance of petroleum," the communiqué read, "and of the fact that nationals of our two countries hold . . . rights to develop extensive oil resources in the Middle East, this Government would welcome informal and preliminary discussions between our two Governments regarding petroleum problems of mutual interest in that area."[1] Its matter-of-fact tone notwithstanding, the invitation indicated a reversal in American oil policy, a shift from aggressive nationalism to conciliatory internationalism.

All the same, Hull's telegram surprised no one. State Department committees had been considering the move for months. So had oil men on both sides of the Atlantic. For almost a year, government and industry officials had been trying to clear the way for an agreement between their two governments covering oil development in the Middle East. That area, they knew, was bound to become the center of world oil production after the war. With valuable economic concessions and national security interests at stake, the major powers might move directly to control oil resources that had once been the province of private companies. On the other hand, unrestrained competition among commercial firms could bring about overproduction and price wars, the twin plagues of the industry. Anglo-American oil talks, petroleum planners in government and business hoped, would generate an under-

1. Hull to Halifax, December 2, 1943, NA, RG 59, 800.6363/1388a.

standing to clarify the future roles of public and private agencies in exploiting the treasures of the Middle East.

Trouble in the Middle East

To fulfill the Atlantic Charter's pledge to establish equal access to trade and raw materials, the State Department in 1942 began looking at the possibility of concluding an international agreement over postwar oil development. Questions about the willingness of countries to accept even a partial surrender of national sovereignty discouraged the effort until the spring of 1943. In March the department's Committee on International Petroleum Policy resurrected the idea in the form of a bilateral agreement with Great Britain to protect American concessions in Saudi Arabia. More ambitious internationalists on the committee used the opportunity to recommend a multilateral accord for pooling global oil resources, so that ample supplies could be made available to all nations. They argued that the United States should exhaust every means of meeting its commitment to international collaboration before attempting to obtain foreign reserves on its own. Although it ultimately favored more direct ways of acquiring oil abroad, the committee did suggest further examination of an international pact. "In this connection," according to its report of March 22, 1943, "it may be pointed out that the committee will include in its study the possibility of there being concluded agreements which are limited to specific regions containing important oil resources. It is not unlikely that agreements of this nature may present fewer difficulties than would broader and more inclusive agreements."[2]

The regional approach led to the Middle East. The area demanded the attention of everyone concerned with foreign oil. Despite low prewar production, the Middle East was one of the world's major oil

2. Ferris memorandum, "Post-War Arrangements Concerning Oil, and Commitments of the United Nations," enclosed in Thornburg to Welles, March 25, 1942, NA, RG 59, 800.6363/579-1/2; Minutes of Committee on International Petroleum Policy, March 15, 1943, NA, RG 48, File 1-188: Petroleum Administration, Folder 2828; "Essentials of an International Petroleum Agreement," March 23, 1943, NA, RG 59, 800.6363/1145; Feis to Hull, "Report of Committee on International Petroleum Policy," March 22, 1943, NA, RG 59, 800.6363/3-2243.

basins, with, as one government expert observed in 1942, "productive potentialities greater than those of the Caucasus, and probably as great as those of the United States."[3] By the fall of 1943 pressures both public and private, abroad and at home, convinced American officials that an agreement with Great Britain over the development of Middle Eastern oil was essential.

Accusations by American oil companies of British intrusion in Saudi Arabia had first turned the eyes of State Department officers to the Middle East in 1941.[4] That episode had revealed the mistrust American oil men felt toward their British competitors. Mistrust surfaced again late in 1942, when the department received information suggesting that British oil interests, in concert with the British government, were seeking commercial advantages at American expense.

In November 1942 executives from the Near East Development Corporation (Near East)[5] and from its parent companies, Jersey Standard and Socony-Vacuum, came to the State Department with a curious story. The British army, they said, had destroyed some of the oil installations they owned through the Iraq Petroleum Company (IPC), a multinational consortium in which Near East held a 23.75 percent interest. In Iraq and on the Arabian peninsula British soldiers had systematically plugged wells and dismantled production equipment at selected drilling sites within the IPC concession. According to the oil men, the operations, normally carried out to deny facilities to enemy troops, had been performed in this instance to strengthen the market position of Anglo-Iranian, which, like Shell and the Compagnie Française des Pétroles (CFP), also owned a 23.75 percent share of the

3. C. Parsons to Ray W. Smith, "The Strategic Significance of Near East Oil," March 23, 1942, NA, RG 169, Box 1613, File 960–5.

4. See chap. 2.

5. The Near East Development Corporation, formed in 1928 to obtain access for American companies to the oil of the old Ottoman Empire, originally included the Standard Oil Company of New Jersey, the Standard Oil Company of New York (reconstituted in 1931 as Socony-Vacuum after merging with the Vacuum Oil Company), the Atlantic Refining Company, the Gulf Oil Corporation, the Sinclair Oil Company, the Texas Company, and the Pan American Petroleum and Transport Company. By the Second World War, all but Jersey Standard and Socony-Vacuum had withdrawn from the corporation. Shwadran, *MEOGP*, p. 238, 249n; John A. Loftus, "Middle East Oil: The Pattern of Control," *The Middle East Journal* (January 1948), pp. 17–32.

consortium. By restricting liftings in Iraq, the American executives pointed out, Anglo-Iranian could control competition from a number of non-British firms. That tactic would also protect outlets for British production in Iran, where Anglo-Iranian monopolized development. At the same time the British could continue to draw extra revenue from the limited yields of Iraq because the army had avoided those areas where Anglo-Iranian, under special arrangement with its partners, received bonus supplies from IPC production.[6]

Oil companies had always told such tales on each other, on some occasions to obtain diplomatic support, on others to record the venality of competitors. What they now expected from the State Department was unclear, but the reasons for their anxiety were obvious. They too were worried about business after the war. Dispossessed by the Japanese of their holdings in the Dutch East Indies, Jersey Standard and Socony-Vacuum looked to the Middle East to furnish requirements for their huge Far Eastern markets, now endangered by their American rivals in Saudi Arabia. Yet throughout Asia Minor and the Arabian peninsula they were obligated by agreement with members of IPC to operate only through the consortium. If IPC restricted output, Jersey Standard and Socony-Vacuum not only risked paying penalties to local rulers for failing to develop the property but also would be deprived of oil that figured heavily in their postwar plans.[7]

6. Murray conversation with Seidel, Foster, and Stuart-Morgan, September 5, 1942, NA, RG 59, 890G.6363/375; Allen conversation with Stuart-Morgan, December 21, 1942, NA, RG 59, 890G.6363/384. As part of the 1928 agreement that allowed American companies to join IPC, Anglo-Iranian surrendered 25 percent of its share in the company and received as compensation a 10 percent overriding royalty on twenty-four plots reserved exclusively for exploitation by IPC. When the concession was revised in 1931 to cover an additional 32,000 square-mile area east of the Tigris River, member companies renegotiated the royalty issue. As a result, Anglo-Iranian received a 7½ percent royalty from the entire revised concession area. The royalty was paid in crude oil delivered to Anglo-Iranian free of cost at the field. Shwadran, *MEOGP*, p. 249n.

7. In the Far East, Jersey Standard and Socony-Vacuum operated through a relatively independent subsidiary, the Standard-Vacuum Oil Company. Both Jersey Standard and Socony-Vacuum suffered from chronic shortages of crude. After the Japanese captured the companies' holdings in the Dutch East Indies, those shortages became acute. For a more elaborate discussion, see Anderson, *Stanvac and U. S. East Asian*

When questioned, British authorities claimed to have based demolition decisions on military necessity, not on commercial considerations. State Department officers, especially those in the Near East Division, where the American share of IPC had always been regarded as something of a public trust, remained skeptical. The pattern of the denials, together with the fact that the British government held majority ownership of Anglo-Iranian, suggested collusion between the British army and the oil company. Without hard evidence, however, the department could do nothing to assist the oil men or to allay their suspicions.[8]

Constraints imposed by its British partner led another American company to Washington in 1943. The Gulf Oil Corporation had obtained a concession in Kuwait during the early 1930s. In order to exploit oil in the British protectorate, Gulf had accepted a partnership with Anglo-Iranian that effectively gave the British company control over development of the concession. As part of the agreement Gulf had also submitted to stipulations prohibiting it from selling its portion of production in Anglo-Iranian's markets, an area covering all the prewar outlets for Kuwaiti oil. As a result Anglo-Iranian had been able

---

Policy. The restrictive agreement, referred to as the ''Red Line Agreement,'' was signed in 1928 and gave the Near East Development Corporation access to oil in the old Ottoman Empire formerly under concession to the Turkish Petroleum Company, jointly held after the First World War by British, French, and Dutch interests. The agreement derived its name from a red line demarcating the area (Asia Minor and the Arabian peninsula, excluding Kuwait) on a map attached to the 1928 compact. Original member companies of IPC (whose name had been changed from the Turkish Petroleum Company in 1929) included Anglo-Iranian, Near East, Shell and the Compagnie Francaise des Pétroles. Calouste Gulbenkian, a British national of Armenian descent who helped to negotiate the original concession, owned the remaining 5 percent. For a discussion of the tortured negotiations leading to the agreement, see Shwadran, *MEOGP*, pp. 219–38.

8. Adolf Berle to H. Freeman Matthews, c. January 1943, NA, RG 59, 890G.6363/388. The State Department did, however, inform its representative in Iraq of the charges. Welles to Wilson, January 12, 1943, NA, RG 59, 890G.6363/378. Near East continued to maintain that Anglo-Iranian was guiding IPC activities, as one Near East executive put it, ''looking to the post-war period and feathering its own nest.'' Murray conversation with Stuart-Morgan, January 6, 1943, NA, RG 59, 890G.6363/405–1/2.

to keep commercial liftings to a minimum, while protecting its markets from Suez to the Pacific.[9]

During the spring of 1943 Gulf executives, eager to make Kuwait a wellhead for the Near and Far East and for Europe after the war, began considering ways to eliminate the restrictive clauses from their agreement with Anglo-Iranian. They saw in the wartime need for petroleum and in American anxiety over postwar reserves an opportunity to increase production in Kuwait. In July they traveled to London to try to convince their British associates that American antitrust laws made the legality of their arrangements doubtful. But Anglo-Iranian found the stratagem transparent and refused to modify the understanding except through an intergovernmental accord that would clarify the scope and jurisdiction of American legislation. Checked in its attempt to reach a private solution, Gulf in September 1943 requested diplomatic assistance from the State Department. Department officials were unwilling to act right away; they preferred to wait for Gulf's response to overtures made by Ickes, who had offered to buy a share of Gulf's holdings.[10]

9. The Kuwait Oil Company, the subsidiary formed by Gulf and Anglo-Iranian, was typical of oil companies operating in British protectorates. The company was registered in Great Britain and had to employ British nationals on its senior staff. Appointment of the company's chief local representative was subject to the approval of the British government, which also retained the right of prior approval for any transfers of company property to firms controlled by non-British nationals. During national emergencies, the British government had preemptive rights to all oil produced by KOC and could take possession of the company's plant and premises. As part of the marketing restrictions, Anglo-Iranian also agreed not to use Kuwaiti oil to injure the commercial position of Gulf. All the same, both parties admitted that the apparent bilateral nature of the agreement was illusory, since Gulf never marketed any oil in the Far East, the natural outlet for Kuwaiti production. In addition to marketing restrictions, Gulf also agreed to obtain oil supplies from Anglo-Iranian's production in Iran and Iraq in lieu of Gulf's requiring KOC to produce oil in Kuwait. John A. Loftus memorandum, "The Petroleum Situation in the Middle East," January 13, 1944, NA, RG 59, Notter File. For a resumé of similar restrictions on American operations on Bahrain, see Shwadran, *MEOGP*, pp. 390–97. Drilling began in Kuwait in 1936, but it was not until 1938 that KOC had any real success with oil development. By 1942, KOC had nine producing wells, which were shut in as a war measure in July of that year. Shwadran, *MEOGP*, pp. 409–10; Mosley, *Power Play*, p. 117.

10. Loftus memorandum, "The Petroleum Situation in the Middle East," January 13, 1944, NA, RG 59, Notter File; Alling to Gray, September 9, 1943, NA, RG 59,

British Reactions

Anglo-Iranian's request for government-level discussions was no ploy for stalling a rambunctious partner. Rather, it was the preliminary step toward heading off trouble in the Middle East. More oil than local markets could possibly absorb would soon be available in the area. Unless private companies were permitted to rationalize production and distribution, competition for concessions and for markets would flood the entire world with oil and send prices plummeting. Anglo-Iranian, planning as it did to increase crude exports from Iran after the war, had to know where the United States government stood on cooperation among private companies.[11]

For several months Basil Jackson, Anglo-Iranian's agent in the United States, had been monitoring American activities with growing concern. As the company's representative on the Foreign Operations Committee of the Petroleum Administration for War, Jackson maintained extensive contacts among public and private oil authorities. Their increased attention to the Middle East led him in May 1943, well over a month before the creation of the Petroleum Reserves Corporation, to recommend bringing London and Washington together. Prime Minister Winston Churchill rejected the move as premature, perhaps for fear that talking now might cost the British too much. Jackson persisted. In August he again urged Sir William Fraser, the craggy, hard-fibered Scotsman who chaired Anglo-Iranian, to press for oil talks with the Americans.

Jackson had reason to press, for he considered the time "most opportune" for agreement on a range of postwar commercial questions, oil development among them. American businessmen, mindful of the need to work with British interests to avoid what Jackson called the "economic and political evils" of uncontrolled competition, had told

---

890F.6363/68; Feis memorandum conversation with J. F. Drake, September 16, 1943, NA, RG 59, 890F.6363/418; Ickes Diaries, vol. 50, 8188.

11. James T. Duce, aide-mémoire conversation with Basil Jackson, August 9, 1943, NA, RG 59, 800.6363/1281. By Jackson's own admission Anglo-Iranian had previously occupied a "minor position in the export market."

him repeatedly of their desire to see commercial discussions opened between the two countries as soon as possible. However, not until Washington clarified its position on American participation in foreign cartels did businessmen feel free to begin planning for cooperation after the war. Conversations with oil men and with federal officials also indicated that aside from a general desire for a petroleum agreement with Great Britain, neither industry nor government had formulated a clear policy regarding foreign oil. With American thinking not yet fixed, Jackson surmised, the British might gain a hold upon affairs through an Anglo-American conference.[12]

According to Jackson, common enemies now gave Allied governments an incentive for cooperating. Should peace come suddenly, that incentive might evaporate, diminishing chances for collaboration. Already he saw signs of Washington's tendency to act alone where foreign oil was concerned: plans for a government-financed refinery in Saudi Arabia had gone ahead without a word to the British; talk persisted of forcing Great Britain to repay Lend-Lease oil with reserves owned by British companies in the Middle East; above all, the Petroleum Reserves Corporation, shrouded in secrecy since its creation, seemed intent on acquiring control of a major American oil company. The trend, Jackson concluded, boded ill for British oil interests in the Middle East unless his country discussed with the United States ways of facilitating cooperation among private companies. "I do not believe," he wrote Fraser on August 25, 1943, "that any scheme offering a reasonable measure of security to British interests could be worked out by the companies until they have received a lead from their Governments. The U. S. Government must indicate broadly what its

12. Ickes first invited Jackson to attend meetings of the Foreign Operations Committee in 1942, Ickes to Basil Jackson, March 19, 1942, NA, RG 48, File 1–188: Petroleum Administration, Folder 2834; Jackson to H. B. Blake-Tyler, "Extracts of a letter dated May 28, 1943, to Sir William Fraser, Chairman of Anglo-Iranian Oil Co., Ltd.," August 31, 1943, PRO, FO 371, A9194/3410/45; Extract from War Cabinet Conclusions, W. C. 99(32)2, July 14, 1943, PRO, FO 371, E4264/2551/65; Jackson to Fraser, August 25, 1943, PRO, FO 371, A9194/3410/65. For an example of one of many conferences Jackson had with American officials regarding the need for an oil agreement between the United States and Great Britain, see Duce aide-mémoire conversation with Jackson, August 9, 1943, NA, RG 59, 800.6363/1281.

Nationals may do in the way of collaboration in foreign trade and the two Governments I hope will agree [on] a common political policy to be followed by each oil producing countries [*sic*] and then lay down certain broad principles within which the commercial interests can get together and work out their salvation.''[13]

Getting the British government to initiate oil talks would be difficult. Despite their sophisticated grasp of political and economic developments during the war, the British so far had declined to discuss postwar oil questions with the Americans. When at the end of 1942 Under Secretary of State Adolf Berle first mentioned Middle Eastern oil as a latent source of trouble between the two countries, Foreign Office officials, uncertain of his meaning, had dismissed the warning. The eccentric Berle, they observed, seemed to be suffering from ''oil on the brain.'' In the spring of 1943 the State Department had approached the British over two issues involving oil: the development of subsoil resources, particularly petroleum, in enemy territory under Allied occupation, and the disposal of wartime oil installations constructed overseas by the United States. Again the British had hedged, replying that such complex questions required further study. Even Jackson's reports generated no positive response from London. The War Cabinet, though worried about the general lack of coordination between British and American policy in the Middle East, saw no need for special conversations over oil.[14]

Contact with Americans and with their own oil men, however, imparted a sense of urgency to British officials stationed in the United States. Harold Wilkinson, the British petroleum representative in Washington, agreed with Jackson that concern about domestic reserves dominated all consideration of oil. As a former oil man, Wilkinson too feared the effects of the Petroleum Reserves

13. Jackson to Fraser, August 25, 1943, PRO, FO 371, A9194/3410/65.

14. H. A. Cacuian minute, April 10, 1943, Neville Butler minute, April 11, 1943, PRO, FO 371, E2035/784/65. For a review of American approaches to the British government concerning these matters, see Butler minute, ''America and Oil,'' October 1, 1943, PRO, FO 371, A9286/3410/45. Hull to Winant, May 27, 1943, NA, RG 59, 800.6363/1190A; Winant to Hull, August 11, 1943, NA, RG 59, 800.6363/1267; Feis to Hull, September 22, 1943, NA, RG 59, 800.6363/1323–1/2.

Corporation—in his words, a "Washington Santa Claus bidding for . . . concessions with the lush money bags of the Treasury and Fort Knox." For him, as for Jackson, cooperation among the international companies was the "only solid basis to a real and lasting United Nations' oil policy."[15]

Wilkinson spent considerable time and energy trying to dissuade Ickes from developing foreign reserves. At the end of August 1943 he saw some sign of success when Ickes suggested that the two governments "get together." Wilkinson implored his superiors at the Ministry of Fuel and Power to accept the informal invitation, because government-level talks seemed the most fruitful way to make private cooperation possible. Not only would they illuminate the relationship between the oil industries of Great Britain and the United States, but they might help to confine the Petroleum Reserves Corporation and to temper American ambitions.[16]

While Wilkinson petitioned the Ministry of Fuel and Power, Ronald Campbell, chargé d'affaires at the British embassy in Washington, was working on the Foreign Office. Campbell had no experience in the oil industry, but he did have the benefit of Jackson's analysis. Never one to neglect opportunity, Jackson had passed some of his correspondence with Sir William Fraser to an acquaintance on the embassy staff, who in turn had given the letters to Campbell. As a result, Campbell's thinking mirrored Jackson's. "The spectre of the entry of the United States government itself into the oil field in the Near East," Campbell wrote to the Foreign Office late in September 1943, "would appear to conjure up complex problems of a political and social nature. Developers of oil concessions in this region have many burdens to bear in connection with the provision of housing, sanitation, etc. for their workmen which would normally be the charge of the country concerned and presumably paid for from oil royalties. United States government projects on the other hand would be under no handicap from lack of funds for these purposes, and might also establish wage scales which would be impossible for private enterprise to follow and remain

15. Harold Wilkinson to Sir William Brown, September 2, 1943, Wilkinson to Brown, September 29, 1943, PRO, FO 371, A9286/3410/45.

16. *Ibid.;* Ickes Diaries, vol. 49, 8117–18.

in a state of solvency.'' Campbell's communiqués contained no new insights, but they buttressed Jackson's accounts with the observations of a government representative working in the United States.[17]

Other developments threatened the British less directly than did the Petroleum Reserves Corporation. Late in September 1943 a group of five American senators, recently returned from a two-month tour of Allied combat zones, charged the British with hoarding their Middle Eastern reserves. It was, recalled Owen Brewster, a Republican from Maine and the most outspoken member on the panel, ''another one of those cases where our reserves were being utilized to win the war, and the British reserves were being reserved to win the peace.''[18]

The charges, reminiscent of those leveled against the British after the previous war, offered another example of the kind of anglophobia that had always made relations between the United States and Great Britain uneasy. In its more benign forms it manifested itself as grudging respect for the dexterity with which Englishmen handled their affairs abroad. When subjected to enough stress (as in the case of American apprehension over oil), it became a deep distrust of all things British—a conviction that British diplomats, devoted to the preservation of the empire, stood ready to cajole Americans into supporting and extending British power and influence.[19]

Such a view, implicit in the allegations of the five senators, probably accounted for their failure to consider less venal motives. Admin-

17. Ronald I. Campbell to Eden, September 28, 1943, no. 822, PRO, FO 371, A9194/3410/45. For similar reports on American activities, see Campbell to Eden, September 28, 1943, no. 819, PRO, FO 371, AN9193/3410/45; Michael Wright to Butler, November 12, 1943, PRO, FO 371, A10650/3410/45.

18. New York *Herald Tribune,* September 30, 1943; *NYT,* September 30, 1943, October 1, 1943. The group included Richard B. Russell (D-Ga.), James M. Mead (D-N.Y.), R. Owen Brewster (R-Me.), A. B. Chandler (D-Ky.), and Henry Cabot Lodge (R-Mass.). For the text of each of the senator's remarks, see U. S., Congress, Senate, Special Committee Investigating the National Defense Program, *Additional Report of the Subcommittee Concerning Investigations Overseas, Section 1—Petroleum Matters,* Report No. 10, Part 15, 78th Cong., 2nd Sess. (Washington, 1944). See also, text of radio address by R. Owen Brewster on ''National Forum'' on October 6, 1943 in FDRL, Oscar S. Cox Papers, Box 67, Five Senators Folder; Blum, *Wallace Diary,* p. 254; *Arabian Oil Hearings,* 25042.

19. McNeill, *America, Britain, and Russia,* p. 268n, 279n, 284, 285. For a clear example of wartime anglophobia, see Owen Brewster, ''Don't Blame the British—Blame

istration spokesmen, even the president himself, wasted no time in providing such explanations to prevent the senators' charges from embarrassing Roosevelt politically or disrupting Anglo-American relations. Responsibility for supplying oil to the Allies, the spokesmen were quick to explain, fell disproportionately to the United States because of wartime circumstance and the strength of the American petroleum industry. In-house investigations revealed that the only considerations governing American supply decisions had been the speed and efficiency with which petroleum and petroleum products could be furnished at the time and place they were needed. With nearly 75 percent of the world's crude oil production and almost 70 percent of available refinery capacity, the United States had proved by far the largest accessible source of supply. The Middle East, on the other hand, produced only about 5 percent of world totals, and despite plans for new pipelines and refineries, existing facilities were inadequate to meet Allied needs, particularly for special items such as aviation fuel. More important, the scarcity of oil tankers, the length of the sea haul from the Persian Gulf to western Europe, and the closing of the Mediterranean to Allied shipping during the early part of the war had confined the usefulness of Middle Eastern oil principally to nearby military operations. American authorities explained that improved transportation conditions would now allow the Allies to draw more heavily on Persian Gulf sources. "The situation," Roosevelt assured reporters at a press conference on October 5, 1943, "is well in hand."[20]

Us!'' *Collier's,* December 25, 1943, pp. 21, 68, 70. Patrick Hurley, a friend of and later special envoy for President Roosevelt, was always wary of the British, and although he claimed deep affection for them, he filed reports to Roosevelt during a tour of the Middle East in 1943 that contained warnings about British efforts to manage Americans in the region. Patrick Hurley memorandum of conversation with Regent of Iraq, April 9, 1943, NA, RG 59, 123 Hurley, Patrick J./104; Hurley to Roosevelt, May 5, 1943, FDRL, Roosevelt Papers, PSF (151). For a brief discussion of the fears of some administration officials over the impact of anglophobia during the war, see Stimson Diary, vol. 41, 101.

20. Though eager to refute the charges themselves, the British decided to allow the Roosevelt administration to, as one British official said, "fight the battle for us." Butler minute, "America and Oil," October 1, 1943, PRO, FO 371, A9286/3410/45. Churchill did inform the State Department that he planned to make a public statement correcting what he believed were factual errors. The administration's response to the charges

Competition in Iran

Though the British were pleased with the alacrity of Roosevelt's defense, they drew no comfort from the enterprise of the Standard-Vacuum Oil Company (Stanvac), a relatively independent subsidiary of Jersey Standard and Socony-Vacuum. The company was busy preparing a bid for a new concession in Iran, Britain's most valuable source of oil. Stanvac had not taken the initiative with the Iranians but was responding to an approach made to Jersey Standard in February 1943 by the Iranian commercial attaché in Washington.

Having been denied a concession in Iran in 1940, the Standard interests at first were reluctant to become involved with Iranian oil again.[21] They knew that more than leasing property had been on the line in earlier negotiations and suspected that such would again be the case. Indeed, State Department officers had speculated in 1940 that the Iranian government, its sovereignty threatened for more than a century by Anglo-Russian rivalry, was using oil to lure American businessmen to the country in an effort to "call forth a corresponding

---

came so quickly that Churchill's statement proved to be unnecessary. Woodward, *British Foreign Policy,* p. 395n; Roosevelt Press Conference, October 5, 1943, FDRL, Roosevelt Papers, Press Conferences, vol. 22, pp. 127–30; *NYT,* October 6, 1943. See also "Reply to Statement of the Five Senators . . .," n.d., FDRL, Cox Papers, Box 67, Five Senators Folder; "Remarks on Statements Made on Petroleum by Senators Mead, Russell and Brewster," October 4, 1943, NA, RG 169, Box 1740, Procedures and Policy Folder; Byrnes to Roosevelt, FDRL, Roosevelt Papers, OF (56); Ickes to James Mead, December 10, 1943, NA, RG 48, File 1–188: Petroleum Administration, Folder 2829. For a list of the steps taken to increase use of British-owned sources in the Middle East, see Andrew F. Carter memorandum, "Use of Oil from British Holdings in the Middle East," February 3, 1944, NA, RG 334, File ANPB: 21/2(d)-Petroleum Reserves, Middle East Folder. For Roosevelt's formal reply to Congress, see Petroleum Division memorandum regarding oil policy, Appendix XIVB, reprint of "Thirteenth Report to Congress on Lend-Lease Operations For the Period Ended November 30, 1943, Chapter 7: Lend-Lease Petroleum in the War," c. March 17, 1944, PRO, FO 371, W4654/34/76.

21. Campbell to Eden, October 11, 1943, no. 876, PRO, FO 371, A9561/3410/45; Wilkinson to Lloyd, December 12, 1943, PRO, FO 371, W357/34/76. Leland Morris to Hull, December 11, 1944, Enclosure "Chronological Summary," NA, RG 59, 891.6363/12–144. The company had responded affirmatively to the inquiry but had expressed a desire to wait before entering into negotiations because of the "Iranian political situation." Hull to Tehran, December 24, 1943, NA, RG 59, 891.6363/811.

interest from the United States government in the welfare and continued independence of Iran." The company too had hoped for closer ties between Iran and the United States to afford protection for its would-be concession. Iran's remoteness from what the department considered legitimate spheres of American interest prevented those ties from materializing, and the venture had fallen through completely. With Russian and British troops now occupying the country, the Iranians again found their national survival imperiled. They turned once more to oil as a way of giving the United States a long-term investment in Iran's political integrity and economic stability.[22]

The prospects for concluding a new concession had improved by 1943. Entry into the war had broadened the scope of American concerns so much that Iran assumed a position of importance. As a major Allied supply route to Russia and as a source of petroleum, a stable Iran was vital to winning the war. The country also presented an opportunity for the United States to carry out the lofty principles of the Atlantic Charter—in effect, to win the peace. American officials thought that as disinterested parties they could make Iran a model for Allied cooperation by shoring up the country's sagging economy, reforming its political institutions, and harmonizing relations between the British and the Russians. The State and War departments had already dispatched several advisory missions to Iran. By the end of 1943 Roosevelt would secure from Prime Minister Churchill and from Premier Stalin a pledge to respect Iranian sovereignty and territorial integ-

22. Murray to Welles, May 7, 1940, NA, RG 59, 891.6363/Standard Oil/430. The Iranians tried to link the 1940 concession to a loan from Standard-Vacuum along with generally closer economic ties to the United States government. Engert to Hull, January 17, 1940, NA, RG 59, 891.6363/Standard Oil/427. On the common practice of tying loans to concession grants, see Wilkins, *Maturing Multinational,* p. 214n. For a discussion of the efforts of American oil companies to exploit Iranian oil during the 1920s and 1930s, see George Lenczowski, *Russia and the West in Iran* (Ithaca, 1948), pp. 83–85. The interpretation offered here conforms to one offered in a recent study of American relations with Iran during the Second World War. Its author maintains convincingly that "the desire to give the United States Government a large stake in Iran's future motivated Iranian enthusiasm for American commercial enterprise." He bases his analysis on patterns first visible in Iranian diplomacy during the nineteenth century. Mark H. Lytle, "American-Iranian Relations 1941–1947 and the Redefinition of National Security" (Ph.D. diss., Yale University, 1973), especially pp. 106–91.

rity and to withdraw their troops soon after the cessation of hostilities. Despite the interest the United States was now evincing, the Iranians realized that continuing commitments from a major power depended less on disinterest than on self-interest. Toward that end they had offered up rich deposits of oil.[23]

American authorities failed to see that promoting American oil ventures would undercut their efforts to nurture Iranian sovereignty. Excited by the prospect of developing new sources of oil, State Department officials encouraged Stanvac to undertake negotiations with the Iranian government. Over the next twelve months, until competition from British and Russian oil interests forced the Iranians to suspend bidding, the State Department supported Standard-Vacuum (and later the Sinclair Oil Company, which also sought the concession) whenever possible. It furnished transportation and communication facilities for oil men. It used diplomatic channels to keep negotiations open. It supplied military personnel and equipment for private surveying teams and passed on to the oil men confidential information about each company's standing with the Iranian government. All the while, department officials refused to look on the services they performed as advocacy. They continued to believe, as they instructed their envoys to tell the British, "that the negotiations now being conducted by American companies are strictly commercial, the companies concerned having neither sought nor obtained our diplomatic support or special privilege."[24]

23. For the most complete statement of this policy, see John Jernegan memorandum, January 23, 1943, *FRUS* (1943), vol. 4, pp. 331–32. See also Hurley to Roosevelt, December 21, 1943, *FRUS* (1943), vol. 4, pp. 420–26; Lytle, "American-Iranian Relations," pp. 61–106, 191–230; "Declaration of the Three Powers Regarding Iran," December 1, 1943, *FRUS* (1943), vol. 4, pp. 413–14.

24. P. W. Parker to State Department, October 20, 1943, Berle to Parker, November 17, 1943, NA, RG 59, 891.6363/808. Under Secretary of State Acheson questioned the propriety of an American company applying for a concession in Iran. He feared that the application might be in conflict with the earlier American proposal to the British for negotiations in regard to seeking concessions in foreign countries. Department experts replied that the proposal had referred only to development rights in territories previously under enemy control and hence did not apply to Iran. Sappington to Acheson, November 2, 1943, NA, RG 59, 891.6363/808. Hull to Dreyfus, December 20, 1943, *FRUS* (1943), vol. 4, p. 627; John Leavell to Hull, July 31, 1944, NA, RG 59,

The possibility of losing any of Iran's oil to the Americans disturbed Whitehall. Most British officials shared the anxieties of Sir Frederick Godber, a genial but sharp-witted director of Shell and an influential member of the industry's petroleum board. Godber maintained that increasing American activity in the Middle East made it, in his words, "necessary to keep the British end up before the Americans get all [the oil] that is left." That fear inspired Shell itself to apply for the Iranian concession. After receiving approval from the British government, the company sent its representative to Tehran in November 1943 to open discussions. Officials in the Treasury and in the Petroleum Division, guardian of the empire's oil interests, smiled upon the move. They knew that Britain, already short of dollars and heavily in debt to the United States, could ill afford to be deprived of another source of sterling oil after the war.[25]

Groping for Agreement: The British Side

Against a backdrop of suspicion and competition, London authorities reviewed recommendations for an agreement with the United States over oil. Efforts to bring the Americans to the conference table centered in the Petroleum Division, where anxiety about the intentions of the United States government ran high. Geoffrey Lloyd, Secretary for Petroleum, and his deputy, Sir William Brown, recognized the

---

891.6363/7-2544. "Petroleum Concessions in Iran," March 16, 1944, NA, RG 59, 740.0011 Stettinius Mission/3-1944. Even after the negotiations had been suspended, American officals continued to see the episode as having been a private commercial enterprise. "The American and British Embassies in Iran," recounted an official American summary of the affair, "were aware of these negotiations but regarded them as private commercial ventures and in no way participated in the negotiations." "The Problem of Oil Concessions in Iran . . .," January 6, 1945, FDRL, Roosevelt Papers, Map Room, Box 165, Folder 4, A-16, Naval Aides File: Crimean Conference.

25. Maurice Peterson to William Brown, September 23, 1943, PRO, FO 371, E5703/545/34; Peterson minute, October 25, 1943, PRO, FO 371, E6387/545/34; R. M. A. Hankey minute, October 23, 1943, PRO, FO 371, E6387/545/34. Peterson minute, September 23, 1943, PRO, FO 371, E5703/545/34; Morris to Hull, "Chronological Summary," December 11, 1943, NA, RG 59, 891.6363/12-1144; Lloyd to Law, October 20, 1943, PRO, FO 371, E6773/545/34. The Petroleum "Division" had only recently acquired that title, when it was shifted in June 1942 from the Board of Trade to the Ministry of Fuel and Power, where it functioned in virtual autonomy under Secretary Lloyd. Payton-Smith, *Oil,* p. 115.

dangers, so carefully enumerated in Wilkinson's letters, of American determination to acquire a greater share of Middle Eastern oil. Even so, they saw no need for conflict with the United States. Their calculations indicated that more than enough oil existed in the Middle East and throughout the world to satisfy the demands of both countries. Rather than seek competitive advantage, Lloyd counseled, British policy "should aim at an orderly development with considerable intertwining of British and American interests." Not only would such a strategy fortify the positions of both countries with respect to oil and help each nation to avoid disagreements with the other; "it might also assist us in diverting American minds from the unduly simplistic plan of helping themselves by taking from us."[26]

Putting that plan into effect required cooperation from the United States government. To ease tensions between the two nations, Lloyd and Brown proposed a joint declaration, broadly fashioned and issued as soon as possible, setting out British and American intentions about oil. During October 1943 Brown drafted a set of principles conciliatory enough to calm Americans and sufficiently general to secure quick approval. At the same time he met the requirements of the Petroleum Division by implying ongoing cooperation between the two governments and among their oil interests.[27]

A larger dose of cooperation to cure the ills of the industry and to tranquilize the Americans seemed an odd prescription coming as it did from the Petroleum Division, which after all had just encouraged Shell to compete for the concession in Iran. As Richard Law, parliamentary under secretary of state for foreign affairs, commented, "I would have thought myself that if the Petroleum Dep[artmen]t are really anxious to have talks with the Americans on the whole subject it was not very prudent to launch this other scheme at this particular moment." The British were aware that an opportunity to relax tensions between the two countries existed in Iran; yet they followed a course that could only distress the Americans. If harmony over oil were the aim, Law implied, the division might have restrained Shell, at least until Britain

26. Lloyd to Churchill, October 22, 1943, PRO, FO 371, A10103/3410/45.

27. Butler minute, "America and Oil," October 1, 1943, P. Mason minute, October 8, 1943, PRO, FO 371, A9286/3410/45; Brown Draft Oil Principles, November 5, 1943, PRO, FO 371, A10101/3410/45.

and the United States had concluded discussions. Better still, as H. M. Hankey of the Near Eastern Department suggested, the Petroleum Division could have proposed that the companies operate the concession together, thereby entwining British and American interests in another Middle Eastern oil field. The Americans might have rejected such a proposal, but no one could fault the British for failing to make pacific overtures.[28]

The Petroleum Division saw things differently. Long-term cooperation could be plotted only at the conference table, where success depended on wit and strength. Confident of their cleverness, division officials felt compelled to parry the American thrust into Iran, lest, as one of them said, "our negotiating position generally . . . be impaired." Others in the department worried that sharing Iran might set a dangerous precedent. "It would be unfortunate," warned Maurice Bridgeman, "if we had to regard it as an accepted principle that no British interest in the Middle East is safe unless an American company is established next door to give it the necessary support."[29]

Lloyd and Brown found support at the Foreign Office. Officials there had a broader view of affairs, and they applauded plans for encouraging greater cooperation between British and American oil companies. Aside from the commercial advantages of collaborating with the market-rich American companies, they expected political dividends from the expansion of American oil operations in the Middle East. In their view such expansion would produce a powerful counterweight to any Russian designs by giving the United States a "highly strategic entanglement" in the area.[30]

28. Law minute, October 15, 1943, PRO, FO 371, E6164/545/34. Hankey minute, October 30, 1943, PRO, FO 371, A9835/3410/45. Discussion of whether to bring the Americans into the new concession continued even after Shell had applied for it. Most officials in the Foreign Office agreed that, if necessary, an Anglo-American consortium could be created after Shell had obtained the right to exploit the field. Officials believed that the Shell bid was imperative because they were convinced that, if the Americans won the concession, American companies would never share it with the British. Hankey minute, January 18, 1944, PRO, FO 371, W1141/34/76; Butler minute, January 26, 1944, PRO, FO 371, W1143/34/76.

29. Butler to Campbell, October 21, 1943, no. 7185, PRO, FO 371, A9286/3410/45; Maurice R. Bridgeman to John LeRougetel, March 17, 1944, PRO, FO 371, W3946/34/76.

30. Butler minute, October 14, 1943, PRO, FO 371, E6164/545/43.

Cooperation over oil also meshed with Foreign Office plans for collaboration on civil aviation, international monetary policy, and collective security. So did the Petroleum Division's recommendations for a bilateral agreement on postwar oil policy. According to Richard Law, recently returned from the United States, an Anglo-American accord was the only way to eliminate friction over oil, which he believed now jeopardized all schemes for economic collaboration after the war.[31]

An oil pact at the government level did have some critics in Britain. "Much of the charm of an Anglo-American oil agreement," observed Sir Maurice Peterson of the Foreign Office, "lies in encouraging the oil interests to make one." His view reflected the traditional European preference for private commercial arrangements. Though usually undertaken with tacit approval of authorities, such arrangements left governments unencumbered by formal commitments. The remark also revealed the aplomb with which Peterson had received news of the Petroleum Reserves Corporation. Perhaps convinced by the recent trend toward nationalization in Latin America or by the new assertiveness of Arab potentates, Peterson believed that state-owned companies such as the Petroleum Reserves Corporation would never again be able to obtain oil concessions in the Middle East. More than competition from government agencies he feared a clash among private companies, which might weaken British oil interests. His solution: have the two governments arrange a conference among the concerned companies and allow them to settle matters while the governments watched from the sidelines. He admitted that American officials, wary of cartel arrangements, might be unwilling to sanction the talks.[32]

Peterson's faith in the industry's capacity to resolve its problems was shared by Sir Frederick Godber. Whenever price wars or quarrels over developing new regions had beset Shell executives before, they had followed the Dutch precept "cooperation means power." Godber, as much as his predecessors, wanted to abide by that injunc-

31. Mason minute, October 13, 1943, D. Scott minute, October 14, 1943, Law minute, October 15, 1943, PRO, FO 371, A9286/3410/45; Foster minute, October 28, 1943, PRO, FO 371, A9873/3410/45.
32. Peterson minute, October 15, 1943, PRO, FO 371, A9286/3410/45; Peterson minute, November 4, 1943, PRO, FO 371, A10104/3410/45.

tion with as little interference as possible from government. In that effort he was no different from the managers of Anglo-Iranian, but he split with them over how best to go about it. Where Basil Jackson had consulted Whitehall to frame general rules for international commercial transactions, Godber wanted first to transact, then to consult—a strategy that typified the less intimate relations his company had always had with Whitehall. The question of greater American participation in Middle Eastern oil development, a Foreign Office official recorded Godber as saying early in October 1943, "is not one in which the Governments of the two countries should plunge, but that it should be in the first instance the subject of negotiations between the British, Dutch and American oil companies."[33]

Had the United States government shown no interest in entering the oil business, the British probably would have left matters in private hands, as Godber advised. Years of cooperation abroad between the British government and its oil industry ensured that a private settlement would do no harm to national interests. In part, that close relationship had accounted for British unwillingness to discuss oil with American authorities in the past. The creation of the Petroleum Reserves Corporation altered British thinking. Direct participation by the United States government threatened to disrupt the complicated system by which private oil companies competed for concessions, marketed their products, and settled their disputes. That system had always supplied Britain with sufficient oil, and Whitehall had learned to work comfortably with it. Whatever political capital might accrue from oil talks, British officials in the Petroleum Division now promoted them primarily to protect the system from government-sponsored competition.

Late in October 1943 Petroleum Secretary Lloyd recommended to Churchill that the British invite the United States government to discuss postwar oil policy. Sensitive to the territorial mentality of Washington bureaucrats, Lloyd suggested approaching the Americans at the highest level to avoid offending agency or department heads. Such a tack would also establish the importance of discussions. Al-

33. Butler minute, "America and Oil," October 1, 1943, PRO, FO 371, A9286/3410/45.

though he had already received endorsement from the Foreign Office, Lloyd found the prime minister hesitant, unwilling to take the initiative. Perhaps he was afraid that eagerness might betray anxiety and place the British at a disadvantage during the conversations. Maybe he hoped that in the face of government procrastination the oil companies would undertake discussions themselves. In any event, Churchill decided to await a formal American approach.[34]

Churchill's reluctance troubled officials at the Foreign Office, for they now regarded any delay as risky. They found some relief, however, in the possibility that oil questions might arise during the visit of a State Department mission to London to discuss Anglo-American problems in the Middle East. When a member of the mission mentioned oil in connection with the upcoming conference, the Foreign Office saw an opportunity to make an advance on its own. On November 20, 1943, Chargé Ronald Campbell informed the Americans that "we and the Oil Board would be very ready to have exploratory talks regarding the general principles which our two Governments would adopt towards oil resources in all parts of the world, if the United States Government cared to send representatives of their Petroleum Administration for War with Mr. Murray [the Near East Division chief who accompanied the group] and his party."[35]

Groping for Agreement: The American Side

On the other side of the Atlantic the idea of an Anglo-American oil pact had been gaining considerable momentum since March 1943,

34. Lloyd to Churchill, October 22, 1943, PRO, FO 371, A10103/3410/45. Neville Butler of the North American Department of the Foreign Office speculated that Churchill had turned down Lloyd's suggestion on the advice of Lord Leathers, who recommended leaving discussions to the companies. Butler minute, "Oil," November 4, 1943, PRO, FO 371, A10104/3410/45. John Summerscale, commercial secretary of the British embassy in Washington, attributed British hesitance to recent criticism in the United States of Great Britain's propensity to advance solutions to Anglo-American problems. Alling to Murray, December 3, 1943, NA, RG 59, 800.6363/1402.

35. Alling to Murray, December 3, 1943, NA, RG 59, 800.6363/1402; Scott minute, November 4, 1943, PRO, FO 371, A10104/3410/45; Campbell to F. O., November 2, 1943, no. 4938, PRO, FO 371, E6647/2551/65; F. O. to Campbell, November 20, 1943, no. 8025, PRO, FO 371, E6756/2551/65.

when the Committee on International Petroleum Policy recommended putting it aside for further examination. The gestation period had proved a fruitful one, owing in equal measure to the persuasiveness of advocates and the difficulties encountered by the Petroleum Reserves Corporation.[36]

Economic Adviser Herbert Feis and his associates at the State Department became the leading promoters of an agreement. Federal ownership, they argued, might upset the delicate pattern of competitive relationships among private companies in the Middle East or might cause anxiety in London or Moscow over American intentions. When their plan for acquiring oil through option contracts had failed to win favor, they seized upon a bilateral accord as a way of safeguarding the reserve position of the United States without causing misunderstandings or reprisals. The agreement also would provide the State Department with a means of establishing its precedence over foreign oil policy, since negotiations would presumably take place under department supervision.[37]

As department officials envisaged it, the understanding would set down general principles for the orderly development of Middle Eastern oil based on sound conservation practices. The objectives of that development would blend international with national concerns by seeking to assure, according to a department memorandum, "freely available supplies on equal terms to the United States and all other peaceful nations, and proper benefits to the countries in the area." With those ends in mind, Feis and his colleagues assumed that discussions leading to the agreement would deal with removing restrictions on exploration, production, and marketing—the chief concerns of the American oil companies operating in Iraq, Kuwait, and other Persian Gulf states. They recognized that in order to eliminate those constraints, provisions would have to be made (though they offered

36. Feis to Hull, "Report of Committee on International Petroleum Policy," March 22, 1943, NA, RG 59, 800.6363/3-2243.

37. "Minutes of Special Committee on Petroleum," June 15, 1943, NA, RG 59, 811.6363/6-1543; "Minutes of Special Committee on Petroleum," July 27, 1943, NA, RG 334, File ANPB: 14/1-Foreign Petroleum Policy, Misc. Folder; Feis, *Three International Episodes,* pp. 134-35.

none at this point) for disposing of large quantities of Middle Eastern oil without disorganizing local markets.[38]

In the minds of advocates the agreement promised far-reaching benefits. Above all, it would reduce the drain on Western Hemisphere reserves by opening the Middle East to greater development. State Department planners projected that after the war the Persian Gulf region would provide western Europe with petroleum supplies previously furnished by the United States and Latin America. Those planners suggested as well that Middle Eastern oil might even be introduced into the domestic market to satisfy postwar demand and to conserve indigenous stocks for security needs. Making Europe the outlet for increased production in the Middle East would also avoid flooding prewar markets with oil and would help to maintain a stable price structure within the industry.

State Department officials saw other, less direct advantages to an agreement. From a political viewpoint, a bilateral pact would serve to stabilize the Middle East by eliminating Anglo-American rivalry over oil and by generating revenue for local governments. At the same time, rational development and increased production would make the concessions themselves more secure. The department assumed that Middle Eastern countries, lacking the funds and technology to exploit their oil, would not cancel the source of their own prosperity. An oil accord might also prove to be a model for international understandings on other raw materials. Finally, an Anglo-American pact had the virtue of being feasible. Despite some tension, wartime relations between Great Britain and the United States had been harmonious, even with respect to oil. The two countries had virtually pooled their petroleum supplies for war purposes. The smooth-running apparatus they had fashioned to superintend the program pointed to a favorable end for oil talks.[39]

38. Murray memorandum, November 24, 1943, *FRUS* (1943), vol. 4, pp. 943-47. State Department memorandum (no. 5), November 20, 1943, NA, RG 59, 800.6363/1397; W. L. Parker memorandum, "The Necessity of the Formulation of an Oil Policy by the Department," December 8, 1943, NA, RG 59, Pasvolsky File.

39. W. L. Parker memorandum, December 8, 1943, NA, RG 59, Pasvolsky File; Feis, *Three International Episodes,* pp. 136-37; James C. Sappington memorandum,

The summer and fall of 1943 found Feis pressing for the agreement. He received help from sources as salutary as they were unforeseen. Basil Jackson of Anglo-Iranian had not confined his wire-pulling to the London headquarters of his company or to the Foreign Office. Early in August 1943 he met in New York with British-born James Terry Duce, a Socal executive on loan to the Petroleum Administration for War. Jackson, as candid with fellow oil man Duce as he had been with his friends at the British embassy, reiterated his plea for government cooperation and guidance in rationalizing oil development along the Persian Gulf. Duce agreed that legal problems, together with personality conflicts among company executives, made it impossible for the oil men to resolve their problems without government intervention. He too favored a bilateral agreement. As soon as Jackson left his office, Duce sent word of the visit to Ickes, along with his personal recommendation for oil talks.[40]

Already in the midst of negotiations with Socal and Texaco, Ickes welcomed the information. "To me," he wrote Hull in mid-August, "these documents are exceedingly interesting and not only justify our formation of the Petroleum Reserves Inc.,[*sic*] but call for the careful formulation of an international oil policy and active proceedings in pursuance of that policy." Ickes awaited neither a reply nor the careful delineation of policy. Instead, he sent Duce's memorandum to Roosevelt that day and urged him to come to an immediate understanding with the British over oil.[41]

Ickes saw no contradition in calling for a multilateral measure while he employed a unilateral one. Like many of his colleagues, he looked on federal ownership of foreign oil operations as compatible with, even necessary to, concluding a petroleum agreement. Aside from the rewards that a piece of the Arabian concession held, Ickes believed

"Memo on the Department's Position with Respect to the Proposal that the Government Purchase Stock Control or Participation in the California-Arabian Standard Oil Company . . .," December 1, 1943, NA, RG 59, 890F.6363/92-1/2.

40. Duce aide-mémoire conversation with Basil Jackson, August 9, 1943, enclosed in Duce to Ickes, August 13, 1943, NA, RG 59, 800.6363/1281.

41. Ickes to Hull, August 18, 1943, NA, RG 59, 800.6363/1281; Ickes to Roosevelt, August 18, 1943, FDRL, Roosevelt Papers, PSF (66).

that the purchase would make Britain more responsive during negotiations by placing the United States on a par with British oil interests in the Middle East. After all, Ickes reasoned, the British government owned a controlling share of Anglo-Iranian. The United States government had every right to do the same with Casoc.[42]

Then and later, British diplomats resented the comparison. They had tried repeatedly and without success to disabuse Ickes of his notion that, as one of them put it, "the interest of H[is] M[ajesty's] G[overnment] in the Anglo-Iranian Oil company has proven to be a magic talisman." Though it owned just over half the company's stock, the government had never been known to interfere with day-to-day commercial activities. Ickes, on the other hand, had already made it plain that he intended to exert some control over company operations. His conversion to the agreement, even while negotiations for the purchase continued, must have come as a relief to the British.[43]

With Ickes now committed to the pact, the way seemed clear for oil talks. In September 1943 Feis sent a draft he had composed to other

42. Ickes wavered momentarily on the question of federal ownership of an oil company operating abroad. After the stock purchase negotiations had fallen through early in November 1943, Ickes spoke to John A. Brown, president of Socony-Vacuum. Brown seemed to have brought Ickes around to the view that purchasing options on American-owned reserves was preferable to purchasing an oil company, because federal ownership of an oil company might disturb United States relations with Latin American countries. When Ickes expressed those doubts at a meeting of the Board of Directors of the Petroleum Reserves Corporation, General Boykin Wright and Commodore Andrew F. Carter, military oil advisers, convinced him to continue pursuing stock purchase possibilities. Minutes of Meeting of the Petroleum Reserves Corporation, November 3, 1943, NA, RG 59, 800.6363/11-343. For Ickes's views of the effect of stock ownership on oil talks with the British, see Ickes to Hull, January 7, 1944, FDRL, Roosevelt Papers, PSF (66).

43. Wright to Eden, March 13, 1944, PRO, FO 371, W4417/34/76. According to the original purchase agreement, the British Admiralty paid £2,000,000 for approximately 51 percent of the company. That interest allowed the government to appoint two directors to the company's board. They had the right of veto. The government assured the company that government directors would exercise that right only on questions of foreign or military policy, or on matters relating directly to Admiralty contracts. Sampson, *Seven Sisters,* pp. 55-57. Because of lack of government interference, British officials came to refer to the arrangements as a "sleeping partnership." See, for example, Sir Reader Bullard to F. O., October 23, 1944, PRO, PREM 3, Operational Papers of the Prime Minister's Office, hereafter cited as PREM 3, 237/5, 34. See also Wilkinson to Brown, September 2, 1943, PRO, FO 371, A9286/3410/45.

departments for review. A meeting with the ubiquitous Basil Jackson in October 1943 convinced Feis that official British reluctance to talk about oil would dissolve if the Americans made more formal advances at higher levels. Two weeks later Assistant Secretary of State Edward R. Stettinius, Jr., proposed to Roosevelt that Feis visit London to prepare the way for future negotiations. Roosevelt at first approved the trip but shortly thereafter reversed the decision. The expedition, he now told Stettinius, was ill timed. Besides, he indicated that he might personally discuss the matter in the near future—a reference to the upcoming Allied conferences in Cairo and Tehran scheduled for late November.[44]

Again, as he once had told Henry Morgenthau, Roosevelt had refused to let his left hand know what his right was doing. It was Ickes who had been responsible for disabling the Feis mission. Ickes's support for an agreement did not extend to backing State Department control of negotiations. Furious over what he regarded as poaching, fearful that the trip would be ''a waste of valuable time'' or, even worse, would produce commitments he could not condone, Ickes had gone directly to the president as soon as he learned of it. Only a fragmentary record of that conversation exists, but Ickes revealed his feelings some weeks later. ''The State Department couldn't handle this job,'' Ickes told a group of oil executives as he disclosed his intention to open negotiations himself. ''They are a lot of cookie pushers. And now they are so befuddled they don't even know how to push cookies.''[45]

Ickes's success in blocking the State Department was short-lived.

44. Feis, *Three International Episodes,* pp. 137–38; Minutes of Meeting of the Petroleum Reserves Corporation, September 13, 1943, NA, RG 250; Wilkinson to Brown, September 2, 1943, PRO, FO 371, A9286/3410/45; Feis memorandum, ''Questions in the International Petroleum Field,'' October 1, 1943, NA, RG 59, 800.6363/1330A; Edward Stettinius to Roosevelt, October 12, 1943, FDRL, Roosevelt Papers, OF (56); Stettinius to Hull, November 29, 1943, NA, RG 59, 800.6363/1388.

45. Schlesinger, *Coming of the New Deal,* p. 583. Feis himself never learned why the president had canceled his trip to London. Feis, *Three International Episodes,* pp. 138–39. After his success with Roosevelt, Ickes could not contain himself, and he repeated the story of his ''showdown'' with the president to Harold Wilkinson, the British petroleum representative in Washington. Wilkinson memorandum for Embassy, November 25, 1943, PRO, FO 371, W357/34/76. For an account of Ickes's meeting with Roosevelt, see Ickes Diaries, vol. 50, 8283–84. Alling to Hull, Stettinius, Murray, December 6, 1943, NA, RG 59, 800.6363/1426.

Hull, who had earlier acquiesced in the stock-purchase plan, would not be denied now. While Roosevelt concluded conversations with Churchill and Stalin in Tehran, Hull took matters into his own hands. On December 2, 1943, he addressed a note to British ambassador Halifax, proposing that the two governments undertake "informal and preliminary discussions regarding petroleum problems in the Middle East." A week later Hull informed Roosevelt of the invitation. To forestall any plans Ickes might have for conducting the negotiations, Hull wrote the president that, "in view of the delicate situation of the Middle East and the close connection between foreign oil questions and the general conduct of our foreign relations, it is extremely desirable that any conversations with the British on oil be under the clear supervision and guidance of the Department of State." Hull suggested that a representative from his department serve as chairman of the negotiating team, which would contain two additional members, one designated by Hull, the other by Ickes. With the invitation already extended, Roosevelt belatedly approved it.[46]

More than the tactical maneuvers of Cordell Hull moved the United States toward an agreement with Great Britain. The Petroleum Reserves Corporation, upon which so many had pinned their hopes for the safety of the nation and for parity with Great Britain, was faltering. Not only had it failed to obtain a share of the Arabian property (or any other concession), but it had ruffled oil men.

Normally broken into factions, the oil industry had closed ranks against the amalgam of public and private interests envisioned by the Petroleum Reserves Corporation. In November 1943 the Foreign Operations Committee of the Petroleum Administration for War delivered the first blow by presenting its own prescriptions for foreign oil policy. They contained no mention of federal ownership. On the contrary, the committee's report stated that private enterprise was the best medium for oil development at home and abroad. Early in December the Petroleum Industry War Council endorsed the general principles set down by the Foreign Operations Committee and specifically called on the federal government to stay out of oil operations overseas. At the

46. Hull to Halifax, December 2, 1943, NA, RG 59, 800.6363/1388a; Hull to Roosevelt, December 8, 1943, NA, RG 59, 800.6363/1423.

same time the council created its own committee to investigate national policy for foreign oil. The National Oil Policy Committee, as it was called, later demanded the dissolution of the Petroleum Reserves Corporation.[47]

Trade organizations followed suit. Despite an impassioned statement by Ickes at the annual meeting of the American Petroleum Institute, its members also condemned the government corporation. In December 1943 the Independent Petroleum Association of America, composed of small producers usually at odds with large companies, passed yet another resolution repudiating government ownership abroad.[48]

There were exceptions. Neither Socal nor Texaco, both with representatives on the Foreign Operations Committee, endorsed its report. To do so would have placed them in the awkward position of repudiating their own actions. Their footing in Arabia remained unsteady, and company plans for making the concession more secure by expanding pipeline and refinery facilities still required kind treatment from federal agencies charged with doling out construction materials and diplomatic assistance. Any swipe at government policy might nettle those upon whose favors the companies depended.

Intimacy with the government inhibited the Gulf Oil Corporation as well. It too had been contemplating a partnership with the Petroleum Reserves Corporation. Negotiations, only at the preliminary stage, were unpromising but remained open in early December 1943. Gulf also had a petition pending at the State Department for aid with its concession in Kuwait. The company therefore sidestepped outright condemnation by qualifying its approval of the Foreign Operations Committee report. While it subscribed to the notion that using tax-

47. Petroleum Industry War Council, "A Foreign Oil Policy for the United States" (Washington, 1944); *NYT,* November 12, 1943; "Resolutions Adopted by the Petroleum Industry War Council Pertaining To A Petroleum Policy For The United States," December 9, 1943, January 12, 1944, found in NA, RG 250, Box 119, Reports on Petroleum Folder; Petroleum Industry War Council, "A National Oil Policy for the United States," especially Petroleum Industry War Council Resolution of February 2, 1944 (Washington, 1944).

48. Nash, *U. S. Oil Policy,* p. 173. The Independent Petroleum Association of America resolution of December 11, 1943 appears attached to "Report of Special Committee on Foreign Oil Policy to the Petroleum Industry War Council," January 10, 1944, found in FDRL, Roosevelt Papers, OF (4435-b).

payers' money to finance federal ownership was unsound, Gulf pointed out that exceptional circumstances would justify such action. Harry Sinclair, whose company bore his name as well as his independent spirit, played his customary lone hand. Claiming that his absence from the country prevented him from taking a stand on the committee's report, he refused to sign it.[49]

The Petroleum Reserves Corporation also suffered attacks from within the administration. Hull had always felt that the corporation would jeopardize American oil interests along the Persian Gulf. Its success, he believed, might offend other powers, which would resent the abrupt intrusion of the United States government into Middle Eastern oil affairs; its failure ran the risk of shaking the confidence of King Ibn Saud in American resolve to develop the concession. The plans of the corporation to aid the expansion of British oil facilities in the Middle East also bothered him. Hull favored the full use of British oil and equipment to relieve the strain on American reserves, but he frowned on wartime construction that, in his view, would strengthen British oil interests at American expense after the war.[50]

Hull and his staff had been sniping at the Petroleum Reserves Corporation since mid-November 1943, when word of its so-far unsuccessful negotiations leaked to the press. He told Ickes early in January 1944 that the efforts of the Petroleum Reserves Corporation were really unnecessary because they duplicated what conversations with the British were designed to accomplish, namely, assuring the United States and other friendly nations access to Middle Eastern oil. Until the direction of the discussions became clear, he added, the corporation should hold in abeyance all negotiations, since they might prove inconsistent with Anglo-American oil policy.[51]

49. Charles Rayner to Stettinius, December 27, 1943, NA, RG 59, 800.6363/ 1404-1/2.

50. Hull to Ickes, November 13, 1943, NA, RG 59, 800.6363/1367A. Among the projects under consideration by the Petroleum Reserves Corporation that particularly disturbed Hull were plans for additional expansion of the Abadan refinery in Iran, a new pipeline to the Mediterranean from Iraq, and a refinery in Bombay.

51. Murray to Stettinius, October 26, 1943, NA, RG 59, 890F.6363/89; Hull to Ickes, November 13, 1943, NA, RG 59, 890F.6363/1367A; Murray memorandum, December 14, 1943, NA, RG 59, 800.6363/1420; Hull to Leahy, December 15, 1943, NA, RG 59, 800.6363/1404; Hull to Ickes, January 5, 1944, FDRL, Roosevelt Papers, PSF (66).

Ickes balked, so the two antagonists sought a ruling from the president. Despite his conciliatory disposition and in the face of industry opposition to the corporation, Roosevelt sided with Ickes. "It is, of course, true," he told Hull in mid-January, "that the State Department should handle, in general, matters relating to foreign affairs—but at the present time I think it vital that we should go ahead with some speed in negotiating with the American companies, in order to find out just where the United States stands before we take the matter up with the British. . . . I feel that time is important—because after the war the American position will be greatly weaker than it is today." Though genuinely committed to multilateralism, Roosevelt, no less than Ickes, preferred to deal from strength. He also was not above using wartime circumstance to secure postwar advantage.[52]

For the time being the Petroleum Reserves Corporation was safe. With support from the White House, it might remain so indefinitely. Still, the criticisms had cast doubt on the ability of the United States government to pursue the course it had plotted. Even if Roosevelt kept the corporation alive, he could do little to ensure its efficacy. More and more, federal authorities came to regard an agreement with Great Britain as the cornerstone of national policy for foreign oil. That shift was monitored carefully by Harold Ickes, who made certain that any such accord would bear his stamp.

The State of Affairs

Each advocate of the pact had his own idea of how it should turn out. On both sides of the Atlantic all agreed that an understanding between the two governments should assure the availability of oil vital to the security of the United States and Great Britain. But in Washington, where self-interest and idealism rarely parted company, loftier ends were foreseen. Hull and his department saw the pact as one of many such agreements that would make internationalism the basis for post-

52. Rayner to Hull, January 6, 1944, *FRUS* (1944), vol. 5, pp. 11–12; Ickes to Hull, January 7, 1944, Hull to Roosevelt, January 8, 1944, FDRL, Roosevelt Papers, PSF (66); Roosevelt to Hull and Ickes, January 10, 1944, NA, RG 59, 800.6363/1431. See also Roosevelt to Hull, January 10, 1944, *FRUS* (1944), vol. 5, pp. 16–17.

war diplomacy. They envisioned a world of free trade in which nations collaborated to prevent wars by guaranteeing equal access to raw materials and to commerce. For Harold Ickes, as well, an oil agreement would ground the peace solidly on the principle of international cooperation. Equally important, it would represent an extension of his public stewardship. The understanding, he hoped, would set down general rules of behavior for governments and for oil companies to ensure that their activities were in harmony with public welfare.

British authorities had a more prosaic outlook. Officials at the Foreign Office believed that a bilateral agreement would dispel American distrust of British intentions in the Middle East without impairing British oil interests. With American suspicions allayed, London and Washington could then set about designing a postwar world to British specifications. Ickes's counterparts in the Petroleum Division entertained equally modest hopes. They wanted to protect British oil companies against competition from the United States government. An oil agreement appeared a useful way to distract the Americans from introducing federal ownership into the international oil industry. A bilateral agreement would also connect British and American oil policy through a public understanding that pointed to continuing cooperation.

American oil companies had other goals in mind. Latecomers to the Middle East, they had suffered because of their tardiness. British restrictions on concession hunting, production, marketing, and incorporation hampered their ventures throughout the region. An oil agreement offered some relief. Once accepted by Britain, broad principles embodying the Open Door might give American companies a freer hand in the Middle East. An agreement might also provide the framework for restructuring the commercial arrangements that hindered Americans in Kuwait and in Iraq. Above all, an oil accord to which the United States government was party would signify to rival companies and to oil-producing nations that American oil men could expect strong support along the Persian Gulf.

British companies also saw the agreement in commercial terms. They realized that the center of world oil production was shifting to the Middle East, where they controlled concessions of enormous value.

Unless ways of rationalizing development could be maintained, the very abundance that promised riches would bring instead overproduction and price wars. Commercial relations woven as intricately as a Persian rug already guarded against such hazards, but American aggressiveness, both public and private, threatened to disrupt the arrangements. An understanding between London and Washington might allow the British to incorporate American companies more equitably into Middle Eastern cartels without overturning the system. At the very least, it would draw the legal boundaries within which companies could resolve their own difficulties.

Hull's request for oil talks with the British government made public the new directions in national policy for foreign oil. The change in course, still incomplete, might have come about in any event. President Roosevelt had already committed the nation to international cooperation after the war. Yet Roosevelt had not instigated the change; indeed, he had resisted it. Rather, it was the improbable combination of the Anglo-Iranian Oil Company and the Department of State that had first pressed for a petroleum agreement. By the time Hull extended his invitation to the British, others had also found the new course suitable. It was unlikely that one agreement could satisfy all their needs.

5 / "A Wrangle about Oil"

Everything was set. Only details remained to be worked out. Or so it seemed in Washington on the eve of 1944. Though the British had yet to accept the American invitation to discuss oil, they had indicated their readiness to talk. American officials expected that readiness to harden into formal acceptance within a few weeks. Only small matters would require attention then: the date and site of the conference; the members of the delegations; the scope of the talks; perhaps even a tentative draft to serve as a working model. From there it would be a short step to the conference itself and to an Anglo-American oil agreement. The new year appeared to mark the beginning of cooperation over oil between the United States and Great Britain.

As it turned out, conflict, not cooperation, characterized oil diplomacy in the early part of 1944. Instead of quick acceptance, Hull's invitation produced months of diplomatic sparring that threatened to escalate into an outright brawl. Details developed importance beyond their worth and became matters of contention between the two governments and within them. Underneath it all power was at stake, though misperception, mutual suspicion, and the pressure of domestic politics in the United States obscured the dimensions of that stake. American officials believed that they were consolidating the position of their oil interests in the Middle East; British officials thought that they were defending theirs. In fact, a transfer of power was beginning—not just in the Middle East and not just with respect to oil, but all over the world and across a range of affairs. The British Empire was in decline, a decline made precipitous by wartime stresses. The United States was in ascendance, also owing largely to the impact of the war. Neither side fully understood how serious was the decline or

121

how sharp the ascendance. The elevation of details to issues offered one indication of what was really happening.

Planning an Anglo-American Agreement on Oil

When Hull cabled the British government early in December 1943 to request talks on oil, his staff had already settled upon the general objectives of American foreign oil policy. The planners recognized the importance of oil to the security of the nation and aimed first at conserving domestic reserves in order to make the United States self-sufficient in time of emergency. Toward that end they sought to shift the burden of supplying Europe with petroleum from the Western Hemisphere to the Middle East. That substitution required greater development of Middle Eastern sources and demanded the protection and extension of American-owned concessions along the Persian Gulf basin. In keeping with the Atlantic Charter, planners also intended to cultivate the economic well-being of producing countries by pledging a fair return on their oil. That concern for the welfare of others, though genuine, would pay dividends to the United States. However it might benefit native populations, a sound economy contributed to the stability of local governments and to the safety of foreign concessions.[1]

Under the direction of Economic Adviser Herbert Feis, State Department planners had already composed a draft of the agreement they hoped to conclude. Though vague and tentative, the draft foreshadowed the understanding that the United States and Great Britain were to work out. Its preamble indicated the importance of petroleum to all nations both during and after the war. It also pointed to the predominance of British and American oil companies along the Persian Gulf and to the necessity of developing the region in an orderly

1. See, for example, unsigned memorandum, November 20, 1943, NA, RG 59, 800.6363/1397; Sappington memorandum, "Memorandum on the Department Position with Respect to the Proposal that the Government Purchase Stock Control or Participation in the California-Arabian Standard Oil Company . . . ," December 1, 1943, NA, RG 59, 890F.6363/93–1/2; W. L. Parker memorandum, "The Necessity of the Formulation of an Oil Policy by the Department," December 8, 1943, NA, RG 59, Pasvolsky File; Loftus memorandum, "United States Petroleum Policy in the Middle East," January 13, 1944, NA, RG 59, Notter File.

fashion—a responsibility that justified Anglo-American cooperation over the acquisition and exploitation of the area's reserves. The two governments, the draft continued, would work together to see that the region was developed according to "sound conservation practices," in order to promote the economic welfare of oil-producing countries and assure adequate reserves for the military forces of the United Nations. That concern about conservation reflected the State Department's appreciation of the mechanisms used by the oil industry to control production. Further, the department's draft, in the spirit of the Atlantic Charter, called for making Middle Eastern oil "freely available to all United Nations and other friendly countries on completely equal terms and conditions."

To effect cooperation, the signatories were to establish a petroleum board, at first limited to the United States and Great Britain but later open to "other directly interested governments"—presumably France and the Netherlands, whose companies shared concessions in the area. Through the petroleum board the two governments would consult regarding all the operations of their oil companies, including construction projects, negotiations for new concessions, joint ventures, and the distribution of production. Such consultation would give neither government a veto over the actions of the other's nationals, but it would provide both with a way of monitoring and influencing each other's oil policies. The function of the petroleum board would be to report periodically to the governments with recommendations for legislative and executive action to accomplish the purposes of the agreement. The board would also assist the two countries in devising an international pact for worldwide oil development.[2]

While other departments and agencies reviewed the draft, Hull and Ickes fought to direct the forthcoming negotiations. Though they agreed that the conversations should take place in Washington and should lead to a pact along the lines of the State Department draft, they

2. Feis, *Three International Episodes,* p. 138; a copy of the draft entitled "State Department Draft Agreement with the British on Petroleum in the Middle East" is contained in Boykin C. Wright to Secretary and Under Secretary of War, "Oil Concessions in the Middle East," November 30, 1943, NA, RG 59, 800.6363/1455. The draft agreement is dated September 16, 1943.

differed over the format of discussions and over who should conduct them. Hull wanted exploratory talks among technicians to precede a cabinet-level conference, with both under the direction of the State Department. His invitation to the British government had already committed the United States to "informal and preliminary" talks, and he believed that any changes might suggest to Whitehall and to the American oil industry confusion within the administration. Even the appearance of such confusion, he maintained, would damage department prestige and jeopardize chances of concluding an agreement. Besides, Hull insisted, the complexity of international oil problems required full-time consideration from technical and political experts who were unhampered by cabinet responsibilities.[3]

Ickes, characteristically eager to direct policy, stressed the importance of speed. He thought staff discussions an unnecessary delay at a time when oil problems demanded immediate attention. With the end of the war in sight, he was also convinced that the United States should press the advantage offered by British concern over the Petroleum Reserves Corporation. After the war, he suspected, London might be unwilling to discuss Middle Eastern oil. He also believed that the approaching presidential election could turn on the rapidity and deftness with which the administration concluded an Anglo-American petroleum agreement. Recent attacks by congressional conservatives against Allied supply decisions and against the Petroleum Reserves Corporation and persistent talk in the press of dwindling American reserves portended an all-out assault against administration oil policy. An oil agreement, Ickes held, would buttress the president's defenses.[4]

Ickes insisted on handling the negotiations. He argued that as petroleum administrator and as president of the Petroleum Reserves Corporation, he was best equipped to deal with oil matters. He was equally certain that he alone could carry the discussions to a successful end. By virtue of his efforts to bring about the conference, he felt that re-

3. Hull to Ickes, January 3, 1944, NA, RG 253, Grey Box II, Ralph K. Davies Folder; Joseph Grew to Roosevelt, FDRL, Roosevelt Papers, PSF (172).
4. Ickes to Roosevelt, January 4, 1944, Ickes to Roosevelt, May 29, 1944, FDRL, Roosevelt Papers, PSF (66).

sponsibility for conducting it belonged to him. "In a sense," he told President Roosevelt late in December 1943, "this is my baby."[5]

During the first few months of 1944 Ickes and Hull took their respective cases to the president, with whom Ickes held the advantage. Over the years Roosevelt had come to rely on Ickes's sharp tongue in political scraps and on his unflagging energy for tough administrative work. Their relationship extended beyond the Oval Office to Ickes's secluded house near Chevy Chase Lake. There Ickes entertained the president and a small group of his advisers with good food, idle conversation, and poker for tiny stakes. Though Ickes, as he put it, never treated Roosevelt "with familiarity," the two played familiar games. In a huff over some slight, Ickes would threaten to resign; Roosevelt, with feigned mendicancy, would charm him back into the administration. Ickes would send the president a stream of letters filled with complaints and recommendations; Roosevelt would put him off. Ickes would persist, and in the end his persistence would produce concessions from the White House.[6]

Hull enjoyed no such access. Roosevelt liked him and his Wilsonian ideals but, during the war as before it, increasingly ignored him. The omission of Hull from the delegation that accompanied Roosevelt to Casablanca, Cairo, and Tehran reflected the extent to which the president had passed him by, doubtless because Roosevelt wished to conduct foreign policy unimpeded by Hull's interpretations of internationalism. Such rebuffs left Hull brooding and bitter, ever more isolated from the conduct of wartime diplomacy.[7]

By February 1944 Ickes had just about convinced Roosevelt of the need for holding cabinet-level talks as soon as possible. British hedging and the appearance of unauthorized newspaper stories about the conference finally moved the president to Ickes's van. For two months

5. Ickes to Roosevelt, December 27, 1943, FDRL, Roosevelt Papers, PSF (89).

6. Schlesinger, *Coming of the New Deal*, p. 579. For an example of Roosevelt's style in dealing with Ickes, see Ickes to Roosevelt, May 29, 1944, Roosevelt to Ickes, May 30, 1944, FDRL, Roosevelt Papers, PSF (66).

7. Schlesinger, *Coming of the New Deal*, p. 192; Drummond, "Cordell Hull," in Graebner, ed., *Uncertain Tradition*, pp. 184–209.

the Foreign Office had delayed accepting Hull's invitation. Initially the British had postponed their reply with a promise to answer after Churchill had met with Roosevelt at Tehran in December 1943. The British were hoping that during the parley Churchill would learn more about American intentions, but a heavy agenda kept the two leaders from discussing oil. A query from Washington early in January still produced no response, this time because the Petroleum Division saw no need to rush matters now that the Petroleum Reserves Corporation was under fire from Congress and the industry. Further inquiries from the State Department finally yielded an acceptance on February 7, 1944. The British, it seemed, were in no hurry to get to the conference table.[8]

In the meantime, stories describing the oil conference and the agreement it was to produce began to appear in the press. British hesitation forced Roosevelt to deny at a press conference early in February any knowledge of a British mission coming to Washington to discuss oil. It was pure Roosevelt—thé denial did have some substance. Although they had consented to talks, the British had yet to agree to hold the conference in the United States. Unconvinced by the president's answer, reporters pressed the question at the State Department, where Under Secretary of State Stettinius admitted that Anglo-American oil talks were to take place and "at an early date."[9]

The date had yet to be set. In part to hasten matters, in part to placate Ickes, Roosevelt in mid-February named him chairman of the negotiating team, which also included other high-ranking officials. Hull, who had been away from Washington, was infuriated when he returned. He reminded Roosevelt that with his consent he had already

8. Halifax to F. O., December 5, 1943, no. 5510, PRO, FO 371, W7686/3710/65; Memorandum by Ministry of Fuel and Power (Petroleum Division), "Anglo-American Oil Policy," c. January 1944, PRO, FO 371, W793/34/76; Winant to Hull, January 3, 1944, NA, RG 59, 800.6363/1416; Law to Lloyd, January 18, 1944, PRO, FO 371, W1361/34/76; Lloyd to Law, January 20, 1944, PRO, FO 371, W1360/34/76; LeRougetel to Law, January 25, 1944, PRO, FO 371, W872/34/76; LeRougetel minute, c. January 1944, PRO, FO 371, W793/34/76; Stettinius to Halifax, January 11, 1944, NA, RG 59, 800.6363/1439b; Halifax to Hull, February 7, 1944, NA, RG 59, 800.6363/1482-1/2.

9. *NYT,* February 11, 1944, February 12, 1944.

advised the British and several executives of American oil companies that the conversations would be conducted on a working level under State Department leadership. To prevent his Secretary of State from losing more face, to preserve the State Department's role in negotiations with foreign governments, and, characteristically, to avoid an open fight within his cabinet, Roosevelt split the differences. He decided that Hull would head a cabinet-level delegation to the oil conference and that Ickes would serve as vice-chairman.[10]

On February 15, 1944, Under Secretary Stettinius informed British ambassador Halifax of the change. The president's thought now, Stettinius said, was to convene a ministerial conference in Washington within the next few weeks. Stettinius would "button up any loose ends" from the Washington talks when he visited London at the end of March to discuss Anglo-American problems in the Middle East. If the British were agreeable, the State Department would issue a press release describing the conference and listing the American delegates. Stunned and irritated by the sudden changes, Halifax replied that the British were not agreeable. Despite that response, three days later Roosevelt told the ambassador that he planned to open the conference himself.[11]

Roosevelt's impatience to convene the oil conference reflected the pressure he felt at home, where domestic politics underscored the desirability of speed. Since returning from their tour of Allied warfronts, the five senators had kept up a barrage of criticism aimed at administration petroleum policies. They continued to point to disparities between British and American contributions to the Allied oil pool, and they called for the formulation of a foreign oil policy to guarantee adequate supplies for the future. Republicans E. H. Moore of Oklahoma and R. Owen Brewster of Maine introduced in the Senate late in January a resolution demanding the dissolution of the Petroleum

10. Those officials included the under secretaries of state, war, and navy, as well as the deputy director of the War Production Board. Hull, *Memoirs*, vol. 2, pp. 1522–23; Stettinius to Roosevelt, February 12, 1944, NA, RG 59, 800.6363/1495a; Hull, *Memoirs*, vol. 2, p. 1523.

11. Halifax to F. O., February 15, 1944, no. 751, PRO, FO 371, W2344/34/76; Halifax to F. O., February 18, 1944, no. 839, PRO, FO 371, W2642/34/76.

Reserves Corporation. Over the years Moore, an independent oil man, and Brewster, as strong and steady a conservative as could be found in Congress, had made opposition to the New Deal their religion. Their demand for disbanding the Petroleum Reserves Corporation could only be viewed as an attack on the administration, especially since Brewster had been among the first to score Roosevelt for failing to monitor British oil contributions to the war effort.[12]

Brewster had also served on the Truman Committee, whose report on overseas petroleum matters, released in the middle of February 1944, took a harsh view of administration oil policy. The report condemned government ownership of concessions abroad, insisted on full diplomatic support of private operations in foreign countries, and suggested that Great Britain recompense the United States by giving up a portion of British-owned reserves. More important, the report added, was an agreement among the Allies for equitable distribution of future discoveries. Most important, it concluded, was the "formulation of a positive, vigorous American policy on the whole subject." That task, the senators assumed, would fall to Congress. But by convening the oil conference quickly and by chairing the opening session himself, Roosevelt planned to serve notice on his critics that he was capable of dealing with the British and of charting national policy for foreign oil.[13]

The British, though aware that domestic as well as bureaucratic politics explained the quickened pace of American diplomacy, were unwilling to follow Washington's lead. "These fits and starts on [the] American side are infuriating," Halifax wrote after his interview with Stettinius. Tall, stoop-shouldered, a gaunt figure with aristocratic

12. R. Owen Brewster, "Don't Blame the British—Blame Us!" *Collier's*, December 25, 1943, pp. 21, 68, 70; *NYT*, February 10, 1944, February 16, 1944; U. S., Congress, Senate, *Congressional Record*, 78th Cong., 2nd Sess. (Washington, 1944), vol. 90, pt. 1, 1135-38, pt. 2, 1466, 1468-71; Minutes of Special Meeting of Directors of Petroleum Reserves Corporation, January 27, 1944, NA, RG 48, File 1-188: Petroleum Reserves Corporation, Folder 2845.

13. U. S., Congress, Senate, Special Committee Investigating the National Defense Program, *Additional Report of the Subcommittee Concerning Investigations Overseas. Section 1—Petroleum Matters*, S. Rept. 10, Part 15, 78th Cong., 2nd Sess. (Washington, 1944).

bearing that befit high station, Lord Halifax was an astute observer of court intrigue. He realized that the new format Stettinius had presented was, in large degree, the result of a "prolonged tussle" between Ickes and Hull. Still, Halifax found the changes unacceptable because they prejudged the site and level of the talks, issues he and his government thought open.[14]

When they received Hull's invitation early in December 1943, British authorities in the Petroleum Division and in the Foreign Office had expected that any discussions about oil would be held in London at the staff level. Unsure of what Hull had in mind, they saw preliminary talks as a way of exploring American thinking without committing either government and with little publicity. They preferred to talk in London because they believed that technicians would there be free from the political pressures endemic to Washington in an election year. Those pressures, they suspected, might generate public demands for the surrender of British rights, which British delegates would have to refuse. Officials at Whitehall also realized that in London they would be able to field a stronger negotiating team, since British participants would have on hand oil experts unavailable in the United States. The symbolic value of the London site did not escape them either. They feared that traveling to the United States to talk about Middle Eastern oil would be a sign of declining British prestige in international oil affairs. Such a journey might leave the Americans with the impression, as one British diplomat commented, that "they can call the tune in the Middle East."[15]

Whether the talks were to be held in London or in Washington, at

14. Halifax to F. O., February 15, 1944, no. 751, PRO, FO 371, W2433/34/76. Halifax continued to urge meeting with the Americans. For a more balanced assessment, see Halifax to F. O., February 20, 1944, no. 865, PRO, F. O. 371, W2863/34/76. On Halifax, see Robert Sherwood, *Roosevelt and Hopkins: An Intimate History* (New York, 1950), p. 237.

15. Hankey minute, January 11, 1944, PRO, FO 371, E225/16/25; memorandum by Ministry of Fuel and Power (Petroleum Division), "Anglo-American Oil Policy," c. January 1944, PRO, FO 371, W793/34/76; LeRougetel minute, January 13, 1944, W964/34/76; Lloyd to Law, January 20, 1944, W1360/34/76; Hankey minute, January 26, 1944, PRO, FO 371, E417/16/65; Law to Churchill, February 19, 1944, PRO, FO 371, W2642/34/76.

the staff or at the cabinet level, was less important to the British than protecting their concession rights in the Middle East. Since British oil companies had already received complaints from their American partners about commercial restrictions imposed by His Majesty's Government in the Middle East, British officials expected American negotiators to insist on a modification of those policies. Given American concern over domestic reserves, given too the political climate in Washington, the British also anticipated a demand for some of their oil concessions in the Middle East as compensation for petroleum supplies furnished by the United States during the war. Any such transfers would prove disastrous for Britain's postwar economy. Lacking indigenous reserves, Great Britain depended on oil from abroad to meet its industrial and military requirements. Oil was also one of the country's most valuable overseas assets. Petroleum sales generated much capital for British firms and for the British government and served as a vital source of foreign exchange, which promised to be in short supply after the war. With American officials determined to hold down British gold and dollar balances, with the further blow of a recent forced reduction in Lend-Lease assistance, and with a great debt already owed to the United States, Great Britain could afford to relinquish neither commercial rights nor oil.[16]

The British had some justification for their fears. Certainly one of the purposes of the State Department in promoting the conference was to persuade Great Britain to relax commercial restrictions on oil operations in the Middle East—to end, for example, the practice of permitting only British incorporated companies with British directors and British staffs to exploit oil in Persian Gulf states and sheikhdoms pro-

16. Memorandum by Ministry of Fuel and Power (Petroleum Division), ''Anglo-American Oil Policy,'' c. January 1944, PRO, FO 371, W793/34/76; Petroleum Division memorandum, ''Anglo-American Oil Policy,'' January 27, 1944, PRO, FO 371, W1384/34/76; Lord Beaverbrook to Churchill, February 14, 1944, PRO, FO 371, W2486/34/76; memorandum by Albert V. Alexander, First Lord of the Admiralty, W. P. (44)126, ''Oil Conference with the United States of America,'' PRO, FO 371, W2932/34/76; Petroleum Division memorandum, ''Anglo-American Oil Policy,'' January 27, 1944, PRO, FO 371, W1384/34/76; John M. Blum, *From the Morgenthau Diaries: Years of War, 1941–1945* (Boston, 1967), pp. 131–37; Petroleum Division memorandum, ''Oil Policy,'' March 17, 1944, PRO, FO 371, W4654/34/76.

tected by the British government. Furthermore, various proposals for transferring British reserves to the United States had been circulated in Washington. In October 1943 the director of the Office of War Mobilization, James Byrnes, had recommended that the British assign to the United States one-third of their interest in the Iranian oil fields as payment for Lend-Lease petroleum products. That plan had gone no farther than the White House, where it died of neglect. Even after the British had accepted the invitation, Harold Ickes in February 1944 suggested to the British petroleum representative in Washington that, as a gesture ''of great political value,'' his government turn over to the Petroleum Reserves Corporation its half-interest in the Kuwait Oil Company. Ambassador Halifax saw the suggestion for what it was, a ''try-on,'' as he described it, designed to test British resolve. He told his colleagues to ignore it, just as he cautioned them against attaching too much significance to the demand for British oil concessions in the Truman Committee report. That congressional accounting, he assured them, had been drafted for ''internal political consumption.'' The ambassador's reassurances notwithstanding, officials at Whitehall remained skeptical about American intentions.[17]

Neither Roosevelt nor Ickes seriously entertained hopes of acquiring British-owned reserves in payment for Lend-Lease oil. Roosevelt had let Byrnes's recommendation drop without a reply. Ickes never again mentioned his proposal for obtaining British holdings in Kuwait. Instead of compensation, what Roosevelt and Ickes really sought was cooperation from the British. At times the earnestness of that wish made the two men extravagant. Roosevelt, in one instance, told Ambassador Halifax in January 1944 that he hoped to devise some system of ''pooling'' oil resources to ensure equitable distribution after the war. He also offered the possibility of securing reserves in the ground for United Nations control, in order to guard against future wars. A month later Ickes followed with a suggestion to an associate at

17. Fred Searles to Byrnes, August 13, 1943, Searles to Byrnes, October 12, 1943, FDRL, Roosevelt Papers, OF (56); Byrnes to Roosevelt, October 15, 1943, reprinted in *Arabian Oil Hearings,* 25430; Halifax to F. O., February 11, 1944, no. 701, PRO, FO 371, W2206/34/76; Halifax to F. O., February 20, 1944, no. 860, PRO, FO 371, W2717/34/76.

the British embassy that the two governments form a "joint Anglo-American Middle Eastern Holding Company" for developing oil resources along the Persian Gulf.[18]

Such notions probably came to both men in the expansive moments to which they frequently succumbed, though the proposals did reflect long-term goals for the development and use of oil. At the same time, they served the more immediate purpose of assuring the British that they had nothing to fear from the oil conference. As Halifax reported after speaking to Roosevelt, "the whole spirit in which they [the Americans] were approaching the oil discussions was that of seeking our joint mutual advantage, and that only."[19]

The Trans-Arabian Pipeline

Ickes and Roosevelt relied on more than kind words to encourage their British allies. On February 6, 1944, the day before Halifax accepted Hull's invitation to the conference, Ickes fired what he called a "blunderbuss shot," which he hoped would shake the British from their lethargy and furnish the United States with an insurance policy. Without warning, he announced that the Petroleum Reserves Corporation had agreed with the American companies operating on the Arabian peninsula to build and to operate a government-owned pipeline from the Persian Gulf across Saudi Arabia to the Mediterranean Sea.[20]

The details of the agreement had yet to be worked out, but according to the "Outline of Principles" that Ickes made public, the government would construct, at a cost of between $130 million and $165 million, a trunk-line system to serve as a common carrier for oil produced on the Arabian peninsula. In return, the companies guaranteed the government an underground reserve of one billion barrels of oil in the area. The government would be able to purchase any of that oil at a discount of 25 percent of the market price in the United States. During wars and

18. Halifax to F. O., January 19, 1944, PRO, FO 371, W942/34/76; Halifax to F. O., February 11, 1944, no. 701, PRO, FO 371, W2206/34/76.

19. Halifax to F. O., February 18, 1944, no. 837, PRO, FO 371, W2641/34/76.

20. *NYT*, February 6, 1944; Halifax to F. O., February 11, 1944, no. 701, PRO, FO 371, W2206/34/76.

national emergencies it would have preemptive rights to buy all the oil produced in the concessions. Charges for pipeline service were to provide enough funds to cover operating and maintenance costs and to amortize the initial investment within twenty-five years. Most important, the companies pledged to notify the State Department of any negotiations to sell to foreign governments petroleum or petroleum products from their concessions in Saudi Arabia and in Kuwait. If the State Department objected to those sales as militating against the interests of the United States, the companies pledged to terminate the transactions. They also agreed to align their commercial practices and policies with official foreign policy.[21]

The pipeline agreement raised government-industry cooperation to a new level. In effect, the companies had given the government a seat in their boardrooms, for federal authorities could now exercise some control over commercial policies. Though the oil companies had always consulted the State Department on an informal basis, they had never before entered into a contractual obligation to obtain official approval for transactions with foreign governments. Their vow to keep company plans in line with foreign policy gave the government still another opportunity to exert influence on commercial developments. And, according to a separate clause in the agreement, the Petroleum Reserves Corporation would have a voice in determining the rate of production in the oil fields, since the companies and the government together were to fix the amount of oil tendered for transport through the pipeline.[22]

As with many of the oil projects proposed by the administration during the war, the pipeline agreement had its origins both inside and outside government circles. As early as 1940 James Byrnes had recommended a similar scheme to the president. With the country not yet at war, such plans must have seemed premature, for no one acted on

21. Halifax to F. O., February 11, 1944, no. 701, PRO, FO 371, W2206/34/76; "Outline of Principles of Proposed Agreement," January 24, 1944, NA, RG 253, Anglo-American Oil Agreement File, Grey Box II, Saudi Arabia Folder.

22. "Outline of Principles of Proposed Agreement," January 24, 1944, NA, RG 253, Anglo-American Oil Agreement File, Grey Box II, Saudi Arabia Folder. For Ickes on degree of federal control, see Ickes Diaries, vol. 52, 8566-67.

the recommendation. Some of Byrnes's aides resuscitated the project in the summer of 1943 as a means of increasing Middle Eastern production to ease the postwar strain on domestic reserves. Again, the proposal met with little enthusiasm, though Byrnes did ask Deputy Petroleum Administrator Ralph K. Davies to prepare an estimate of the cost and time that would be involved in constructing the line.[23]

There matters stood until December 1943, when the Arabian American Oil Company (Aramco) informed the State Department of its plans to build a trans-Arabian pipeline. The venture, former petroleum adviser Max Thornburg told an old colleague at the department, had strategic importance for the future but was of no such value now because the company would be unable to complete construction in time for use during the war. As a result, Thornburg saw no need for federal participation, except to help secure the necessary transit rights in countries through which the pipeline would pass.[24]

Although he claimed to have visited the State Department "to renew personal acquaintances and to discuss informally" the work he now performed for Socal and Texaco, Thornburg was really there to

23. Mosley, *Power Play,* p. 155n. There were actually several pipeline proposals, among them facilities to connect the Kuwait fields to the Mediterranean Sea and to connect the Iranian fields to Haifa, Searles to Byrnes, August 13, 1943, FDRL, Roosevelt Papers, OF (56); Minutes Meeting of the Foreign Development Operations Committee Box, Folder 744; Searles to Byrnes, October 12, 1943, Davies to Searles, October 12, 1943, A. H. Chapman memorandum, "Pipelines to Connect Iranian Oil Fields to the Mediterranean," October 12, 1943, FDRL, Roosevelt Papers, OF (56). Davies had also suggested to Ickes the possibility of constructing a pipeline across Arabia before Byrnes approached him. See Ickes Diaries, vol. 46, 7474, vol. 47, 7631.

24. In 1943 the name of the California-Arabian Standard Oil Company was changed to the Arabian American Oil Company, Shwadran, *MEOGP,* p. 344n. Rayner memorandum conversation with Thornburg, December 4, 1943, NA, RG 59, 800.6363/1387-1/2. Thornburg's estimate of the time it would take to complete the pipeline was later supported by a study conducted by the Office of Strategic Services. Completed in May 1944, the report took a dim view of the pipeline scheme as a wartime project and argued that the facility would not be completed soon enough to furnish oil for the war effort. That, in addition to commercial and security considerations, led the authors of the report to advocate dropping the project as a war measure. "The Relation of the Proposed Saudi Arabian Pipeline to United States Interests in Middle Eastern Oil," May 5, 1944, NA, Records of the Office of Strategic Services, Record Group 226, hereafter cited as RG 226, O. S. S. Report no. 109155S.

test official sentiment before Aramco made a more formal approach. That bid came three weeks later, when Aramco president Fred A. Davies asked the department if the company could expect diplomatic assistance with the project. "We believe," he added, "that the Department will not need to be reminded of the importance which Saudi Arabian oil, available in large quantities in the Mediterranean and completely under the control of American nationals, would have on our own domestic oil reserves decline." Nor did he need to explain, as he made sure to point out, that his company had already assured the State Department that Aramco plans squared with official policy.[25]

State Department officials replied in terms inviting enough to indicate interest but tepid enough to suggest their reluctance to embrace a project that might upset the approaching oil talks. Of course, they wrote Davies early in January 1944, they welcomed projects that would increase the development of American-owned concessions anywhere in the world, and they looked with favor on this one. They commended Davies for soliciting the view of the department but warned him that "there are now certain questions and developments relating to oil in the Middle East area to which a project of this nature must be properly related." They made no commitments to the company other than a promise to consider the proposal "in light of military requirements and the materials situation." But they did ask to be kept abreast of the progress of the venture.[26]

While the company discussed its pipeline project with the State Department, Ickes was trying to revitalize the beleaguered Petroleum Reserves Corporation. That task seemed all the more urgent in view of promising reports from an exploratory oil mission he had sent to the Middle East in November 1943. The survey team, headed by prominent oil geologist Everett Lee DeGolyer, confirmed in January 1944 what Ickes had long suspected. In its preliminary report it stated that "the center of gravity of world oil production is shifting from the Caribbean

25. Rayner memorandum of conversation with Thornburg, December 4, 1943, NA, RG 59, 800.6363/1379–1/2; F. A. Davies to Murray, December 27, 1943, NA, RG 59, 890F.6363/91.

26. Rayner to F. A. Davies, January 7, 1944, NA, RG 59, 890F.6363/91.

area to the Middle East—to the Persian Gulf area.'' DeGolyer expected that for the foreseeable future the shift would be permanent. He estimated that the region contained reserves of about 26 billion barrels of oil (already more than the 22 billion barrels within the United States) and concluded that, with much territory still unexplored, ''reserves of great magnitude remain to be discovered.''[27]

The news strengthened Ickes's determination to secure a share of the new treasure. Unfortunately, it came at a time when he found himself without a strategy for doing so. He floundered only for a moment. Soon after DeGolyer began filing his reports, Commodore Andrew F. Carter, the ambitious executive officer of the Army-Navy Petroleum Board, came up with the solution. Carter, another oil man pressed into wartime service, had recently returned from a trip to Saudi Arabia. After conferring with representatives of local governments and of the interested oil companies, he proposed that the United States build and own a pipeline across the peninsula. In exchange for constructing the line, the government would receive an option to buy at favorable prices or to keep in reserve at least one billion barrels of oil from the concessions in Arabia and in Kuwait. In addition, Carter recommended that the administration release the steel and equipment necessary for Aramco to build a refinery in Arabia and that the State Department undertake negotiations with the British to remove all restrictions on production and on marketing in the area.[28]

Here, Carter argued, was the way to encourage development of the

27. Accompanying DeGolyer on the mission were Dr. W. E. Wrather, director of the United States Geological Survey, and C. S. Snodgrass, director of the Foreign Refining Division of the Petroleum Administration for War. The breakdown DeGolyer reported of proven and indicated reserves within each country were: Iran, six to seven billion barrels; Iraq, five billion barrels; Saudi Arabia, four to five billion barrels; Kuwait, nine billion barrels; Qatar, one billion barrels. E. L. DeGolyer, ''Preliminary Report of the Technical Oil Mission to the Middle East,'' February 1, 1944, NA, RG 253, Anglo-American Oil Agreement File, Grey Box I, Folder 1. As DeGolyer foresaw, reserves ''of great magnitude'' remained to be discovered. Recent estimates have located in Saudi Arabia alone proven reserves of 167 billion barrels, *NYT,* October 5, 1976.

28. Carter to Knox, January 17, 1944, NA, RG 334, File ANPB: 14/1-Foreign Petroleum Policy, Misc. Folder; Carter memorandum, January 17, 1944, *FRUS* (1944), vol. 5, pp. 17-20.

region and to safeguard American concessions without putting Washington in competition with the oil industry. Carter, who had often represented the military services at meetings of the Petroleum Reserves Corporation, had himself been an early proponent of purchasing stock in Aramco, but he had come to realize that the industry would never permit such an arrangement. He now offered an alternative that skirted the dangers of federal participation in company ownership by combining earlier proposals for options on Arabian oil with a government construction project that still put the United States unequivocally in the Middle East.[29]

Ickes liked the scheme so much that he made it his own. In one stroke, as he noted, "a pipeline would give an outlet for American oil, would be to the decided benefit of Saudi Arabia, as well as Kuwait, and would block further British encroachment in the Near East oil fields effectively." It would also justify diplomatic or even military intervention to protect the American-owned concessions. All along Ickes had been worried about the willingness of the American people to defend privately owned concessions in far-off countries. A government pipeline would be "a national interest that the people would be willing to protect." It had the further advantages of increasing the importance of American companies in Middle Eastern oil development and of ensuring greater harmony between the foreign policy of the United States and the commercial policies of Aramco and Gulf. At the same time it would impress London with the potency of the Petroleum Reserves Corporation.[30]

As soon as he read Carter's proposal, Ickes advised the Joint Chiefs of Staff to support Aramco's request for permission to build a refinery in Saudi Arabia. That request, which Ickes once had used unsuccessfully to induce Texaco and Socal to sell Aramco, had become an integral part of the pipeline project. Without it, as James Terry Duce earlier pointed out, the pipeline would be of little use. Ickes then approached Socal, Texaco, and Gulf. Prepared for the initiative by a visit

29. Carter memorandum, January 17, 1944, *FRUS* (1944), vol. 5, pp. 17–20.
30. Ickes Diaries, vol. 52, 8557–58, 8534, 8566–67, 8630.

from Carter and in need of funds for their own pipeline project, company executives greeted the proposal warmly.[31]

Negotiations were conducted in secret, since Ickes wished to present the British and the Saudis with a fait accompli. Open discussions, he knew, would be slow and clumsy, especially if domestic producers raised the specter of government control in foreign fields. On January 24, 1944, after only five days of bargaining, company officials signed the "Outline of Principles," which Ickes made public early in February. Two days later the Joint Chiefs of Staff authorized the construction of a privately owned refinery in Arabia.[32]

Almost without exception, Ickes's colleagues applauded the pipeline agreement, as did the president. The day after Ickes signed the tentative contract, the Joint Chiefs of Staff approved it as vital to the prosecution of the war. That commendation satisfied the secretaries of war and navy, who also endorsed the project. Navy secretary Frank Knox must have been especially pleased with the new-found life of the Petroleum Reserves Corporation. Though no advocate of government incursions into the private sector, Knox had argued against freezing the activities of the corporation when Hull had earlier demanded it. "The best way," he had told Hull, "to get serious consideration from the British in the prospective negotiations with them about oil resources is to have some ace up our sleeve." Knox's "ace" was to have been the government's share of an oil company, but a government-owned pipeline would serve his purpose just as well. James Byrnes, conscious of the shady deals oil men sometimes made, noted that the pipeline scheme bypassed a danger posed by federal stock ownership. "If the government were in business with the oil companies," Byrnes explained, "and the oil companies competing with the nationals of other governments should show favors to local officials, the Byrd Committee, or some other [congressional] commit-

31. Ickes to Admiral Ernest J. King, Chief of Naval Operations, January 18, 1944, NA, RG 59, 800.6363/1468; Minutes Meeting of Foreign Development Operations Committee, October 8, 1943, NA, RG 253, Foreign Development Operations Committee Box, Folder 744.

32. Minutes of Special Meeting of Directors of the Petroleum Reserves Corporation, January 27, 1944, NA, RG 48, File 1–188: Petroleum Reserves Corporation, Folder 2845; Leahy to Hull, January 26, 1944, NA, RG 59, 800.6363/1494.

tee, would demand an accounting." Only Hull, among top officials, had reservations. He was still unwilling to involve the government in any part of the oil industry. Overwhelmed, however, by the pipeline's military honor guard, he finally acquiesced, though not before he wrung from Ickes pledges to review the question of future ownership and to have the oil companies operate the facility.[33]

The pipeline scheme provoked other doubts. Some internationalists within the State Department charged the agreement with violating the equal-access clause of the Atlantic Charter. In their view guaranteed reserves and preferential price arrangements could be viewed as attempts to corner a substantial quantity of oil. Some in the diplomatic corps rightly questioned the practicability of an option on oil in Saudi Arabia, where reserves would be vulnerable to local attack. In that case, warned Leo Crowley of the Foreign Economic Administration, the responsibility of the United States for defending both its oil and its pipeline would far exceed its military capability in the region. Crowley added to that drawback a host of political problems. "The agreement," he observed, "may be interpreted in some quarters as an exclusive arrangement for the defense of the United States discriminating against the access of other countries to important reserves, qualifying the independence of local states, and burdening the United States with important political responsibilities in Arabia." Ickes took no notice of those criticisms. Heady with the promise of the pipeline and dazzled by the ease of preliminary negotiations, he was blind to the weaknesses of the project.[34]

On the Hill, where Republicans and southern Democrats were already upset with government encroachments on the oil industry, the

33. Byrnes to Roosevelt, January 25, 1944, FDRL, Roosevelt Papers, OF (56); Knox and Stimson to Ickes, January 26, 1944, NA, RG 334, File ANPB: 21/2(a)-Petroleum Reserves, General Misc. Correspondence Folder; Knox to Hull, January 11, 1944, NA, RG 59, 800.6363/1437; Byrnes to Roosevelt, January 25, 1944, FDRL, Roosevelt Papers, OF (56); Hull, *Memoirs,* vol. 2, p. 1522; Minutes Special Meeting of Directors of the Petroleum Reserves Corporation, January 27, 1944, NA, RG 48, File 1-188: Petroleum Reserves Corporation, Folder 2845.

34. B. F. Haley to Hawkins, February 3, 1944, NA, RG 59, 800.6363/1505; Leavell to Alling, February 3, 1944, NA, RG 59, 800.6363/1511; Leo Crowley to Cox and Stettinius, February 15, 1944, FDRL, Cox Papers, Box 67, F. E. A. Chronological File.

pipeline aroused considerable protest. Oklahoma senator E. H. Moore, in words that recalled the rhetoric of early opponents of the New Deal, denounced the project as another scheme of "White House planners," who visualized "the socialization of the oil business and other basic industries." Moore, an oil man himself, told Ickes on a radio debate that the pipeline was "needless, useless and impractical," a reckless venture in imperialism "fraught with international complications, dangers and hazards," Along with Owen Brewster, he called early in February 1944 for the creation of a special Senate committee to investigate and to recommend national policies for oil development. Meanwhile, in the House, Republican Howard Buffett of Nebraska put to his war-weary colleagues the frightening prospect of conscripted Americans sent by their government "in a few short years . . . to fight, bleed and die on the trackless sands of Arabia to defend this pipeline."[35]

The pipeline received a chilly reception in the press. Liberal and conservative newspapers alike repeated the charges of unfriendly congressmen and added accusations of their own. They depicted the pipeline as everything from a "sellout to the oil companies" to undue interference with private enterprise. More measured but no less hostile was the assessment of Herbert Feis, who had served as midwife at the birth of the Petroleum Reserves Corporation. Feis, no longer with the State Department, cautioned against the commercial and political embroilments the pipeline would bring, just as he had earlier warned of the dangers of federal ownership of an oil company.[36]

35. *NYT*, February 10, 1944, March 17, 1944; *Washington Post*, February 7, 1944; U. S., Congress, Senate, *Congressional Record*, 78th Cong., 2nd Sess. (Washington, 1944), vol. 90, pt. 2, 1466, 1468-71. The Senate approved the resolution in March 1944, and a special eleven-member committee was appointed, *Congressional Record*, 78th Cong., 2nd Sess., vol. 90, pt. 2, 2489-90, 2559-60. *Congressional Record*, 78th Cong., 2nd Sess., vol. 90, pt. 8, A1036. For further comments, see *Congressional Record*, 78th Cong., 2nd Sess., vol. 90, pt. 8, A1070, A1158-59, A1468-69.

36. *PM*, February 6, 1944; *Washington Evening Star*, February 9, 1944; *Memphis Press Scimitar*, March 1, 1944; *Houston Texas Post*, March 4, 1944; *San Francisco Chronicle*, March 4, 1944; *LaFayette Journal*, March 7, 1944; *Columbia Record*, March 7, 1944; *Tulsa-Oklahoma Tribune*, March 13, 1944; *New York Sun*, March 14, 1944; *Newsweek*, March 20, 1944; *New York Herald Tribune*, March 23, 1944. See also "Public Attitudes on Foreign Policy: U. S. Arabian Oil Policy," March 18, 1944, NA, RG 59, 711.00 Public Attitudes, Report no. 15. Herbert Feis, *Petroleum and Foreign Policy* (Stanford, 1944), pp. 40-50.

Among oil men the pipeline agreement produced venomous responses. On March 1, 1944, the Petroleum Industry War Council passed a resolution reiterating its demand for the abolition of the Petroleum Reserves Corporation and urging abandonment of the pipeline project. All but the three companies party to the project voted for the resolution; those three alone defended the plan. John A. Brown, president of competitor Socony-Vacuum, fought the pipeline in the name of free enterprise—and in the interest of his stockholders. Cheap Arabian crude on the eastern shore of the Mediterranean would provide stiff competition in Europe for his company's oil from Iraq and from the Caribbean. Jersey Standard, with a considerably larger share of the European market, had vice-president Eugene Holman point out that the United States no longer needed to be concerned about Middle Eastern oil. According to Holman, estimates now showed that the country had reserves enough "for more than a thousand years to come."[37]

Fearing a collapse of domestic prices should foreign oil enter the country, independent producers joined the attack. George A. Hill, Jr., president of the Houston Oil Company and a spokesman for independents, called the project "fascist" and accused it of "shackling . . . American free enterprise, not to better serve, but to displace private enterprises." In March 1944 those charges received the approval of the Petroleum Industry War Council and the Independent Petroleum Association of America. The president of the latter organization, Ralph T. Zook, denied assertions, as independents had done all along, that the United States was running out of oil. He stressed the damage that an influx of foreign oil would do to domestic producers. As for the pipeline, Zook branded it "a threat to national security," indefensible in wartime, and hence useless when needed most.[38]

37. "Resolution Adopted by the Petroleum Industry War Council," especially resolution of March 1, 1944, found in FDRL, Roosevelt Papers, OF (4436-b); *NYT,* March 3, 1944. For a defense of the pipeline scheme, see W. S. S. Rodgers's editorial, *Texaco Star,* Spring 1944, pp. 4-9; *NYT,* May 5, 1944; "Ickes' Arabian Nights," *Fortune,* June 1944, pp. 123-28, 273-74, 280; *NYT,* April 7, 1944.

38. Petroleum Industry War Council, "United States Foreign Oil Policy and Petroleum Reserves Corporation: An Analysis of the Effect of the Proposed Saudi Arabian Pipeline" (Washington, 1944) and appended "Resolutions Adopted by the Petroleum Industry War Council," especially resolution adopted on March 1, 1944; "The Pro-

At stake in the fight was more than the pipeline, more even than the fate of the Petroleum Reserves Corporation. Every critic in the industry had condemned the plan, in the words of Ralph Zook, as "an entering wedge by the Government into the private oil business."[39] The oil industry had not always looked with such displeasure on interference from Washington. Majors and independents had been ready to cooperate with the government in the war effort; they had even helped to erect a regulatory system during the New Deal. But those were endeavors over which they had exerted substantial influence. The pipeline was a different matter. It threatened to deprive the industry of its commercial independence as well as its preeminent role in setting national policy for foreign oil. Through the pipeline agreement the government could influence directly the production, marketing, and pricing arrangements throughout the Middle East and the world.

Not only principles but profits hung in the balance. Postwar Europe was a prize worth fighting for, and majors such as Socony-Vacuum and Jersey Standard refused to permit government planners to underwrite their competition even for the sake of national security. Independents as well stood to lose from the project, which in their view might flood the domestic market with inexpensive oil from the Middle East. Only tariffs and import quotas could protect them in that event, but so far Roosevelt had given every indication of abandoning such devices after the war. Better to ensure now that the pipeline was stillborn than to attempt to build trade barriers later.

British Reactions

The British received news of the pipeline with indignation. Again, they felt, the Americans had behaved badly by not consulting them on a matter of such importance to British interests. They projected that the pipeline would pump 300,000 barrels of oil daily across the Arabian

---

posed Arabian Pipe Line: A Threat to Our National Security," publication of an address by Ralph T. Zook, April 28, 1944 [n.p., n.d.].

39. Zook to Ickes, March 3, 1944, NA, RG 48, File 1–188: Petroleum Reserves Corporation, Folder 2845.

peninsula. That petroleum would compete directly with British production in Iraq and in Trinidad for European markets, which had absorbed no more than 850,000 barrels per day before the war. More irritating still, the Americans would need British assistance to obtain transit rights through countries with treaty obligations to His Majesty's Government. They would even have to receive special dispensation from London before completing negotiations with the oil companies, since the British government owned preemptive rights to all the petroleum produced by the Kuwait Oil Company. Perhaps most infuriating of all, the British were pleading for American material to add new pipelines to already existing lines in Iraq. For months the United States had rejected British petitions, in spite of criticism that the British were hoarding oil in the Middle East. Now Ickes announced his plan to build a pipeline more than twice the length of the British facility, a project that would increase production in Arabia at the expense of the Iraq Petroleum Company.[40]

Even so, some officials in London saw advantages for Britain in the plan. The Admiralty and the Chiefs of Staff argued that the American pipeline would furnish an alternative route to the lines in Iraq, which were open to attack from the north, and would help British armed forces to build up reserves in the eastern Mediterranean. They also maintained that the project would increase the likelihood of American assistance in policing local sea-lanes, though the British could probably expect aid in any event because American tankers were bound to use the Mediterranean after the war. At the Foreign Office, the Near Eastern Department raised no objections at all. Neville Butler of the North American Department even detected political benefits in the scheme. A pipeline terminus "as attractive as possible for the United

40. *NYT*, March 23, 1944; Wilkinson to H. E., The Ambassador, February 16, 1944, PRO, FO 371, W3282/34/76; Petroleum Division memorandum, "Oil Policy," March 17, 1944, especially pt. 7, PRO, FO 371, W4654/34/76. For figures on absorptive capacity of prewar European markets, see "The Relation of the Proposed Pipeline to United States Interests in Middle Eastern Oil," May 5, 1944, NA, RG 226, O. S. S. Report no. 1091558. Memorandum by the Ministry of Fuel and Power (Petroleum Division), O. C. B. (43)83, "Development of Oil Supplies in the Middle East," January 11, 1943, PRO, FO 371, E6682/3710/65; Cheetham to LeRougetel, March 6, 1944, PRO, FO 371, W3761/34/76.

States,'' Butler believed, might induce the Americans "to share in maintaining peace in the Mediterranean.''[41]

Even so, most British observers held the view of the Petroleum Division, which hoped, as ever, to avoid the participation of the United States government in the international oil business. The division counseled Whitehall to ignore the project, at least until it became clear that the Americans really were going to build the pipeline. To the relief of the British, that remained to be seen. As one official noted early in March 1944, criticism of the pipeline had grown so poisonous that the project might "be killed stone dead.''[42]

In public, where British newspapers railed against the pipeline, Whitehall and industry leaders kept silent. To reveal private anxieties would serve no purpose except to confirm Washington in its course. Foreign Secretary Anthony Eden was appropriately discreet in response to questions raised in Parliament early in February 1944. He told the House of Commons that, since he had received no official word from the United States, he had nothing to say about the pipeline project. He also assured the members of his certainty that Washington would consult all interested governments before it moved ahead.[43]

Despite that seeming indifference, neither Eden nor his colleagues could escape feeling the pressure the Americans were applying. Congressional criticism of British and American oil policies, Roosevelt's demands for a high-level conference, leaks to the press about the oil talks, and the pipeline agreement left the British concerned about Anglo-American relations and about oil. In a debate within the War Cabinet early in February 1944, Eden reminded his associates of how heavily the British leaned on the United States for wartime oil supplies

41. Report by the Chiefs of Staff, W. P. (44)187, "Strategic Aspects of the Discussion on Oil Policy," April 5, 1944, PRO, FO 371, W5803/34/76; Hankey minute, February 5, 1944, PRO, FO 371, W1748/34/76; Butler minute, February 24, 1944, PRO, FO 371, W1384/34/76.

42. Petroleum Division memorandum, "Oil Policy," March 17, 1944, especially pt. 7, PRO, FO 371, W4654/34/76; Hankey minute, March 7, 1944, PRO, FO 371, W3761/34/76; Cheetham to LeRougetel, March 6, 1944, PRO, FO 371, W3761/34/76.

43. See, for an example of newspaper attacks, "America in the Middle East," *The Economist*, March 11, 1944. *Parliamentary Debates* (House of Commons), 396, Col. 1744, February 9, 1944. As late as the end of April 1944, Eden had to report to Commons that he had still received no information about the pipeline, *Parliamentary Debates* (House of Commons), 399, Col. 786, April 26, 1944.

and for equipment essential to the future of their oil industry. As his aides at the Foreign Office observed, important questions about international monetary policy, civil aviation, and Lend-Lease were about to be settled. "In these circumstances," Eden reported to the War Cabinet on February 19, 1944, "to deny the United States Government an opportunity even to discuss oil problems would almost certainly prejudice the development of our oil industry after the war . . . and would also play into the hands of all enemies of Anglo-American cooperation."[44]

Accompanying Eden's defense of the oil talks was a plea for quick action that came as much in response to criticism within the London government as to the American pipeline project. William Maxwell Aitken, the press baron now Lord Beaverbrook and Lord Privy Seal, had set himself against the oil conference from the start. A sturdy defender of empire interests and private enterprise, a strong friend to Winston Churchill, Beaverbrook always proved to be a tough antagonist. He was as compact as a billiard ball and possessed of the self-assurance that attends poor boys who have become millionaires. Overlapping careers as newpaper magnate, financier, politician, and master organizer had made him adviser to prime ministers for over twenty years. Even in his late sixties, he bubbled with ideas and energy. As for the oil talks, he thought them part of a general assault launched by the United States to strip Britain of its assets. He believed, as one of his colleagues described it, "that if you talk you must give way." He refused to share British oil with the Americans, and his fear that Washington would make such demands seemed confirmed early in February, when the State Department sent a tentative agenda to London that included concession rights among the topics for discussion. After reading the wire Beaverbrook recommended putting the American invitation "in a pigeon hole," a move Eden rejected as difficult and dangerous.[45]

44. Eden memorandum, W. P. (44)119, "Oil," February 19, 1944, PRO, FO 371, W2920/34/76.

45. A. J. P. Taylor, *Beaverbrook* (New York, 1972); Lord Beaverbrook to Churchill, February 14, 1944, PRO, FO 371, W2486/34/76; Beaverbrook to Churchill, February 24, 1944, PRO, PREM 3, 332/6, 236; Beaverbrook dictaphone notes, February 1944, Beaverbrook Library, London, Papers of William Maxwell Aitken, Lord Beaverbrook, hereafter cited as Beaverbrook Papers, Cabinet Papers Box, Oil Folder; Law to Eden,

Diplomatic Haggling

Aware that the United States could act alone in the Middle East and having already agreed to an oil conference, the British could scarcely back out now. But they could try to make the Americans meet British terms. Lord Halifax had been attempting to do so for days. In meetings with Roosevelt's men and with the president himself, Halifax had continued to insist on holding the talks in London at the staff level. He also had asked repeatedly, in accordance with Foreign Office instructions, to bar from the conference questions involving "existing rights over oil property or products."[46]

Neither Roosevelt nor his subordinates would bend. They balked at eliminating the consideration of concession rights, not because they wanted to divest the British of oil but because they envisioned freewheeling discussions that would cover a wide range of oil problems. Nor would they consent to technical talks in London, even when Halifax explained that planning for the impending invasion of France had left the British without ministers to spare for an oil conference abroad. Domestic politics, in Roosevelt's view, required a high-level meeting in Washington.[47]

The Americans did show some sensitivity to British concerns. The State Department had earlier granted British requests to extend the scope of the talks beyond the Middle East. It had been a shrewd appeal. The British made their request in order to include Central and South America, where American companies dominated the oil busi-

---

February 19, 1944, PRO, FO 371, W2919/34/76; Hull to Halifax, February 10, 1944, NA, RG 59, 800.6363/1482; Beaverbrook memorandum, February 11, 1944, PRO, FO 371, W2486/34/76; Eden memorandum, W. P. (44)119, "Oil," February 19, 1944, PRO, FO 371, W2920/34/76.

46. Halifax to F. O., February 15, 1944, no. 751, PRO, FO 371, W2433/34/76; Halifax to F. O., February 18, 1944, no. 837, PRO, FO 371, W2641/34/76; Halifax to F. O., February 18, 1944, no. 839, PRO, FO 371, W2642/34/76.

47. Rayner memorandum conversation with Halifax, February 18, 1944, NA, RG 59, 800.6363/2-1844. Other participants in that conversation included Acting Secretary of State Edward Stettinius and Michael Wright, First Secretary of the British embassy in Washington. Also present were James Dunn, Acting Director of Special Political Affairs, and Wallace Murray, chief of the Office of Near Eastern and African Affairs.

ness. With the oil of the world under consideration, the British could balance any American claims to a larger share of Middle Eastern production with calls of their own for greater access to Latin America. Even if American negotiators made no such claims, the British saw profit in including Latin America. British oil policy, as determined by the Petroleum Division, dictated that on the basis of security considerations, "British oil interests should be able to maintain, and if possible, increase, their position in the Western Hemisphere." That end, petroleum planners in London believed, would be well served by talking about ways to cooperate more closely with Washington over Latin America. Such cooperation, they also hoped, might avert the uncoordinated diplomacy that had hurt British oil companies during the Mexican expropriation of 1938.[48]

In smaller measure, Roosevelt too tried to calm British fears. One evening about two weeks after Ickes announced the pipeline agreement, the president called Halifax to the White House for a special briefing on Middle Eastern oil. Roosevelt pointed to a rough sketch of the Persian Gulf that he had drawn. Iran, he told the British ambassador, is yours; we share the oil of Iraq and Kuwait, and Saudi Arabia is ours. The new pipeline, he added reassuringly, should become a common carrier for both of our supplies.[49]

The gesture proved insufficient. On the next day, February 20, 1944, Churchill wired the president. He told Roosevelt that official telegrams from Washington had left him more and more disturbed. "A wrangle about oil," he cautioned, "would be a poor prelude for the tremendous joint enterprise and sacrifices to which we have bound ourselves." He appreciated Roosevelt's difficulties at home, but the president had to understand that he too faced problems. "There is

48. Halifax to Hull, February 7, 1944, NA, RG 59, 800.6363/1482–1/2. Even with that concession, the Americans hedged. "This government," Hull wrote Halifax, "believes that it may be found desirable to extend the scope of the conversations beyond a discussion of the problems concerning Middle Eastern oil but that a determination of whether that should be done and to what extent can be made best in light of the progress of the discussions on Middle Eastern oil." Hull to Halifax, February 10, 1944, NA, RG 59, 800.6363/1482. Memorandum by Ministry of Fuel and Power (Petroleum Division), "Anglo-American Oil Policy," c. January 1944, PRO, FO 371, W793/34/76.

49. Halifax to F. O., February 20, 1944, no. 846, PRO, FO 371, W2667/34/76.

apprehension in some quarters here,'' Churchill explained, ''that the United States has a desire to deprive us of our oil assets in the Middle East . . . that we are being hustled and may be subjected to pressure.'' He pleaded with Roosevelt for a guarantee that would tranquilize anxieties in Parliament about losing British oil property, and he implored the president to reexamine the possibility of convening technical discussions as a prelude to ministerial talks.[50]

Roosevelt was impatient with Churchill's appeals. Instead of reassuring the prime minister about American intentions, Roosevelt replied that he was ''disturbed about the rumor that the British wish to horn in on Arabian oil reserves.'' He refused to reconsider the level and location of the talks, but he did agree that during the cabinet conference, ''actual working technical discussions should be at the expert level.'' He still planned to preside over the opening session of the conference, which, he assured Churchill, would lead to a ''mutually satisfactory [oil] agreement.''[51]

Now the prime minister stiffened, in a true reflection of growing irritation and suspicion within the War Cabinet. After reviewing Roosevelt's telegram, cabinet members had agreed that it was necessary to resist American demands. They were willing to talk about oil, Churchill reported to Roosevelt on February 24, but initially at the technical level and only if no changes in concession ownership were proposed. Further, Churchill warned the president to withhold public pronouncements about the conference until the War Cabinet had finished reviewing the matter, ''because I am by no means sure that we could endorse [them].'' After a week without futher word from London, Roosevelt asked Churchill to accept his pledge that ''we are not making sheeps eyes at your oil fields in Iraq or Iran.''[52]

That declaration softened the British mood. So did assurances from Under Secretary of State Stettinius, who daily told the British that the Americans had no intention of extorting oil. Churchill responded in

50. Churchill to Roosevelt, February 20, 1944, no. 583, PRO, PREM 3, 332/6, 258.

51. Roosevelt to Churchill, February 22, 1944, NA, RG 59, 800.6363/1514b.

52. Churchill to Roosevelt, February 24, 1944, *FRUS* (1944), vol. 3, pp. 102–103. See also, W. M. (44), 24th Conclusions, Minute 1, February 23, 1944, PRO, PREM 3, 332/6, 233. Roosevelt to Churchill, March 3, 1944, FDRL, Roosevelt Papers, OF (56).

kind on March 4 by disavowing any desire to raid American reserves in Arabia: "We have no thought of trying to horn in upon your interests or property in Saudi Arabia." Two days thereafter, he waived British objections to meeting in Washington and promised to send a delegation to the United States. "We still feel," he added, "that this delegation should be official and expert, and once the ground is clear and facts established, that higher authorities should then intervene." He also reserved the right to advise Parliament that no question of transferring property or rights should arise during the conference.[53]

By this time the Americans were inclined toward compromise. Almost a month had passed since Stettinius had divulged word of the conference, and speculation about a breakdown over oil between the Allies had lately begun to appear in the press. Eager to quash the rumors, Stettinius was ready to accept Churchill's terms. Roosevelt must have been ready too. On March 7 the State Department issued a press release announcing that the United States and Great Britain would hold "preliminary and exploratory discussions on petroleum questions." Included also was a list of the American delegates appointed for further talks on a higher level at an unspecified future date.[54]

Preliminary bargaining over oil was characteristic of negotiations on many troubled issues between the two allies in the first few months of 1944. Sterling-dollar balances, occupation currency policy, the Jewish refugee problem, policy toward Argentina, preliminaries to Dumbarton Oaks and Bretton Woods—all became matters of serious discussion. The decisions, few of them final, tended like oil to go now

53. Halifax to F. O., March 2, 1944, no. 1069, PRO, FO 371, W3417/34/76; Churchill to Roosevelt, March 4, 1944, *FRUS* (1944), vol. 3, p. 103; Churchill to Roosevelt, March 6, 1944, PRO, FO 371, W3697/34/76. See also, W. M. (44), 28th Conclusions, Minute 2, March 6, 1944, PRO, PREM 3, 332/6, 204.

54. Halifax to F. O., February 23, 1944, no. 920, PRO, FO 371, W2884/34/76; Halifax to F. O., March 2, 1944, no. 1069, PRO, FO 371, W3417/34/76; Halifax to F. O., March 3, 1944, no. 1079, PRO, PREM 3, 332/6, 213; Stettinius to Winant, March 5, 1944, NA, RG 59, 800.6363/1514c; Hull, *Memoirs,* vol. 2, p. 1524; U. S., Department of State, *Bulletin,* March 11, 1944, p. 238. To Ickes's great dismay, Roosevelt claimed to have told Churchill by phone that the United States had no interest in present British concessions. Ickes Diaries, vol. 53, 8724.

one way, now another. The British successfully resisted American pressure to freeze Argentinian assets and to embargo wheat and meat shipments from the country, both part of an American attempt to break the fascist regime then in power. Less successful, though not without positive results, were British efforts to maintain current levels of Lend-Lease assistance and to avoid forced reductions in gold and dollar balances. Here the British were able to work out compromises that reduced aid at rates lower than the Americans had originally wanted. The question of gold and dollar balances, which the Americans were also bent on cutting, was deferred. On other matters the British met with mixed results, but on all of them they did remarkably well considering the weak hand they held.

As for the Americans, they found early bargaining over oil alarming and frustrating. Administration officials and even the president himself had come to see the oil conference as a way of silencing domestic critics of foreign oil policy, of asserting the rights of American oil companies in the Middle East, and of demonstrating mastery over the complexities of postwar planning, at least with respect to petroleum. The obduracy of the British took them by surprise. They had expected a smooth trip to the conference table. Instead they found every step subject to dispute, disputes aggravated by bureaucratic rivalries within their own camp. Faced with what they regarded as stiff necks in London, Hull and Ickes pressed the British in their own separate ways. Hull relied on diplomatic channels, his staff on public disclosures. Ickes typically used a blunter instrument, the trans-Arabian pipeline. In the end Roosevelt and Churchill had to intervene to soothe hard feelings across the Atlantic and within their own governments. That intervention was at once a mark of the importance oil had assumed and a measure of the necessity for cooperation.

6 / The Anglo-American Oil Agreement: Security and Order on Public Terms

"Tell me the sort of agreement that the United States will reach with respect to the world's petroleum resources when the war is over," wrote Harold Ickes early in 1944, "and I will undertake to analyze the durability of the peace that is to come."[1] For Ickes, as for Cordell Hull and the petroleum planners at the State Department, oil was as indispensable to lasting peace as it was to Allied victory. Modern wars, they held, were largely struggles for the control of vital resources. They believed that by inducing other nations to cooperate in removing barriers to the equitable distribution of those resources, the United States would go a long way toward obviating the need for war. They also calculated that the nation would advance its own interests. A durable peace that offered ready access to raw materials would assure the country prosperity and safety.

The kind of internationalism that Ickes and Hull sought for oil touched all nations, looked first to the United States and Great Britain to frame guidelines for developing the world's reserves, and envisioned ultimately a multilateral pact to guarantee sufficient supplies to consuming countries and to ensure rightful benefits to producing countries—especially to those whose underdeveloped economies depended on oil revenues. In pursuit of those goals, conscious always of the limits of political feasibility, Ickes and Hull sponsored an oil conference with Great Britain. From that conference they expected the United States and American oil companies to profit. They assumed as

1. Harold Ickes, "We're Running Out of Oil," *American Magazine* (January 1944), pp. 26–27.

well that the agreement they would negotiate would make the United States government, and not those companies, chief architect of national policy for foreign oil.

Preliminaries

The Americans began at once to prepare for the preliminary meeting. By mid-March they had picked their negotiating team. Ickes wanted to put his deputy, Ralph Davies, in the chairman's seat. Hull, now in control of preparations, blocked the move. He installed Charles Rayner, the newly appointed petroleum adviser to the State Department, as chairman, while Davies filled the vice-chairman's slot.[2]

Rayner solicited industry points of view in advance of the conference. Earlier in his career he had served with Socony-Vacuum in the Far East. Later, in 1922, he became an independent producer in the Texas fields. He was therefore comfortable with all kinds of oil men, appreciated their concerns, and spoke their language. He already knew that the industry approved of concluding an agreement with Great Britain. As early as November 1943 industry leaders had recommended such an accord, first in a report on national oil policy submitted by the Foreign Operations Committee of the Petroleum Administration for War, later in meetings with Secretary Ickes, and finally

2. Ickes to Hull, March 30, 1944, NA, RG 253, Anglo-American Oil Agreement File, Grey Box II, R. K. Davies Folder; Minutes Meeting of Technical Oil Committee, April 4, 1944, NA, RG 334, File ANPB: 14/2-Foreign Petroleum Policy, British Conversations (1st sess.) Folder; Minutes Meeting of President's Committee on Oil, April 10, 1944, NA, RG 253, Anglo-American Oil Agreement File, Grey Box I, Folder 3. Other members of the negotiating team included Middle Eastern expert Paul Alling and economist Leroy Stinebower from the State Department; Davies's special assistant George Walden and chief of the Refining Division C. S. Snodgrass from the Petroleum Administration for War; and petroleum officers General Howard Peckham and Commodore Andrew Carter representing the War and Navy departments. For revisions of draft petroleum agreement, which were completed by mid-April, see "Draft Agreement with the United Kingdom with Particular Reference to Near and Middle Eastern Petroleum," March 30, 1944, NA, RG 253, Anglo-American Oil Agreement File, Grey Box II, Folder 8; "Draft Agreement with the United Kingdom on Petroleum (revised)," April 7, 1944, NA, RG 48, File 1-188: Petroleum Reserves Corporation, Folder 2845; "Memorandum of Understanding with the United Kingdom on Petroleum," April 17, 1944, NA, RG 253, Anglo-American Oil Agreement File, Grey Box II, Folder 8. The draft dated April 17, 1944 served as the working copy for the preliminary conference.

through endorsements from the National Oil Policy Committee of the Petroleum Industry War Council. Still, Rayner wished to consult oil men in order to make sure that the agreement had their support.[3]

Early in April 1944 he invited leaders from a cross section of the industry to attend technical meetings to be held just before the British arrived. At the meetings the oil men maintained that they still favored an agreement on general principles with Great Britain, but they told the American delegation that they had reservations about the extent of government intervention entailed in the pact. In order for the understanding to win industry approval, it would have to leave domestic producers untouched. They would suffer no interference with their activities from foreign governments. The industry advisers also sought in more serious ways to limit the role of both governments once the agreement went into effect. They suggested the formation of a joint petroleum commission, which would be larger and have greater industry participation than the commission Feis had envisioned. They recommended that responsibility for calling a multilateral oil conference rest not with the governments, as federal authorities wanted, but with the joint commission, where oil men would carry more weight. Finally, they insisted on taking part directly in negotiations with the British.[4]

3. Report of the Foreign Operations Committee of the Petroleum Administration for War, "A Foreign Oil Policy for the United States," November 5, 1943, FDRL, Roosevelt Papers, OF (4435-b); Sappington to Murray, December 13, 1943, NA, RG 59, 800.6363/1466; Wilkinson to Starling, December 3, 1943, no. 690 ELFUNCOOP, PRO, FO 371, E7792/3710/65; Report of the National Oil Policy Committee of the Petroleum Industry War Council, "A National Oil Policy for the United States," February 28, 1944, NA, RG 253, Anglo-American Oil Agreement File, Grey Box II, Folder 2. On Rayner, see "Biographical Data," n.d., NA, RG 59, 800.6363/1611A.

4. Minutes Meeting of United States Technical Group Appointed to Conduct Preliminary Conversations with the United Kingdom on Petroleum, Meeting nos. 2, 3, 4, April 12, 1944, April 13, 1944, NA, RG 253, Anglo-American Oil Agreement File, Grey Box II, Folder 5. Industry representatives included John A. Brown, president of the Socony-Vacuum Oil Company; W. Alton Jones, president of the Cities Service Oil Company; Alfred Jacobsen, president of the Amerada Petroleum Corporation; W. S. S. Rodgers, president of the Texas Oil Company; J. F. Drake, president of the Gulf Oil Corporation; Ralph T. Zook, president of the Sloan and Zook Company and of the Independent Producers Association of America; and Orville Hardin, vice-president of the Standard Oil Company of New Jersey.

Rayner accommodated the oil men where he could. He made no changes in the size or composition of the petroleum commission, but he did accept textual revisions that clarified the meaning of the understanding. More important, he assured the oil men that domestic activities would remain outside the jurisdiction of the agreement. At the same time, he obtained permission for a small group of industry representatives to serve as advisers and to observe deliberations during the preliminary conference.[5]

The British encountered no difficulties with their oil industry. The composition of their delegation mirrored the close cooperation that typified contact between government officials and oil men in Great Britain. Even before they had chosen their technicians, British authorities assumed that Sir William Fraser of Anglo-Iranian and Sir Frederick Godber of Shell would serve as delegates. Their knowledge of the industry and their experience as negotiators, in the view of the War Cabinet, were essential to the success of the mission. Sir William Brown, head of the Petroleum Division of the Ministry of Fuel and Power, served as chairman of the group, which also included representatives of the Foreign Office, the Treasury, the Petroleum Division, and the service departments.[6]

5. Minutes Meeting of United States Technical Group Appointed to Conduct Preliminary Conversations with the United Kingdom on Petroleum, Meeting nos. 2, 3, 4, April 12, 1944, April 13, 1944, NA, RG 253, Anglo-American Oil Agreement File, Grey Box II, Folder 5. Brown, Rodgers, and Jacobsen were designated as industry advisers to the American delegation, Minutes Meeting of United States Technical Group, Meetings nos. 6, 7, April 17, 1944, April 19, 1944, NA, RG 253, Anglo-American Oil Agreement File, Grey Box II, Folder 5. For their contributions, see Minutes Meeting of United States Technical Group, Meetings nos. 8, 9, n.d., May 3, 1944, NA, RG 253, Anglo-American Oil Agreement File, Grey Box II, Folder 5. At the final meeting (no. 9) of the American technical delegation, all those industry representatives invited to meeting no. 2 attended. Also present were George A. Hill, president of the Houston Oil Company, and William R. Boyd, president of the American Petroleum Institute. For a summary of the criticisms of the industry group regarding the preliminary draft agreement, see "Report on the Comments of the Industry Advisors . . .," May 20, 1944, NA, RG 253, Anglo-American Oil Agreement File, Grey Box II, R. K. Davies Folder.

6. "Report by the Ministerial Oil Committee," W. P. (44)179, April 5, 1944, PRO, FO 371, W5619/34/76. Those representatives were career diplomat John LeRougetel, chief of the General Department of the Foreign Office; Frederick Harmer, a bright young treasury official who specialized in currency exchange; Commodore A. W. Clarke, representing the three service departments; and Frederick C. Starling and V. S.

Though contrary to custom, the Foreign Office, under pressure from the State Department, released in April a list of their negotiators. They described the delegates by name only. Conscious of the suspicions most Americans harbored about contact between government and industry, the British wished, as the Foreign Office described it, "to avoid discussion as to the proper description to be attached to . . . Fraser and Godber, though there must be no doubt about their status as members of the official delegation."[7]

The Technical Conference

The British technicians met their American counterparts for two weeks in mid-April 1944 in Washington, D.C. They came with instructions from the War Cabinet that reflected the defensive posture Britain had taken from the start. They were to make no commitments. They were to refuse even to consider proposals involving existing rights or property, or the transfer of oil products without reimbursement. They were to see that discussion moved beyond the Middle East and that the conference produced no impediments to British oil production that might compromise military or economic security. Their purpose, the War Cabinet reminded the delegates, was to frame general principles for the orderly development of oil resources throughout the world. Those principles were also to include terms under which the two governments would support the activities of their nationals as well as pledges to furnish each other with oil supplies during wars and to uphold each other's concessions in peacetime. That last stipulation, of course, was an attempt to commit the United States to stronger support of British concessions than it had shown in Mexico.[8]

The technicians worked together in good temper. From the opening

---

Butler of the Petroleum Division. For brief biographies of the members of the British delegation, see "Thumbnail sketches of British delegation," n.d., NA, RG 253, Anglo-American Oil Agreement File, Grey Box II, Folder 3.

7. Winant to Roosevelt, March 19, 1944, *FRUS* (1944), vol. 3, p. 107; Hull to Winant, March 29, 1944, NA, RG 59, 800.6363/1563c; Blake-Tyler to Rayner, April 1, 1944, NA, RG 59, 800.6363/4-1444.

8. "Washington Discussions on Oil: Instructions to Official Delegation," W. P. (44)179, April 5, 1944, PRO, FO 371, W5629/34/76; W. M. (44), 45th Conclusions, Minute 1, PRO, FO 371, W5619/34/76.

session, Rayner adopted a conciliatory tone that heartened British delegates. They had expected acrimony, coupled with demands for British oil to replenish depleted stocks in the United States. Instead, Rayner offered them friendship, emphasized the common problems confronting both countries, and ignored the issue of repayment for American oil supplies. He welcomed the British delegation by talking about the future, not the past, about surpluses and not shortages. He described the outlook of the international oil industry in terms of its "expanding markets and expanding supplies." "It is not a rationing of scarcity with which we shall be faced in the post war world," Rayner said, "but the orderly development and orderly distribution of abundance in an economy of plenty." How best to deal with that abundance, in accordance with the principles of the Atlantic Charter, was the question Rayner hoped the conference would answer. His emphasis on a postwar oil glut revealed his concern for maintaining order under government guidance within the industry.[9]

By the first week in May the conferees had drawn up a tentative agreement acceptable to both delegations. As with many of the Anglo-American negotiations carried on in the closing years of the war, the American draft served as the working model. Since the Americans generally had a stronger economic hand, the finished product followed primarily American lines, although the British were able to obtain some of the assurances they were seeking. By design, the document was general, because its authors wished to ensure the broadest possible support when they converted the interim agreement into a multilateral one.

The "Memorandum of Understanding," as it was called, opened with a preamble acknowledging common convictions held by both governments.[10] They recognized that ample supplies of oil were essen-

9. Text of Rayner's opening remarks in Minutes of Anglo-American Exploratory Discussions, Joint Session no. 1, April 18, 1944, NA, RG 253, Anglo-American Oil Agreement File, Grey Box II, Folder 7.

10. All analysis of the draft agreement refers to the "Draft Memorandum of Understanding Between the Government of the United States and His Majesty's Government in the United Kingdom on Petroleum," May 31, 1944, NA, RG 48, File 1-188: Petroleum Reserves Corporation, Folder 2845. For an annotated agenda of the talks prepared by the American delegation, see "Proposed Agenda for British Conversations," n.d., NA, RG 253, Anglo-American Oil Agreement File, Grey Box II, Folder 6.

tial to the safety and economic welfare of all nations. They assumed that for the foreseeable future global petroleum reserves were sufficient to assure necessary supplies. The British scored a victory in the insertion of that clause, for they believed it removed any suggestion that a scramble for scant supplies might follow the war, a possibility that had already embittered public discussion of postwar oil policy.[11] The delegates also agreed that, in developing oil resources and allocating supplies, consideration should be given to "available reserves, sound engineering practices, relevant economic factors, and the interests of producing and consuming countries." Such supplies, they added, should also be made available along the lines prescribed by the Atlantic Charter. In those last sections of the preamble the drafters were establishing the global scope of the agreement. More important, they were enumerating the factors to be taken into account in developing world reserves and were also indicating their intention to encourage shifts in production and marketing that served the national interests of both consuming and producing countries. In the case of the United States, American delegates made plain, that meant greater exploitation of areas outside the Western Hemisphere.[12]

After the preamble followed the heart of the agreement—a set of rules to govern the behavior of the signatories and of their nationals in the international petroleum trade. Those guidelines undertook to remove many of the irritants that had arisen from the competitive conduct of the international oil business. They looked, too, toward the orderly development of world oil resources according to the considerations set down in the preamble.

First, the delegates proposed that the governments cooperate to ensure that oil would be "available in international trade to the nationals of all peace-loving countries in adequate volume, at fair prices and on an equitable and non-discriminatory basis." That provision revealed the limits of the agreement by restricting the understanding to oil in-

11. Report of the Ministerial Oil Committee, "Oil Discussions with the United States Government at Washington," W. P. (44)269, May 24, 1944, PRO, FO 371, W8641/34/76.

12. Minutes Exploratory Discussions, Joint Session nos. 1, 2, 3, April 18, 1944, April 19, 1944, April 20, 1944, NA, RG 253, Anglo-American Oil Agreement File, Grey Box II, Folder 7.

volved in international commerce. The qualification was designed to protect domestic producers in the United States from the interference of foreign governments party to the agreement. In addition, the provision gave substance to the "equal access" clause of the Atlantic Charter. All buyers would have equal opportunity to purchase oil supplies without quantitative restrictions and would be able to obtain oil at prices that reflected costs plus a reasonable profit. That principle, utopian without strict means of enforcement, at least made integrated companies aware that both governments frowned on their pricing methods, which often concealed special discounts on oil sold by one branch of a company to another. Purchases would also be limited to "peace-loving countries," a reference later amplified by a pledge to make oil available "subject to the provisions of such collective security arrangements as may be established." The pact thereby sanctioned collective action over oil, which might result in withholding supplies from aggressive nations.

That provision did not satisfy the British delegates. They wanted the availability of oil to be governed not only by collective security arrangements but also by the amount of petroleum with which each country was naturally endowed. Wholly dependent on overseas oil, the British feared that the understanding might limit the development of British sources of supply, while the Americans remained free to develop indigenous reserves in the United States without any restrictions. As a result, British delegates sought clear recognition of their country's position as an oil importer. They wanted special assurances that they would be able to draw from abroad supplies adequate for national security and for their industrial and commercial well-being.[13]

The Americans rejected that request. They maintained that the whole purpose of the accord was to guarantee ample supplies of petroleum to all consuming countries. To grant Great Britain extraordinary allowances, as the Americans saw it, would violate the nonpartisan character of the agreement and would only duplicate assurances already given earlier in the text. Faithful to his instructions from London,

13. Minutes Exploratory Discussions, Joint Session nos. 2, 7, 8, April 19, 1944, April 25, 1944, April 26, 1944, NA, RG 253, Anglo-American Oil Agreement File, Grey Box II, Folder 7.

Sir William Brown officially refused to drop the demand. Outside the conference room, however, where his freedom was less restricted, Brown told Rayner that in fact he was satisfied and would urge his superiors to accept the provision as it appeared in the draft.[14]

Next came an assurance to producing countries that the development of their oil would encourage "sound economic advancement" at home. An astute reader would recognize in that promise the hand of Franklin Roosevelt, who had insisted on similar guarantees in almost every transaction the Petroleum Reserves Corporation had conducted. This assurance, like the earlier ones, was aimed at more than calming oil-rich countries that might turn to nationalization to avoid being cheated by foreigners. It promised, so far as signatory governments could, that revenues from oil concessions held by foreign companies would be sufficient to meet requirements for an expanding scale of services that included education, public health, agricultural development, and public improvements. Satisfying those needs, the conferees realized, would help to make the concessions more secure, host governments more stable, and prospects for lasting peace greater.[15]

Oil executives had no quarrel with any of those goals. They had always been willing, Sir William Fraser told delegates, to assume responsibilities larger than those imposed by concession contracts, and they were ready to accept guidance from their governments about how best to improve living standards in areas where they operated. Fraser thought it unwise, however, to add any stipulation that might appear to fix royalty rates, since those were the result of contractual negotiations that varied with the prospects of the concession and the vigor of the competition. The warning was really unnecessary. Neither govern-

14. *Ibid.*; Rayner, "Report on Petroleum by the Expert Technical Group to the President's Committee on Petroleum," May 10, 1944, NA, RG 253, Anglo-American Oil Agreement File, Grey Box II, Folder 6.

15. Minutes Exploratory Discussions, Joint Session no. 1, 5, 6, April 18, 1944, April 22, 1944, April 24, 1944, NA, RG 253, Anglo-American Oil Agreement File, Grey Box II, Folder 7. The British asked for and received minor revisions in this clause, which, they believed, had originally implied that producing countries had heretofore been denied an equitable share of the proceeds from oil development. Such an impression, the British feared, might invite demands for more generous financial returns from concessionary governments. The American delegates disagreed with that reading but accommodated the British nonetheless.

ment had contemplated setting rates. Nonetheless, it defined more sharply for all concerned the boundaries within which they had to work.[16]

The "open door" principle received affirmation in two separate provisions. Both came in response to complaints lodged by British and American oil interests, each charging the other with attempts to secure exclusive rights over important oil-bearing regions.[17] The signatories promised to direct their efforts so that with regard to "the acquisition of exploration and development rights in areas not now under concession, the principle of equal opportunity shall be respected." They also vowed to see that "the exploration for and development of petroleum resources, the construction and operation of refineries and other facilities, and the distribution of petroleum shall not be hampered by restrictions imposed by either Government or its nationals" in violation of the purposes of the agreement.

Together the provisions represented an exceptional and commendable pledge to apply self-restraint in the pursuit of national advantage. Never again, it seemed, would Great Britain or British oil interests attempt to exclude American companies from such areas as the Netherlands East Indies or the Middle East. Nor would they try to dictate the terms under which American companies might operate, as they had done in Kuwait. By the same token, the Americans would have to show for British oil interests the same tolerance in Latin America, where Shell had complained recently about rumors that the Petroleum Reserves Corporation was trying to corner exploration rights in Peru. As for restrictive arrangements now in operation, both delegations agreed that those would have to be reconsidered once the agreement was in effect. None of the conferees, however, was sure exactly how such situations would be remedied.[18]

A final provision carried national self-restraint one step further.

16. Minutes Exploratory Discussions, Joint Session no. 3, April 20, 1944, NA, RG 253, Anglo-American Oil Agreement File, Grey Box II, Folder 7.

17. For complaints of American oil companies, see chap. 4. British companies, specifically Shell, reported that American oil companies and the United States government were trying to keep them out of Latin America. John London to Frank J. Hopwood, March 3, 1944, PRO, FO 371, W4344/34/76.

18. London to Hopwood, March 3, 1944, PRO, FO 371, W4344/34/76; Wright to South American Department of Foreign Office, March 9, 1944, PRO, FO 371,

Both governments affirmed their intention to respect each other's concession contracts and acquired rights, and to refrain from direct or indirect interference with either. That pledge was aimed at easing American concern over Saudi Arabia, though it had wider implications. By establishing the rule that neither government could induce a breach of contracts held by nationals of the other, the agreement lessened the likelihood of political crises arising in connection with the protection of oil rights.

To that rule the British gave hearty assent, for it protected their preemptive rights to oil production in countries such as Kuwait. But the British delegates sought more assurances. They wanted, in addition, to obligate both governments to ensuring that all parties, including producing countries, observed the terms of their concession contracts. Armed with that kind of commitment from the United States, the British believed they could protect their oil property in South America from expropriation. The Americans demurred, replying that such a commitment was tantamount to a military alliance. Further, they refused to make the United States responsible, especially in Latin America, for policing commercial contracts in defense of British interests. In recent years the State Department had been disinclined to act in such a manner even on behalf of American oil companies, so seriously had government authorities taken the proscriptions implicit in the Good Neighbor policy and the need for hemispheric solidarity.[19]

To carry out its principles and to consider problems of mutual inter-

---

W4344/34/76. The State Department and the Petroleum Reserves Corporation denied those rumors as being, according to Wright, "completely absurd." In fact, the Bristish later learned, Socony-Vacuum, which had been trying to obtain a concession in Peru, had complained to the State Department that the company had received no support from the American embassy in Lima, while the British embassy was "lending every support to Shell." Wright to F. O., April 16, 1944, PRO, FO 371, W8250/34/76; Washington to F. O., May 4, 1944, no. 2339, PRO, FO 371, W7157/34/76; McQuillen memorandum, May 9, 1944, PRO, FO 371, W7157/34/76; Minutes Exploratory Discussions, Joint Session no. 9, April 29, 1944, NA, RG 253, Anglo-American Oil Agreement File, Grey Box II, Folder 7.

19. Minutes Exploratory Discussions, Joint Session nos. 4, 5, 6, 7, April 21, 1944, April 22, 1944, April 24, 1944, April 25, 1944, NA, RG 253, Anglo-American Oil Agreement File, Grey Box II, Folder 7. For an excellent discussion of emerging United States oil policy toward Latin America, see Wood, *Good Neighbor Policy*, pp. 159–282.

est, the agreement established a Joint Petroleum Commission in the mold of the Interstate Oil Compact, which regulated oil development in the United States. The functions of the commission, advisory like those of the compact, were to prepare long-range estimates of world demand for petroleum, to suggest ways of satisfying that demand on an equitable and orderly basis, and to analyze short-term problems involving oil production, processing, transportation, and distribution. The commission was also supposed to recommend action to both governments, to report regularly on its own activities, and to make additional reports and recommendations "as may be appropriate to carry out the purposes of this Memorandum." The two governments pledged to make available to the commission whatever information it required about the activities of their nationals.

Like the compact, the commission was to have no executive authority. The Americans had originally contemplated giving it limited power to execute its recommendations after both governments had approved them. The British disagreed. Pointing to the harmonious relations the British government enjoyed with its industry, the British delegates argued that the strength of the commission should rest on its composition, not on any arbitrary powers with which signatory governments invested it. The caliber of its staff alone, the British maintained, would be enough to inspire the confidence necessary to obtain compliance from the oil companies. Anything more might undercut the commission's effectiveness by creating hostility and suspicion in an industry known to resist regulation from without. Anything more, they might have added, would also make British oil companies liable to even greater interference from abroad.[20]

The Americans, though less trusting of their companies, recognized the merit of the British position. Any attempts to bully oil men would

20. "Memorandum of Understanding with the United Kingdom on Petroleum," April 17, 1944, NA, RG 253, Anglo-American Oil Agreement File, Grey Box II, Folder 8. In that draft, the working model for the conference, the commission was empowered, among other things, to execute approved recommendations, Minutes Exploratory Discussions, Joint Session nos. 2, 5, April 19, 1944, April 22, 1944, NA, RG 253, Anglo-American Oil Agreement File, Grey Box II, Folder 7.

spell disaster, since industry support was essential for administering the agreement. For that reason, as well as to safeguard national sovereignty, the delegates decided against giving any power to the commission. If oil companies needed encouragement, it would have to come from their governments rather than from the commission. In a carefully worded clause the two countries vowed to "endeavor, in accordance with their respective constitutional procedures, to give effect to such approved recommendations and, wherever necessary and advisable, to ensure that the activities of their nationals will conform thereto."

Even without executive functions the Joint Petroleum Commission could still wield power. Its statistical research services, like those of the Interstate Oil Compact, could furnish data for planning oil policy on an aggregate basis. It could correlate supply with demand by recommending suitable levels of output for producing areas and by suggesting appropriate sources of supply for specific markets. Those efforts could serve, as they did for members of the Interstate Oil Compact, to control production, to restrict competition, and to maintain prices. All that, of course, depended on cooperation from the oil companies, both with their governments and with the commission. Again, each delegation approached that problem within the context of its own national experience.

British suggestions for the composition of the Joint Petroleum Commission, which would bear so much of the responsibility for inducing industry compliance, reflected the closeness between public and private oil policy in the United Kingdom. British delegates envisioned an eight-man body with four representatives appointed by each government. The British members, their delegation proposed, would consist of three oil men, who would retain their positions with private companies, and one civil servant. The Americans showed less faith in the consonance of national and private interests. They insisted on a board of ten members of whom their half, Secretary Hull later recommended, would contain only government officials, with industry representatives serving as unofficial advisers. In the end the British yielded, but only temporarily and at small cost. They agreed, pending review by senior officials, to a ten-man board. Even so, London could still appoint whomever it liked.[21]

Over one final matter the British exhibited greater stubbornness. The Americans were anxious to convene an international conference as soon as possible after bringing the bilateral agreement into effect. They wanted to avoid giving other countries the impression that the pact represented an Anglo-American partnership to dictate terms for oil development throughout the world. The British counseled against haste. They feared that a promise to establish immediately a multilateral organization might force the United Kingdom and the United States to move without proper preparation. This first postwar venture in commodity organizing might thus come to an untimely end. Instead, British delegates advised approaching the international stage at a reduced pace that would give the interim agreement a longer test run. Such caution, they asserted, would allow both countries to acclimate themselves to the accord and to prepare thoroughly for the multilateral conference. As a compromise, the two governments pledged to propose to other nations an international oil agreement ''as soon as practicable.'' They also gave themselves an escape way should the pact prove unbearable: either government could terminate the agreement after six months notice.[22]

British and American Reactions

The British delegates returned home early in May 1944 with an oil accord they pressed their government to endorse. For the most part, reported Sir William Brown, the draft agreement more than met the

21. Minutes Exploratory Discussions, Joint Session no. 5, April 22, 1944, NA, RG 253, Anglo-American Oil Agreement File, Grey Box II, Folder 7; Rayner, ''Report on Petroleum by the Expert Technical Group,'' May 10, 1944, NA, RG 253, Anglo-American Oil Agreement File, Grey Box II, Folder 7. Rayner originally proposed that the five American representatives on the Joint Petroleum Commission consist of three government officials and two industry representatives. Hull, unwilling to give the industry such representation, insisted that only government men serve as official members, Minutes United States Cabinet Committee on Petroleum, August 3, 1944, NA, RG 59, 800.6363/8–344.

22. Minutes Exploratory Discussions, Joint Session nos. 6, 7, April 24, 1944, April 25, 1944, NA, RG 253, Anglo-American Oil Agreement File, Grey Box II, Folder 7.

wishes of the War Cabinet. At the moment, it committed the British government to nothing, since the technicians had conducted negotiations subject to inspection by their superiors. The draft preserved British commercial rights and in no way obligated the United Kingdom to use British property to compensate the United States for oil received through Lend-Lease. In a larger sense, observed Frederick Starling, who had represented the Petroleum Division on the delegation, the agreement indicated the willingness of the United States to take in British interests as equal partners over future petroleum questions all over the world. Given the expansionist tendencies of American oil companies, such a partnership, Starling held, could only bring benefit to Great Britain by reducing the chances of conflict. Best of all, the preliminary conference and the understanding it produced had succeeded, as Sir William Brown put it, in "lowering the temperature on this important matter." In order to keep the heat down, he advised the cabinet to take steps now to seal the agreement.[23]

On two matters, Brown admitted, his delegation had been unable to persuade the Americans. First, the agreement contained no pledge of mutual support for each other's concession contracts. However, Brown reassured his colleagues that, as the Americans had told him, such episodes as the Mexican expropriation could have been forestalled had there existed an international forum for discussing petroleum problems.[24]

A more important problem was the lack of recognition of Britain's dependence on foreign oil. Without such an acknowledgment, the British foresaw the possibility of future reductions in petroleum output in areas controlled by their nationals. To meet demand in the United Kingdom, Britain would then be forced to make up the difference with more expensive oil from dollar sources. Even more distressing, especially to the Treasury, was the prospect of being unable to use British-controlled oil to solve exchange problems after the war. Treasury offi-

23. Report by the Chairman of the United Kingdom Delegation, "Oil Policy," May 15, 1944, PRO, FO 371, W7889/34/76; Minutes Ministerial Oil Committee, M. O. C. (44), 6th Meeting, May 16, 1944, PRO, FO 371, W7970/34/76; Minutes Ministerial Oil Committee, M. O. C. (44), 5th Meeting, May 8, 1944, PRO, FO 371, W7877/34/76.

24. Minutes Ministerial Oil Committee, M. O. C. (44), 6th Meeting, May 16, 1944, PRO, FO 371, W7970/34/76.

cials anticipated for Great Britain a postwar world characterized by large imports of foodstuffs and essential raw materials, slow recovery in export trade, and heavy indebtedness abroad. Such circumstances, they calculated, would produce shortages in foreign currencies and would force reductions in nonessential imports. To meet those difficulties, the Treasury had contemplated selling sterling oil in dollar areas or barring dollar oil from sterling areas. Such action, the Treasury now feared, could be construed as a violation of the petroleum agreement, under whose terms oil involved in international trade would be supplied to consuming countries only to satisfy industrial and military needs, not to serve commercial purposes.[25]

Brown countered those objections with claims that he already had made the Americans aware of the importance of oil to currency exchange. As he understood it, the necessary commercial prerogatives were covered by references to "relevant economic factors" in the text of the agreement. Treasury authorities found that insurance inadequate. They continued to urge that Britain reserve expressly the right to make any provision for oil under its control in the interest of military, industrial, or commercial security. That reservation they saw as only fair; it afforded Great Britain self-sufficiency comparable to that of the United States, whose domestic production fell outside the scope of the understanding.[26]

25. *Ibid.;* Report of Ministerial Oil Committee, "Oil Discussions with the United States Government at Washington," W. P. (44)269, May 24, 1944, PRO, FO 371, W86/34/76; Edward E. Bridges to T. L. Rowan, March 3, 1944, PRO, PREM 3, 332/6, 224; T. L. Rowan note, March 3, 1944, PRO, PREM 3, 332/6, 225; LeRougetel minute, June 15, 1944, PRO, FO 371, W9535/34/76. For the clearest explanation of this problem, see Minutes Anglo-American Conversations on Petroleum, Joint Subcommittee Session no. 1, July 26, 1944, NA, RG 48, File 1–188: Petroleum Reserves Corporation, Folder 2845. British economic problems were enormous. By the end of 1944 British exports had fallen to a third of their prewar volume. During the war, even with aid from the United States, Great Britain had lost a quarter of its prewar assets and had been forced to liquidate one-half or $8 billion worth of foreign investments. Through the first three years of the postwar period, Great Britain would have to contend with a balance of payments deficit of $5 billion. Paterson, *Soviet-American Confrontation,* p. 161. For a fuller discussion of British finances as they related to Anglo-American diplomacy, see Richard N. Gardner, *Sterling-Dollar Diplomacy: Anglo-American Collaboration in the Reconstruction of Multilateral Trade* (Oxford, 1956).

26. Minutes Ministerial Oil Committee, M. O. C.(44), 5th Meeting, May 8, 1944, PRO, FO 371, W7877/34/76; Report of the Special Oil Committee, "Oil Discussions

By and large, the War Cabinet favored the draft agreement, although debate over the need for some additional safeguards postponed endorsement for over a month.[27] In addition to the Treasury, the Admiralty and Lord Beaverbrook registered complaints. As usual, the Admiralty wanted to make certain that the final agreement left Great Britain free to blockade belligerents and to engage in economic warfare without first having to consult other signatories. Lord Beaverbrook had more serious problems with the pact. In his view the understanding established a "monster cartel" run by the Americans to protect their producers at British expense. If adopted, it would lock the United Kingdom into a static market system that preserved American dominance and restricted British expansion. Worse still, the agreement would lead to higher petroleum prices in Great Britain by limiting the production of cheap oil in the Middle East.[28]

At first, Beaverbrook argued for rejection of the accord. Faced with the insistence of his colleagues, however, he drew back. As long as the final version met the objections of the Treasury, which covered many of his own, and preserved the right of British oil companies to compete for a larger share of the international market, Beaverbrook was willing to carry through negotiations.[29]

In Washington, President Roosevelt was so pleased with the preliminary agreement that he shelved the pipeline scheme. With his exquisite talent for political bargaining he thereby turned a liability into an asset. Soon after the technical conference had opened, Roosevelt assured Senator Francis Maloney, chairman of the special Senate committee appointed early in March to investigate national oil policy,

---

with the United States Government," W. P.(44)313, June 14, 1944, PRO, FO 371, W9880/34/76.

27. See, for example, W. M.(44), 70th Conclusions, Minute 1, May 31, 1944, PRO, PREM 3, 332/6, 149.

28. Minutes Ministerial Oil Committee, M. O. C.(44), 7th Meeting, May 24, 1944, PRO, FO 371, W8613/34/76; Alexander, "Note by the First Lord on the draft Memorandum of Understanding with the United States Government," n.d., PRO, PREM 3, 332/6, 164; Memorandum by Lord Privy Seal (Beaverbrook), "Oil Discussions," W. P.(44)281, May 30, 1944, PRO, PREM 3, 332/6, 158; Beaverbrook to Eden, June 1, 1944, PRO, FO 371, W8879/34/76; Memorandum by Lord Privy Seal, "Oil Discussions," W. P.(44)324, June 14, 1944, FO 371, W9880/34/76.

29. W. M.(44), 79th Conclusions, Minute 1, PRO, PREM 3, 332/6, 149.

that the pipeline deal would not be consummated without review by Congress. Early in June the president made that commitment firm by promising to give Maloney thirty days notice to examine any pipeline contract that the Petroleum Reserves Corporation was about to conclude. In return, Roosevelt received Maloney's word that he would suspend consideration of the pipeline and that he would hold off hearings on the preliminary oil agreement until after the cabinet conference.[30]

Roosevelt paid only a small price for defusing Congress. He upset Ickes, who realized that congressional review might bring an end to the pipeline scheme. At the very least, Ickes contended, interference from Congress would deny the executive the power of quick action, which had already proved so helpful in bringing the British to the United States. Ickes believed that without the threat of the pipeline the British would be slow to return. In that event, he wrote Roosevelt on May 29, 1944, the final agreement might come too late to influence the impending election.[31]

Roosevelt was shrewder than Ickes knew. The pipeline was already tied to the oil agreement. At the last session of the technical conference Rayner had informed the British delegates that if the pact were executed within the next month or two, the pipeline project would be forwarded to the Joint Petroleum Commission for consideration. On the other hand, if no understanding were reached, "it would be difficult, if not impossible, to postpone decisions on the proposed pipelines beyond such period."[32]

As for the pipeline agreement itself, Roosevelt had done little to damage its prospects, which had faded considerably in past months. Not only had it ignited congressional and industry criticism, it had

30. Minute Meeting Petroleum Reserves Corporation, April 3, 1944, NA, RG 250, Petroleum Reserves Corporation Minutes; U. S., Congress, Senate, *Congressional Record,* 78th Cong., 2nd Sess. (Washington, 1944), vol. 90, pt. 3, 3615–16; Ickes to Roosevelt, May 29, 1944, Roosevelt to Maloney, June 12, 1944, FDRL, Roosevelt Papers, PSF (66); *NYT,* June 15, 1944.

31. Minutes Meeting Petroleum Reserves Corporation, May 12, 1944, NA, RG 250, Petroleum Reserves Corporation Minutes; Ickes to Roosevelt, May 29, 1944, Roosevelt to Ickes, May 20, 1944, FDRL, Roosevelt Papers, PSF (66); Stettinius memorandum conversation with Ickes, June 8, 1944, NA, RG 59, 890F.6363/6–844.

32. Minutes Exploratory Discussions, Joint Session no. 9, April 29, 1944, NA, RG 253, Anglo-American Oil Agreement File, Grey Box II, Folder 7.

failed to move beyond the preliminary stage. Since the announcement of the "Outline of Principles" early in February 1944, negotiation of the formal contract had proceeded at a languorous pace, owing largely to the inability of the oil companies to assign among themselves satisfactory shares of the pipeline. By the time the staff conference adjourned in May, negotiations were at a standstill, with little hope of a speedy end. Neither congressmen nor British officials understood how dismal the outlook really was, so Roosevelt could trade on their fears even though the project stood little chance of succeeding.[33]

With the threat of the pipeline Ickes had hoped to accelerate British decisions, which were still coming too slowly to suit him. He had planned on concluding the oil agreement by the middle of June, well in advance of the Republican and Democratic national conventions. Roosevelt could then accept his party's nomination for a fourth term as president with an international oil pact already in hand. In the November election, such early success abroad would undercut Republican criticism of his oil policies, demonstrate his ability to conduct postwar diplomacy, and furnish, along with other agreements on monetary policy and civil aviation, a foundation for lasting peace.[34]

Churchill showed no enthusiasm for a quick decision, which he believed would subordinate British interests to American electoral politics. He wanted instead to postpone final negotiations until after November, when Roosevelt, free from the pressures of reelection, might look more kindly on British needs. So far, the Allied invasion of France and debate within the War Cabinet over the preliminary agreement had allowed Churchill to put off the Americans for over a month. But on June 7 Roosevelt again intervened. "I personally hope

33. Mortimer Kline to Ickes, April 19, 1944, NA, RG 253, Anglo-American Oil Agreement File, Grey Box II, Middle East Folder; Minutes Meeting Petroleum Reserves Corporation, May 12, 1944, NA, RG 250, Petroleum Reserves Corporation Minutes. Even if the scheme had been agreed to, government reports maintained that the facility could not have been completed in time to be of value during the war. "The Relation of the Proposed Saudi Arabian Pipeline to United States Interests in Middle Eastern Oil," May 5, 1944, NA, RG 226, O. S. S. Report no. 109155S.

34. Ickes to Roosevelt, May 29, 1944, FDRL, Roosevelt Papers, PSF (66). See also Minutes Ministerial Oil Committee, M. O. C. (44), 5th Meeting, May 8, 1944, PRO, FO 371, W7877/34/76. Though Ickes used his fear of Roosevelt's defeat in November to pressure the British, his concern over the impact of oil on the election was genuine. See Ickes Diaries, vol. 53, 8747–48, 8845, 8861.

much,'' he wrote the prime minister, ''that they [the British ministerial delegation] can come as quickly as possible, as the situation is becoming embarrassing.''[35]

Roosevelt's plea underscored for Churchill and for his staff the need to avoid further delays. The day after receiving Roosevelt's message, Foreign Secretary Anthony Eden informed Churchill of the views of the Foreign Office, which had earlier warned against postponement. ''The President and others in his Administration,'' Eden said, ''would be profoundly resentful if they thought we were leading them up the garden path by entering on negotiations, to which they attached great importance, with no intention of concluding them until we had seen which way the cat jumped in November.'' Under those circumstances, the Foreign Office noted, Roosevelt might revive the pipeline, thereby denying Great Britain equipment essential to its petroleum industry, or he might drive stiffer bargains in other collaborative efforts. A week later, on June 16, 1944, the War Cabinet authorized ministerial talks for the purpose of concluding the oil pact.[36]

Churchill could stay the conference no longer, but he could protect British interests by naming a tough negotiating team. He chose Lord Beaverbrook to lead the delegation. Though Beaverbrook was already on his way to the United States to attend an international civil aviation conference, his selection was more than a matter of convenience. Beaverbrook's skill as a negotiator, his devotion to protecting British interests and private enterprise, and his opposition to the oil accord guaranteed that he would sacrifice nothing to the Americans.[37]

35. Churchill personal minute, June 5, 1944, PRO, FO 371, W9348/34/76. All along, Halifax continued to insist on a hasty conclusion of the agreement, Halifax to F. O., May 1, 1944, no. 2249, PRO, FO 371, W6870/34/76; Halifax to F. O., June 2, 1944, no. 2931, no. 2932, PRO, FO 371, W9348/34/76. Beaverbrook, on the other hand, counseled for delay, Lord Privy Seal to Churchill, June 9, 1944, PRO, PREM 3, 332/6, 139; Roosevelt to Churchill, June 7, 1944, PRO, PREM 3, 332/6, 142.

36. Eden to Churchill, June 8, 1944, PRO, FO 371, W9348/34/76; LeRougetel to Law, May 31, 1944, PRO, FO 371, W8798/34/76; Butler minute, LeRougetel minute, Law minute, June 6, 1944, PRO, FO 371, W9348/34/76; W. M. (44), 79th Conclusions, Minute 2, June 16, 1944, PRO, PREM 3, 332/6, 119.

37. For Beaverbrook's position on the British posture at the ministerial conference, see Note by Lord Privy Seal, ''Oil Discussions in Washington,'' W. P. (44)394, July 17, 1944, PRO, FO 371, W11418/34/76; Taylor, *Beaverbrook,* p. 557.

Joining Beaverbrook were Minister of State Richard Law; Ben Smith, Minister Resident in Washington and the only representative of the Labour Party on the delegation; Ralph Assheton, Financial Secretary to the Treasury and, as Beaverbrook described him, a "true and blue" Conservative; Parliamentary Secretary to the Ministry of Fuel and Power and chairman of the Oil Control Board, Geoffrey Lloyd; and Sir William Brown, who served as chief adviser to the ministers.[38]

No oil men appeared among the British delegates this time, although Sir William Fraser of Anglo-Iranian had been asked to come along. It was not that Fraser disapproved of the agreement; on the contrary, both he and Sir Frederick Godber of Shell had lobbied strenuously for concluding the understanding. Rather, Anglo-Iranian feared that Fraser's presence, in the words of company managers, "might prove an acute embarrassment." Anglo-Iranian expected that at the conference the British would reserve the right, as the War Cabinet had discussed, to claim a larger share of world markets. Any talk of market distribution in front of Fraser, executives explained, might damage Anglo-Iranian's commercial prospects by leaving the impression that the company was a government agency. For that reason they declined the War Cabinet's invitation.[39]

The American delegation also contained no oil men. Since a small panel of industry representatives had attended the preliminary conference and had already made their objections known to the State Department, government officials saw no reason to invite them to the cabinet conference. The American delegation included Cordell Hull as chairman; Harold Ickes as vice-chairman; navy secretary James

38. U. S., Department of State, *Bulletin,* July 16, 1944, p. 62. For a discussion of the basis on which the delegates were chosen, see Churchill to Beaverbrook, June 29, 1944, Beaverbrook Library, Beaverbrook Papers, Oil Conversations File; Beaverbrook to Eden, July 3, 1944, Beaverbrook Library, Oil Correspondence File.

39. Secretary, Anglo-Iranian Oil Company, to John Anderson, Chancellor of the Exchequer, July 7, 1944, PRO, PREM 3, 332/6, 86; Anderson to Beaverbrook, July 7, 1944, PRO, PREM 3, 332/6, 85. For Fraser's and Godber's attitudes toward the preliminary agreement, see Minutes Ministerial Oil Committee, M. O. C. (44), 6th Meeting, May 16, 1944, PRO, FO 371, W7970/34/76; LeRougetel to Law, May 31, 1944, PRO, FO 371, W8798/34/76; Godber to Beaverbrook, July 7, 1944, PRO, PREM 3, 332/6, 88.

Forrestal; Under Secretary of War Robert F. Patterson; Foreign Economic Administrator Leo Crowley; Charles E. Wilson, vice-chairman of the War Production Board; Deputy Petroleum Administrator Ralph Davies; and State Department petroleum adviser Charles Rayner. A group of experts from the State Department's Office of Economic Affairs and from its Petroleum Division assisted the negotiators.[40]

The Oil Conference

The conference opened at the State Department on July 25, 1944. It was a typical midsummer day in the Capitol—sweltering, sticky, suffocating. Half an hour of picture taking under the superinduced heat of klieg lights turned the room into a steam bath, barely tolerable for the delegates. For Harold Ickes it was intolerable, but not because of the heat. Cordell Hull occupied the chairman's seat, while Ickes sat to Hull's right in the spot reserved for the vice-chairman. The arrangement galled him, and he sulked through that first meeting, consoling himself with private complaints about the way Hull handled protocol and the welcoming address. As it turned out, he had to endure Hull only for a short time. Illness forced Hull to step down immediately, whereupon Ickes assumed the chairmanship. The president, who had planned to convene the conference himself, failed to attend the opening or any other session. An upcoming election campaign and the demands of the Allied assault on Europe now preoccupied him. Even so, the conference would furnish the gesture he sought.[41]

The cabinet conference proved less easy and agreeable than the earlier meeting. American delegates were suspicious of their British counterparts from the outset. The trouble partly involved the manner of Lord Beaverbrook, whom his friend Joseph Kennedy in a mo-

40. "Report on the Comments of the Industry Advisors," May 20, 1944, NA, RG 253, Anglo-American Oil Agreement File, Grey Box II, R. K. Davies Folder. See, for example, J. A. Brown to Rayner, May 4, 1944, Zook to Rayner, May 5, 1944, NA, RG 253, Anglo-American Oil Agreement File, Box I, Folder 3; U. S., Department of State, *Bulletin,* July 16, 1944, p. 62. Advisers included Harry C. Hawkins, Director of the Office of Economic Affairs; James C. Sappington, Assistant Chief of the Petroleum Division; and John A. Loftus, Petroleum Division.

41. Ickes Diaries, vol. 54, 9126; Minutes Anglo-American Conversations on Petroleum, Plenary Session no. 1, July 25, 1944, NA, RG 59, 800.6363/7-2544.

ment of exasperation had once called "a treacherous little bastard." Ickes too sensed deception. For a man who had, in Ickes's words, "bludgeoned his way into prominence," Beaverbrook seemed over-eager to make court. "He certainly has a technique," Ickes observed at their first meeting, "but it seems to me that he lays his flattery on with a trowel. One would have thought that I was one of the great men of the world and that he had been observing me closely from London." But it was more than Beaverbrook's blandishments that worried the Americans. The long delay between the preliminary and final conferences convinced Americans that something had gone amiss in London. The arrival of a delegation that contained no fewer than four cabinet-rank ministers confirmed that feeling. Such heavy artillery, American delegates believed, must be intended to make some breach in the draft agreement, which everyone in Washington thought would require only minor revisions.[42]

Despite those apprehensions, the British turned out to be flexible. They withdrew their demand for mutual support of concessions and accepted instead the American view that the agreement itself would promote the stability of proprietary rights. They also accepted without quarrel assurances that the pact contravened neither their belligerent nor their preemptive rights over oil. They consented to textual changes proposed by American conferees, changes designed chiefly to satisfy industry criticism in the United States. And they agreed to restricting membership on the Petroleum Commission to government representatives, with oil men confined to advisory roles. In turn, the Americans went along with the British desire for an eight-man board, which all recognized to be more manageable than the ten-man board originally contemplated.[43]

Over one issue the British proved intractable, and on that matter the

42. Arthur M. Schlesinger, Jr., *Robert Kennedy and His Times* (Boston, 1978), p. 48n; Ickes Diaries, vol. 54, 9121, 9135; Campbell to LeRougetel, with enclosed minute of conversation with Sappington on August 17, 1944. August 30, 1944, PRO, FO 371, W13044/34/76; Campbell to Halifax, August 24, 1944, PRO, FO 371, W12956/34/76.

43. Minutes Anglo-American Conversations on Petroleum, Joint Subcommittee Session no. 1, 2, 4, 5, July 26, 1944, July 27, 1944, July 31, 1944, August 1, 1944, Plenary Session no. 4, August 3, 1944, NA, RG 48, File 1-188: Petroleum Reserves Corporation, Folder 2845; Minutes Anglo-American Conversations on Petroleum, Plenary Session no. 2, July 27, 1944, NA, RG 59, 800.6363/7-2544.

conference nearly floundered. The British established early their need to protect explicitly what they called their "economic security." That meant, as they explained it, the freedom to introduce with regard to oil, as well as with other matters, measures needed to strengthen Britain's general foreign exchange position. Such measures might take the form of requiring distributors to supply the United Kingdom and the colonial market with oil drawn from sterling sources or of seeking an enlargement of sterling oil production just to generate exchange. In effect, they argued, Great Britain was claiming the same discretion for its oil that the United States would exercise over its domestic reserves.[44]

The Americans denied the claim and ignored the analogy, even though the State Department generally agreed with the British position on dollar balances and foreign exchange. With Roosevelt and the treasury unsympathetic, American conferees told the British that, if they wanted special attention for their exchange problems, it would have to come through petitions to the Joint Petroleum Commission, which was charged specifically with considering "relevant economic factors" and "short-term problems." The United States would even instruct American representatives on the commission to give added consideration to foreign-exchange difficulties confronting the United Kingdom. But under no circumstances could the Americans permit Great Britain to reserve in the text the right to use oil to solve exchange problems, because such recognition would contradict the ideals of free and flexible trade framed in the agreement. More to the point, such a revision would condone the establishment of a British monopoly over the United Kingdom market by affirming Britain's right to import only oil controlled by British nationals. That restriction not only would disrupt the flow of international trade, but, the Americans declared, it would mean political ruin for the agreement in the United States. Neither the oil companies nor congressional leaders would endorse an understanding that sanctioned the exclusion of American oil from the

44. Minutes Anglo-American Conversations on Petroleum, Plenary Session no. 2, July 27, 1944, NA, RG 59, 800.6363/7-2544; Minutes Anglo-American Conversations on Petroleum, Plenary Session no. 3, August 1, 1944, NA, RG 48, File 1-188: Petroleum Reserves Corporation, Folder 2845.

United Kingdom. Without support from the industry, there would be no compliance; without approval from Congress, there might be no agreement at all.[45]

There matters lay, each side unyielding. Some in the British delegation, like Minister Resident Ben Smith and Financial Secretary Ralph Assheton, saw no way out except to break off negotiations. Others, like Lord Beaverbrook, pressed for delay until after the election, when the Americans might be more responsive. But most British delegates, along with the War Cabinet, shared the views of Minister of State Richard Law and Parliamentary Secretary Geoffrey Lloyd. They were convinced that failure to reach an understanding on oil would seriously damage future cooperative efforts. If the conference were successful, that cooperation would ease all of Britain's postwar difficulties.[46]

With the Americans also anxious to avoid rupture, the conferees finally reached a compromise. They appended to the minutes of the final plenary session a statement, available for publication. In it both delegations agreed that the terms of the accord allowed for consideration by the Joint Petroleum Commission of the exchange position of each country. The United Kingdom affirmed its prerogative, during the transition to a peacetime economy, "to take into account the exchange which it would lose or gain by the purchase or sale of petroleum in deciding sources from which the petroleum it required should be drawn." The United States took note of the reservation but cautioned that such unilateral action would be inconsistent with the purposes of the agreement. Both countries pledged to seek solutions through the Petroleum Commission before they acted alone. Should the commission find no acceptable solution, either country could now terminate the understanding on three months notice, instead of the six months required in the preliminary pact. On August 8, 1944, after two weeks of what one delegate described as "arduous" negotiations,

45. Minutes Anglo-American Conversations on Petroleum, Plenary Session no. 3, August 1, 1944, NA, RG 48, File 1–188: Petroleum Reserves Corporation, Folder 2845; Campbell to F. O., August 2, 1944, no. 4137, PRO, PREM 3, 332/6, 50; Campbell to LeRougetel, with enclosed minute of conversation with Sappington on August 17, 1944, August 30, 1944, PRO, FO 371, W13044/34/76.

46. Campbell to F. O., August 2, 1944, no. 4136, PRO, FO 371, W11844/34/76. See also Campbell to Eden, August 3, 1944, no. 4170, PRO, FO 371, W11931/34/76.

Lord Beaverbrook, on behalf of the United Kingdom, and Acting Secretary of State Edward Stettinius, on behalf of the United States, signed the Anglo-American Oil Agreement.[47]

Both sides were pleased. Although they had failed to carry their main points, the British believed that they had protected themselves adequately by obtaining at least tacit recognition of their exchange problems and by halving the time needed to withdraw from the agreement. More important, as British chargé d'affaires Ronald Campbell observed, "this agreement on petroleum . . . is a most constructive and forward step toward long range collaboration between the two countries in the international economic field." And that, after all, had been Britain's primary objective.[48]

For the Americans, as well, the negotiations were a success. The pact, substantially the same as the preliminary draft, embodied many of the principles upon which the United States hoped to construct a stable and secure peace. Those principles, Ickes and Hull knew, would serve private as well as public interests. American oil companies would have wider access to production and to markets without running the risk of surpluses and price wars. They would also be able to cooperate with foreign companies and with governments without fear of prosecution under antitrust laws. Such cooperation, guided by the signatory governments, would assure the United States and other nations enough oil to maintain their safety and prosperity. Just as important, the understanding created mechanisms through which governments could exert greater influence over the development of re-

47. Minutes Anglo-American Conversations on Petroleum, Joint Subcommittee Session no. 5 (with attachments A, B, and C), August 1, 1944, Plenary Session nos. 3, 4, 5, August 1, 1944, August 3, 1944, NA, RG 48, File 1–188: Petroleum Reserves Corporation, Folder 2845; Campbell to F. O., August 3, 1944, no. 4179, PRO, FO 371, W11910/34/76. For reaction and approval of War Cabinet, see W. M.(44), 100th Conclusions, Minute 1, August 3, 1944, W. M. (44), 102nd Conclusions, Minute 3, August 4, 1944, PRO, FO 371, W12003/34/76. For unofficial negotiations outside the conference room, see Campbell to Halifax, August 24, 1944, PRO, FO 371, W13956/34/76. Ickes to Roosevelt, August 7, 1944, NA, RG 59, 800.6363/8–2144. For text of agreement signed on August 8, 1944, see U. S., Department of State, *Bulletin*, August 13, 1944, p. 153. See also Hull to Roosevelt, August 24, 1944, NA, RG 59, 800.6363/8–2444.

48. Campbell to F. O., August 9, 1944, no. 4292, PRO, FO 371, W12094/34/76.

serves and the allocation of supplies. Those same mechanisms also provided an international forum for nations and for oil companies to discuss problems and to seek peaceful solutions.

On the eve of Allied victory the oil agreement removed an irritant to the Anglo-American alliance. It also furnished a fresh sign that the wartime brand of cooperation—one in which the British were steadily unable to participate as equal partners—would continue after the war. The arrangement suited Roosevelt and his advisers as well as it did American oil executives. Though in 1944 few of them anticipated how great an imbalance between the two countries lay ahead, they all recognized that such a lopsided partnership served their needs. To private oil companies, the arrangement guaranteed more opportunities for exploiting and marketing oil abroad, especially in the Middle East and in western Europe. To government planners, those developments promised greater conservation and security at home.

Even so, the Anglo-American Oil Agreement had a long way to go. It had yet to run the gamut of congressional hearings and votes, and it had still to suffer the scrutiny of the oil industry. In midsummer 1944 the United States had taken but a first step toward assuring security for the nation and order for the industry.

7 / Security and Order by Private Arrangement

A year later, almost to the day, the war was over. Its end left unresolved important questions of policy, among them assistance to China, collective security, and support for Great Britain. So it was with oil. Fears of scarcity that had impelled government authorities to action in 1943 still animated them, though the world now enjoyed surpluses rather than shortages of oil. That abundance came as no surprise to Washington planners, who had anticipated a postwar glut at least since 1944. It was the more distant future that worried them. Regardless of conditions at the end of the war, the United States faced diminishing petroleum stocks that would leave Americans more and more dependent on foreign sources of oil, more and more vulnerable to intimidation from abroad. The safety of the nation still required prudent use of Western Hemisphere reserves. It also demanded continued expansion of Middle Eastern oil development.

Harold Ickes expected to have a voice in that expansion. He believed that Washington had every right to exert greater control over oil because the security of the country was at stake. So too, he assumed, was the peace. Recognizing the interdependence of all nations, he reasoned that cooperation over resources was the only way to avoid war. The petroleum pact was his means of protecting the world, and of course the United States, from destruction in a scramble for oil.

Oil companies were less high-minded. Their managers, naturally more concerned with profits than with national security, looked to Washington for support, not direction. As the United States moved with uncertainty through the early postwar years, oil companies turned back to private ways of settling what they again saw as private problems. In a world that generated disputes more vexing than many the war had brought, Washington officials had neither the energy nor the inclination to argue. Instead, they returned to assisting the oil men, who by then had seen wisdom and profit in exploiting Middle Eastern oil.

Trouble Back Home

The intervening year had brought on signal changes for both the country and the oil agreement. Roosevelt's reelection in November 1944 had diminished the urgency that originally produced the oil conferences. Four more years in office held promise of time to effect his peace. Roosevelt attacked the task with customary vitality, though more and more, body lagged behind will. The Allied summit at Yalta, together with attendant conferences before and after, found him alert but left him tired and old. By April he was dead, the victim of a brain hemorrhage that deprived so many Americans of the only president they had ever known. Within a month Germany surrendered, and by mid-August the Japanese had sued for peace.

The personal deprivation that touched the nation struck Harold Ickes and the oil agreement with particular force. With peace at hand, Americans now had a world of problems to solve. The more immediate questions of occupation policy, aid to China, and Lend-Lease arrangements threatened to crowd the agreement from view. Roosevelt, though never really interested in the details, had nonetheless served as its most valuable patron. Without him no one could be confident of its future.[1]

Even with him that future had been chancy. Ickes and his colleagues at the State Department initially had planned to put the pact into force as an executive agreement. Aware that it might set a precedent for

1. For a discussion of the range of postwar issues facing the United States, see Herbert Feis, *Churchill, Roosevelt, Stalin: The War They Waged and the Peace They Sought* (Princeton, 1957); Feis, *Between War and Peace: The Potsdam Conference* (Princeton, 1960); John Lewis Gaddis, *The United States and the Origins of the Cold War, 1941-1947* (New York, 1972), especially pp. 95-243; Blum, *Years of War,* especially pp. 375-463.

future commodity arrangements, they were anxious to avoid the ordeal of congressional ratification. Congress would tolerate no such evasion. With the oil pact, as with other international arrangements like Bretton Woods and the United Nations Relief and Rehabilitation Agency, the Senate was determined to minimize the use of executive agreements, so that it could play a significant role in framing policy abroad. In the case of oil, Tom Connally, the senior senator from Texas and chairman of the Foreign Relations Committee, naturally took the lead.[2]

With a ten-gallon style and an ego to match, Connally had long been one of the most knowledgeable and effective operators on Capitol Hill. Early in the war he had turned his influence to foreign policy. Upon his appointment in 1943 as chairman of the Foreign Relations Committee, he had become an important sponsor of American participation in a collective security organization after the war. Such participation, according to Connally, should come only with constant advice and consent from the Senate. The dictum applied to all internationalist impulses.

Connally's interest in the oil pact reflected more than concern for the preservation of senatorial prerogatives. For years a promoter in Congress of Texas oil interests, he had been responsible for that essential prop to the Interstate Oil Compact, federal regulation of oil transport across state lines. He now served on a special Senate committee to investigate petroleum resources. If the oil agreement ever were to come into effect, it first had to pass Connally's inspection, conducted always with the interests of producers back home in mind.[3]

In a series of meetings with officials from the State Department late in August 1944, Connally had demanded submission of the pact for review. With several international agreements soon to come before the Senate, the administration could ill afford to refuse. Roosevelt, conscious as he was of the price Woodrow Wilson had paid for snubbing

2. Ickes to Roosevelt, August 16, 1944, FDRL, Roosevelt Papers, OF (5588); Acheson to Stettinius, June 9, 1944, NA, RG 59, 800.6363/6-944; Maloney to Hull, May 24, 1944, NA, RG 59, 800.6363/602; Henry S. Fraser to Tom Connally, NA, RG 59, 800.6363/8-1744.

3. For general background on Connally, see Tom Connally, with Alfred Steinberg, *My Name is Tom Connally* (New York, 1954). See also Engler, *Politics of Oil*, pp. 140–41; Blum, ed., *Wallace Diary*, p. 202, 488; Israel, ed., *Long Diary*, p. 219, 346.

that proud chamber, succumbed. On August 24, 1944, he sent the Anglo-American Oil Agreement to the Hill for approval.[4]

For the next five months it languished there, "gathering dust and cobwebs in a cubby-hole," as Ickes later observed. In the meantime, resistance in the press and among industry leaders grew. Some newspapers, like the *Wall Street Journal,* were basically carrying on an old antipathy toward the New Deal. Others, especially in the Midwest and Southwest, were taking their cues from local producers. Those oil men saw in the agreement a plot to invest federal officials and foreign governments with wide-reaching powers over domestic activities—a view that conformed to the general political attitudes of 1944, scarcely liberal when it came to further expansions of government authority.[5]

Even some major oil corporations, normally at odds with independents and smaller companies, regarded the pact as dangerous. Of

4. Breckinridge Long memorandum of meeting with Senate Foreign Relations Committee, August 15, 1944, NA, RG 59, 800.6363/8–1644. For attitudes of Senators Francis Maloney and E. H. Moore, see Maloney to Hull, May 24, 1944, NA, RG 59, 800.6363/602; *Washington Times-Herald,* August 10, 1944. Long memorandum meeting with Senate Foreign Relations Committee, August 16, 1944, NA, RG 59, 800.6363/8–1644; Rayner memorandum meeting with Foreign Relations Committee, NA, RG 59, 800.6363/8–1744; Long memorandum conversation with Connally, August 24, 1944, NA, RG 59, 800.6363/8–2444; Hull, *Memoirs,* vol. 2, p. 1526; Hull to Roosevelt, August 24, 1944, NA, RG 59, 800.6363/8–2444; U. S., Congress, Senate, *Congressional Record,* 78th Cong., 2nd Sess. (Washington, 1944), vol. 80, pt. 6, 7304–305.

5. Ickes to Roosevelt, December 1, 1944, FDRL, OF(56); *Wall Street Journal,* October 27, 1944; *Newsweek,* August 21, 1944; *Los Angeles Examiner,* August 26, 1944. For reaction typical of middle and southwest press, see *Houston Press,* September 19, 1944; *Houston Post,* September 19, 1944; *Tulsa Tribune,* September 26, 1944. The views of local trade journals such as the *Texas Oil Journal, Oil Weekly,* and *Oil and Gas Journal* were collected by the Petroleum Administration for War in "Views of the Petroleum Industry and Others on the Anglo-American Oil Agreement . . .," n.d., NA, RG 253, Anglo-American Oil Agreement File, Box I, Folder 7. "Resolution unanimously adopted by the oil producers attending a state-wide meeting of the Railroad Commission of Texas . . .," September 19, 1944, found in NA, RG 253, Anglo-American Oil Agreement File, Grey Box, Folder 2; J. A. Carmical, *The Anglo-American Petroleum Pact* (New York, 1945), p. 28; Independent Petroleum Association of America, Report no. 30, October 31, 1944, found in NA, RG 253, Anglo-American Oil Agreement File, Box I, Folder 7; Francis C. Wilson, "Interstate and State Control of the Petroleum Industry and the Anglo-American Petroleum Agreement," paper delivered before the annual meeting of the New Mexico Bar Association in Albuquerque, New Mexico, October 14, 1944, in Independent Petroleum Association of America, *The Anglo-American Petroleum Agreement* (Washington, 1944), pp. 23–27. For the reactions of other independent oil men, trade organizations, and local officials,

182

moderate size among corporate giants, the Sun Oil Company proved the most poisonous critic. Its president, Joseph Pew, was a conservative Republican who had bankrolled a flock of anti–New Deal campaigns. He regarded the petroleum pact as another of Roosevelt's schemes to enlarge government, this time into "a super-state cartel" that would threaten all of free enterprise.[6]

Pew and the independents had found ample support in the Petroleum Industry War Council. After two stormy sessions in the fall of 1944, members stood fixed to recommend against Senate ratification. Ickes stopped them. His essential strategy was to avoid the damage of public repudiation by demanding that the oil men revise, not scrap, the pact. It worked. By December the council had produced its own version, whose message was clear: oil men would accept no penetration of American borders from without and no extension of federal authority from within.[7]

By then Ickes had reckoned that the agreement as it stood would never be brought to a successful end. Accordingly, he had advised Roosevelt to retrieve it from the Senate for revision and renegotiation.

see Petroleum Administration for War, "Views of the Petroleum Industry and Others . . . ," n.d., NA, RG 253, Anglo-American Oil Agreement File, Grey Box, Folder 2. *NYT,* October 10, 1944. For text of the resolution of Independent Petroleum Association of America, see Independent Petroleum Association of America, *The Anglo-American Agreement,* pp. 28–29.

6. Joseph Pew to Connally, August 17, 1944, NA, RG 59, 800.6363/8–2344; *NYT,* October 26, 1944. For Pew's political activity, see Engler, *Politics of Oil,* p. 353, 362. For other examples, see Joseph E. Pogue, "The Purpose of an International Agreement," address before the Interstate Oil Compact Commission, October 7, 1944, NA, RG 253, Anglo-American Oil Agreement File, Grey Box, Folder 2; Dana Hogan to Thomas W. McManus, October 7, 1944, NA, RG 253, Anglo-American Oil Agreement File, Box I, Folder 7. Hogan describes W. S. S. Rodgers of Texaco and Harry Collier of Socal as opposing the agreement in treaty form. Both of those executives remained quiet during the autumn fight, although in August 1944, the press reported Rodgers in favor of the pact, *NYT,* August 10, 1944.

7. J. H. Thatcher, Jr., to Davies, Summary of minutes of meetings of Petroleum Industry War Council of July 19, 1944, September 13, 1944, October 25, 1944, December 2, 1944, NA, RG 253, Anglo-American Oil Agreement File, Box I, Folder 7; Ickes to William R. Boyd, October 24, 1944, reprinted in Frey and Ide, *PAW,* p. 282. See also "Copy of Resolution Presented as Minority Report of the National Oil Policy Committee to the Petroleum Industry War Council, October 25, 1944," in "Action by PIWC on the Anglo-American Oil Agreement," December 6, 1944, NA, RG 253, Anglo-American Oil Agreement File, Grey Box, Folder 1. For the text of the

The State Department agreed. So did the president, and in mid-January 1945, upon his request, the Senate returned the document. A special interdepartmental committee, solely under Ickes's control now that illness had forced Hull into retirement, had then begun the process of redrafting. Despite continued bickering between Ickes's office and the State Department, by late spring the committee had arrived at a version that seemed acceptable both to the Senate and to the oil industry, whose representatives had been consulted throughout.[8]

The new draft, an amalgam of the original agreement and the industry revision, closely resembled its predecessor in form and substance. The most significant changes involved the explicit exemption of domestic operations and severe restriction of the duties of the Petroleum Commission. "No provision," read a newly inserted clause, "... shall be construed to require either Government to act upon any report or proposal made by the Commission, or to require the nationals of either Government to comply with any report or proposal made by

---

industry draft, see "Petroleum Industry War Council Suggested Revision of an Anglo-American Oil Agreement," in "Action by PIWC on the Anglo-American Oil Agreement," December 6, 1944, NA, RG 253, Anglo-American Oil Agreement File, Grey Box, Folder 1.

8. Ickes to Roosevelt, November 29, 1944, NA, RG 59, 800.6363/12-344; Ickes to Roosevelt, December 1, 1944, FDRL, Roosevelt Papers, OF (56); Rayner memorandum, "Recommended Action Regarding the Anglo-American Oil Agreement," ECA-11 with appendix, November 13, 1944, NA, RG 59, Notter File; Stettinius to Roosevelt, December 27, 1944, NA, RG 59, 800.6363/12-2744; U. S., Congress, Senate, *Congressional Record,* 79th Cong., 1st Sess. (Washington, 1945), vol. 91, pt. 1, pp. 179-80, 259; U. S., Department of State, *Bulletin,* January 14, 1945, p. 63. Along with Ickes, Stettinius, Rayner, and Davies, the interdepartmental committee included Leo T. Crowley, Foreign Economic Administrator; Under Secretary of War Robert Patterson; and Navy Secretary James Forrestal. Administrative obligations of the original members often forced them to miss meetings, attended instead by their representatives. See, for example, Minutes Meeting President's Oil Committee, January 20, 1945, NA, RG 253, Anglo-American Oil Agreement File, Box I, Folder 3. For a description of the first meeting of the committee, see Freidman to Ernst, January 26, 1945, NA, RG 169, Box 1715, Anglo-American Conversations on Petroleum Folder. For continued bickering between the State Department and Ickes, see C. F. Darlington memorandum, "The Anglo-American Oil Agreement: Comments on Recent Developments and the Present Position," February 2, 1945, NA, RG 59, 891.6363 A. I. O. C./2-245; Edward Mason to Will Clayton, February 6, 1945, Clayton to Acheson, February 18, 1945, NA, RG 59, 891.6363 A. I. O. C./2-245.

the Commission, whether or not it is approved." That sensitivity to industry fears found further demonstration in the prominence given to petroleum trade rather than petroleum development. Government drafters had struck from the text descriptions of market conditions that the oil men found objectionable. The resulting emphasis on trade seemed to contravene a primary purpose of the original pact, which had been to increase the amount of oil pumped from the Middle East. The impression was misleading. With distribution and exploitation as intertwined as they were, changes in one would necessarily bring changes in the other. Oil men, like wartime procurement officers, followed the short-haul principle in shipping goods to outlet. Once the European market showed signs of revival and growth, nearby well-heads along the Persian Gulf would fill demand. Orderly conduct of the petroleum trade could not help but influence the tempo and sources of petroleum exploitation.

In most essential respects the new draft retained the flavor of the original, along with the concrete concessions won from Great Britain. After all, winning those concessions had been a prime objective of the oil companies and government officials who promoted the pact. Even the Petroleum Industry War Council had left them intact. Oil was still to be accessible on a nondiscriminatory basis, still to serve the interests of producing countries, still to be developed in accordance with the purposes of the agreement. Those purposes remained tied to first intentions: ensuring national safety and prosperity, maintaining peace and preventing aggression, and encouraging rational development of international petroleum. More important, especially for Middle Eastern oil, the draft preserved pledges to respect concession contracts and to observe the principle of equal opportunity in securing rights of exploration and exploitation.[9]

The Second Anglo-American Oil Agreement

Support from the president, valuable under any circumstances, was now critical for Ickes and the oil agreement. But, like other members

9. "Suggested Revisions of the Agreement on Petroleum between the Government of the United States and the Government of the United Kingdom of Great Britain and Northern Ireland" that accompanied Ickes to Roosevelt, March 12, 1945, FDRL,

of the cabinet, Ickes hardly knew Roosevelt's successor, Harry S Truman. Unlike them, he had some idea of how the new president would receive his pet project. The Missouri Democrat had earned his reputation as a muckraking senator by heading a series of wartime probes into the national defense program. Those investigations had put him in touch with petroleum affairs inside and outside the United States. His committee had examined gasoline rationing, fuel oil conditions, and pipeline projects. It had also sponsored the tour of combat zones taken in 1943 by those five senators who returned so miffed about wartime oil policy. Truman himself had endorsed their 1944 report, which had called for an oil agreement with Great Britain. Late in June 1945, to Ickes's great delight, Truman renewed the endorsement and authorized the oil committee to arrange a conference with the British.[10]

The British, forewarned by Ickes and Charles Rayner of a new advance, accepted the formal invitation to reopen talks in London, a site settled upon as a courtesy to their well-traveled delegates. They re-

---

Roosevelt Papers, PSF (113). The original redraft contained an antitrust immunity clause, inserted at the request of the industry to prevent prosecution of oil companies if they complied with petroleum commission recommendations. The clause was dropped because of objections from the State and Justice departments. For that and other objections, see Joseph Grew to Roosevelt, March 21, 1945, FDRL, Roosevelt Papers, PSF (113); Frey and Ide, *PAW*, p. 283. For early Justice Department concern, see Memorandum meeting of Edward Levi, Herbert Berman, Charles Rayner, and Donald Hiss, October 27, 1944, NA, RG 59, 800.6363/10-2744. J. F. McGurk memorandum, "The Anglo-American Oil Agreement," March 6, 1945, NA, RG 59, 800.6363/3-845; Haley to Clayton, March 19, 1945, NA, RG 59, 800.6363/3-1945; "Objections of the State Department to the Proposed Revision of the Anglo-American Petroleum Agreement," NA, RG 250, Box 143E, State Department folder. For industry support, see B. Brewster Jennings to Davies, May 7, 1945, A. C. Mattei to R. Owen Brewster, May 15, 1945, NA, RG 253, Anglo-American Oil Agreement File, Box I, Folder 7; Minutes Meeting of Petroleum Industry War Council, May 16, 1945, NA, RG 59, 800.6363/9-1345. For Foreign Relations Committee, see Minutes Meeting President's Oil Committee, June 5, 1945, NA, RG 169, Box 1736, Anglo-American Agreement Oil Folder.

10. U. S., Congress, Senate, Special Committee Investigating the National Defense Program, *Additional Report of the Subcommittee Concerning Investigations Overseas. Section 1—Petroleum Matters*, S. Rept. 10, Part 15, 78th Cong., 2nd Sess. (Washington, 1944); Minutes Meeting President's Oil Committee, June 6, 1945, NA, RG 169, Box 1736, Anglo-American Agreement Oil Folder; Ickes Diaries, vol. 60, 9812; Frey and Ide, *PAW*, p. 283.

fused, though, to meet the American timetable calling for a summer meeting. The British were not seeking to evade the agreement or to harass the Americans for forcing them to consider it a second time. Once again, domestic politics set the pace of diplomacy. An impending national election had left them barely enough time to prepare for the high-level Allied meeting at Potsdam in mid-July. The oil conference would have to wait until September.[11]

In July British voters replaced Winston Churchill's wartime coalition with the Labour government of Clement Atlee. Like other aspects of British foreign affairs, oil policy suffered no appreciable change. Cabinet officers continued to worry about protecting Britain's exchange position, maintaining the bilateral nature of the agreement, and excluding all sources of empire oil. They still regarded oil as connected intimately to Lend-Lease, a matter of high anxiety since its abrupt end in August 1945. As Churchill had confessed a year earlier, the British were broke. Without further aid they faced economic collapse. In hopes of obtaining that aid, the Treasury wanted to postpone oil talks until Lend-Lease was sorted out. But officials there were overruled by those who feared that delay would have an adverse effect on any Lend-Lease negotiations.[12]

11. Law memorandum conversation with Ickes, Davies, Rayner, January 26, 1945, PRO, FO 371, W1350/12/76; Ickes to Law, February 20, 1945, NA, RG 48, File 1-188: Petroleum Reserves Corporation, Folder 2845. For Law reaction, see Law to Ickes, February 5, 1945, NA, RG 48, File 1-188: Petroleum Reserves Corporation, Folder 2845; Ickes to Law, March 1, 1945, NA, RG 48, File 1-188: Petroleum Reserves Corporation, Folder 2845; R. A. Gallop minute for Secretary of State, August 28, 1945, PRO, FO 371, W11773/12/76. Rayner had promised the British a formal approach no later than April 1, 1945, but difficulties with the revised draft postponed the invitation until June, Halifax to F. O., March 16, 1945, no. 1720, PRO, FO 371, W3835/12/76. See also, Gallop minute for Secretary of State, August 28, 1945, PRO, FO 371, W11773/12/76; "Anglo-American Oil Agreement: Historical note on what has happened since the agreement was signed in Washington last year," August 28, 1945, PRO, FO 371, W11774/12/76; Winant to Secretary of State, September 1, 1945, NA, RG 253, Anglo-American Oil Agreement File, Box II, Folder 14.

12. Minutes Ministerial Oil Committee, M. O. C.(45), 1st Meeting, September 12, 1945, PRO, FO 371, W12258/12/76; Minutes Ministerial Oil Committee, M. O. C.(45), 2nd Meeting, September 22, 1945, PRO, FO 371, W12900/12/76; Minutes Ministerial Oil Committee, M. O. C.(45), 1st Meeting, September 14, 1945, PRO, FO 371, W12258/12/76. On the British economic situation, see Blum, *Years of War,* pp. 306-26.

Emanuel Shinewell was largely responsible for the decision. A passionate socialist, he had just replaced Gwilym Lloyd George as minister of fuel and power. The appointment had disturbed some observers in Washington, who were made nervous by his left-wing credentials. Further, as a member of the loyal opposition during the war, Shinewell had been critical of British inclinations to align policy too closely with the United States. For the oil agreement, however, those views had less relevance than did his steady concern for safeguarding British oil operations against discrimination and nationalization abroad. Shinewell, always sober in thought and action, actually welcomed new oil talks. As he saw it, they foreshadowed collaboration for the protection of British and American oil companies and for the support of empire interests throughout the Middle East. "At the same time," he told cabinet colleagues, "under the terms of the Agreement, we should have equal opportunities with the Americans to secure new openings in South America."[13]

The second oil conference opened on September 18, 1945. Ickes led the American delegation. Experience and knowledge, as well as devotion to the agreement, made him the logical choice. He brought with him oil specialists from the State Department and from the Petroleum Administration for War, along with an assortment of industry advisers mainly representing domestic operators. They included some of the harshest critics of the agreement. The choice, baffling to British conferees, revealed the necessity of satisfying the oil industry, in particular, domestic companies. Ickes hoped to stamp the conference and the agreement with a mark of cooperation between government and industry and so co-opt further criticism. If he succeeded, congressional ratification was bound to follow.[14]

13. Sappington memorandum, August 31, 1945, NA, RG 59, 841.6363/8-3145; Minutes Ministerial Oil Committee, M. O. C.(45), 2nd Meeting, September 22, 1945, PRO, FO 371, W12900/12/76.
14. Other members of the American delegation included Robert E. Hardwicke, chief counsel for the Petroleum Administration for War; Gordon M. Sessions, Foreign Relations assistant to the Petroleum Administration for War, and Samuel Botsford, also of the Petroleum Administration for War; Robert Loftus from the Petroleum Division of the State Department; Victor Barry, petroleum attaché from the American embassy; and James Sappington, observer for the American embassy. Industry advisers included Pe-

Under Shinewell's expeditious chairmanship, the delegates agreed in short order on a pact that differed little from the draft Ickes had carried across the Atlantic. The British were generally pleased with the results, though they again failed to secure full compensation for the paucity of their indigenous reserves. They had tried without success to exclude from the agreement all essential petroleum that either country obtained from wells controlled by its nationals, regardless of where they set their rigs. Still, the new version improved on the original by considering British possessions and protectorates, many rich in oil, as part of the United Kingdom. There was also new precision and clarity of phrasing. The Petroleum Commission, stripped of any hint of executive power, now had the limited mandate pressed for earlier by the British. Best of all, the new agreement promised the British greater fiscal flexibility. An import-limitation clause, inserted by domestic oil men to protect American markets from invasion, gave the British the right to restrict the entrance of dollar oil. Petroleum was thereby restored to the list of commodities that Britain might use to rebuild its economy.[15]

---

troleum Council chairman William R. Boyd and five members of the council's National Oil Policy Committee: Alfred Jacobsen, George A. Hill, W. Alton Jones, Joseph E. Pogue, and Ralph T. Zook. Frey and Ide, *PAW,* pp. 283–84. Starling to Butler, September 11, 1945, PRO, FO 371, W12038/12/76; Ickes Diaries, vol. 61, 10016. The British delegation consisted of Shinewell; Phillip Noel Baker, Minister of State; Sir Norman Duke and F. C. Starling of the Ministry of Fuel and Power; Sir David Waley and D. B. Pitbaldo of the treasury; R. A. Gallop from the Foreign Office; Victor Butler, British petroleum representative in Washington; J. E. S. Fawcett, Foreign Office legal adviser; and K. L. Stock from the Ministry of Fuel and Power, who served as secretary. Frey and Ide, *PAW,* p. 283.

15. Minutes Ministerial Oil Committee, M. O. C.(45), 2nd Meeting, September 22, 1945, PRO, FO 371, W12900/12/76. See also Dominion Office to Canada, Australia, New Zealand, and South Africa, September 24, 1945, no. 1792, September 28, 1945, no. 1825, PRO, FO 371, W10115/12/76. For complete text of revised agreement, see Raymond F. Mikesell and Hollis B. Chenery, *Arabian Oil: America's Stake in the Middle East* (Chapel Hill, 1949), pp. 185–90. For key sessions of conference, see Anglo-American Conversations on Petroleum, Minutes of Plenary Sessions 1 and 2, September 18, 1945, September 20, 1945, Minutes of Joint Official Subcommittee Meetings 1 and 2, September 19, 1945, September 20, 1945, PRO, FO 371, W13140/12/76. Minutes Ministerial Oil Committee, M. O. C.(45), 2nd Meeting, September 22, 1945, PRO, FO 371, W12900/12/76.

The conference adjourned in October 1945 amid the breathless conviviality that accompanies the end of long negotiations. At a reception late in the day each side extolled the other with warmhearted toasts. Only the British could truly afford to relax. Their share of the business was over. Since broad treaty-making powers were vested in the Crown, they would be spared the incertitudes of parliamentary ratification. Besides, the indispensable approval of Shell and Anglo-Iranian had already been bestowed upon the pact.[16]

Ickes was still on the job. When he raised his glass, he took care to commend the assistance rendered by his advisers. He had taken similar care throughout the proceedings. In fact, he had turned so often to the oil men that British delegates complained about feeling their presence at every plenum, even though they had been barred from the conference room. Such solicitude had been extended to Congress as well. As key members of the Senate Foreign Relations Committee, Tom Connally, fellow Democrat Joseph Guffey of Pennsylvania, and Republican Arthur Vandenberg of Michigan received special attention. So did Owen Brewster, who had just embarked on yet another investigation of wartime oil affairs. After several handholding sessions, Ickes's lieutenants reported in mid-October that they had "not heard any real adverse sentiment and with the industry's apparent accord, the treaty, if submitted to the Senate at once, should receive prompt approval."[17]

Despite Ickes's exertions, consideration, let alone approval, remained elusive. Through 1946 matters large and small occupied the Senate: a well-deserved recess, the continuing problems of reconversion, a nasty fight over an important loan to Great Britain, an early cold war crisis in Iran, and finally a mid-term election that gave both houses to the Republicans for the first time since 1930. The second oil pact did not come under review until the summer of 1947. By then it

16. Ickes Diaries, vol. 61, 10015–16.

17. *Ibid.;* G. M. Fuller to Davies, October 11, 1945, NA, RG 253, Anglo-American Oil Agreement File, Box II, Folder 13; Minutes of the Petroleum Industry War Council, October 24, 1945, NA, RG 48, File 1–188: Petroleum Reserves Corporation, Folder 2835.

was too late. The world had passed the agreement by, and with it, the first serious effort to fashion national policy for foreign oil.[18]

The Demise of the Oil Pact

Senate review turned out to be an anticlimax. Although major trade organizations had voted their confidence in the revised agreement, independents in the Southwest, particularly in Texas, could not be won to it. They still believed, in spite of all attempts to accommodate them, that the pact would condone cartels abroad, flood the home market with cheap foreign oil, and worst of all, provide an avenue for federal control of domestic operations.[19]

Texans proved, as ever, the most enterprising and ornery critics. As the leading oil-producing state in the country and a stronghold of independents, Texas could marshall an impressive phalanx of faultfinders. The powerful Texas Railroad Commission had good reason to contest any federal encroachment, real or imagined, since it was the agency charged with regulating oil operations throughout the state. Under the guidance of its chairman, Olin Culberson, local oil men had banded together in a statewide committee to oppose the agreement almost as soon as Ickes had returned from London. Governor Beauford Jester,

18. Truman submitted the agreement to the Senate on November 1, 1945. *NYT,* November 2, 1945; Mikesell and Chenery, *Arabian Oil,* p. 97. On matters occupying the Senate during 1946, see Acheson to Forrestal, April 5, 1946, NA, RG 59, 811.6363/2-546; Rayner memorandum, June 10, 1946, NA, RG 59, 800.6363/5-946; Rayner memorandum conversation with Davies and Clayton, June 26, 1946, NA, RG 59, 841.6363/6-2646. For excerpt from speech of House Majority Leader John D. McCormick on British loan, see *NYT,* July 13, 1946. For discussion of loan to Great Britain, see McNeill, *America, Britain and Russia,* pp. 685-90. See also, Acheson note, May 20, 1946, NA, RG 59, 800.6363/5-946.

19. The Senate hearings ran from June 2, 1947 through June 25, 1947, *AAOA Hearings.* The Independent Petroleum Association of America endorsed the new pact in October 1945. That same month the Petroleum Industry War Council also gave its approval. The American Petroleum Institute followed suit in November 1945. Frey and Ide, *PAW,* pp. 286-87. See also Minutes Meeting Petroleum Industry War Council, October 24, 1945, NA, RG 48, File 1-188: Petroleum Administration, Folder 2835; *NYT,* November 4, 1945, November 15, 1945. A year later, the Independent Petroleum Association of America withdrew its support and approved a resolution condemning the pact, *NYT,* November 1, 1946.

himself a former chairman of the Railroad Commission, was enlisted in the cause, as were local schoolteachers. They shared Jester's opinion that the agreement threatened the economy of the state by facilitating the importation of oil from abroad. Any reduction in oil-generated revenues, their petitions maintained, would diminish funds available for education.[20]

Although most corporate giants made no signs, independents in Texas and elsewhere did find reinforcements among some larger companies. When Joseph Pew of Sun Oil renewed his attack on the agreement, Harry Sinclair lent his hand by dispatching his representative to testify against it. As president of the Sinclair Oil Company and chairman of Richfield Oil, Sinclair was doubtless concerned about his domestic holdings. All the same, his persistent craving for Middle Eastern oil betrayed his private fears that the oil pact would establish a cartel along the Persian Gulf, one immune from antitrust action and impervious to smaller companies.[21]

20. East Texas Oil Association, "America No Longer Dependent Upon British Shipping To Move Petroleum and Other Products," n.d., in NA, RG 59, 890F.6363/10-2945. See also H. P. Nichols, vice-president East Texas Oil Association, to Truman, October 24, 1945, Nichols to Ickes, November 20, 1945, NA, RG 253, Anglo-American Oil Agreement File, Box I, Folder 7; *Texas State House Reporter,* December 18, 1945. D. W. Hovey of Houston served as chairman of the committee. See also *NYT,* January 16, 1946. Beauford T. Jester to Connally and Vandenberg, June 3, 1947, Library of Congress, Washington, D. C., Papers of Tom Connally, hereafter cited as Connally Papers, Box 101, Anglo-American Oil Treaty Folder; H. L. Foster to Connally and W. Lee O'Daniel, February 6, 1946, NA, RG 59, 800.6363/2-646. For other similar examples, see LC, Connally Papers, Box 101, Anglo-American Oil Treaty Folder.

21. Some corporate giants did make signs of support. See remarks of Eugene Holman of Jersey Standard and Harry Collier of Socal, *AAOA Hearings,* 188-89; *Arabian Oil Hearings,* 24847. Others left support to trade organizations. See American Petroleum Institute Resolution adopted at Chicago meeting, November 13, 1946, NA, RG 59, 800.6363/12-246; American Petroleum Institute Resolution adopted by Board of Directors, January 22, 1947, NA, RG 59, 800.6363/2-347. The second resolution came in response to a "University of the Air" broadcast on August 17, 1946. Participants included Charles Rayner; John A. Loftus, chief of the State Department's Petroleum Division; and Colonel G. H. Vogel, Executive Officer of the Army-Navy Petroleum Board. On the broadcast, Loftus had suggested the possibility of a more ambitious international commission than envisioned in the Anglo-American Oil Agreement. That commission, Loftus had hinted, might not be "purely advisory." For a transcript of that broadcast, see "Oil and International Relations," August 17, 1946, NA, RG 59,

Such opposition found the agreement bereft of resolute defenders. By the time hearings began, the pact had already lost its most persuasive and powerful advocate. In February 1946 Harold Ickes had quit the cabinet, another victim of the presidential succession. Characteristically, it was a question of honor that drove him from government; ironically, it was the appointment of an oil man on which the question hinged.

Ickes's row with Truman resulted from the nomination of Edwin Pauley as Under Secretary of the Navy. Pauley, a West Coast oil executive, had been an able and aggressive fundraiser for the Democratic Party. He excelled at tapping money from oil and other corporate sources. Because his industriousness had netted him several positions on the Democratic National Committee, among them secretary, assistant treasurer, and finally treasurer, he had naturally come to influence party politics. At the national convention in 1944 Pauley had opposed the renomination of Vice-President Henry Wallace, the visionary liberal who already had become a pariah among fellow Democrats. Pauley had thrown his support to Harry Truman, and when Truman came to the presidency, Pauley found himself on his way to the Navy Department.[22]

The appointment rankled Ickes, who had known Pauley for years. Ickes had relied on Pauley's expertise in organizing the Petroleum Administration for War and had followed his suggestion to make Ralph Davies deputy administrator. He had even used him as a special envoy during the war. Still, Pauley was an oil man, and Ickes, though

---

800.6363/11–1346. For Rayner's efforts to meet industry criticism of the remarks, see "Statement . . . before the annual meeting of the Independent Petroleum Association of America," October 29, 1946, NA, RG 59, 800.6363/1–947. For Pew's attack, see *NYT*, November 15, 1946. For Sinclair, see "Statement by H. F. Sinclair," February 4, 1946, LC, Connally Papers, Box 101, Anglo-American Oil Treaty Folder. Sinclair had been interested in obtaining a concession in Iran since the 1920s. During the Second World War Sinclair had competed unsuccessfully for a concession in the northern section of the country. Lenczowski, *Russia and the West in Iran*, p. 84; Lytle, "American-Iranian Relations," pp. 128–49.

22. For background material on Edwin Pauley, see *NYT*, January 19, 1946; Harry S Truman, *Memoirs*, vol. 1, *Year of Decisions* (Garden City, 1955), pp. 553–55; Engler, *Politics of Oil*, pp. 341–50.

sometimes impressed by his talents, never completely trusted him. He had earlier objected to Pauley's becoming party treasurer because of his cozy relationship with big oil. "You are going to have a scandal on your hands," he later claimed to have warned Roosevelt. When Truman made the nomination Ickes repeated the warning and backed it with charges that Pauley was peddling influence, in this case to California oil interests then fighting a federal suit to determine owner- ship of offshore deposits. Truman, who was as stubborn as Ickes had been in opposing several of his policies, stuck with Pauley. Early in 1946, after thirteen years of service, Harold Ickes left the government. Thereafter he had to satisfy himself by cheering the oil agreement from the sidelines through his syndicated column.[23]

Ickes's resignation left the pact without a friend at court. His own department had no enthusiasm for it. Doubts about the support it might offer cartels and about the opportunities it might present for bullying host countries—doubts perhaps suppressed in Ickes's presence—now made the Department of the Interior an uncertain and therefore ineffec- tual promoter. The State Department was worse. Ickes's success in capturing responsibility for the agreement had long since stopped de- partment officers from thinking of it as their property. Now that it was, they were no longer sure they wanted it. "Now the orphan is on our doorstep," one of them remarked upon Ickes's departure. "Shall we smother it or adopt it?"[24]

As it happened, they made it a foster child, neither abandoned nor

23. On Ickes's early dealings with Pauley, see Ickes, *Secret Diary,* vol. 3, p. 58, 392, 624–25. See also Ickes, "Why I Chose to Resign," *Vital Speeches,* March 15, 1946, pp. 351–52; *NYT,* February 1, 2, 6, 8, 14, 15, 19, 21, 1946; U. S., Congress, Senate, *Congressional Record,* 79th Cong., 1st Sess. (Washington, 1945), vol. 91, pt. 2, 1893, 2090; Ickes Diaries, vol. 60, 9847–48, vol. 62, February 17, 1946, 12–13. Ickes, "Man to Man," April 3, 1946, April 6, 1946, NA, RG 253, Anglo-American Oil Agreement File, Box II, Folder 10. See also Ickes, "An Oil Policy: An Open Letter by Harold L. Ickes to the Members of the Congress," May 30, 1947, LC, Connally Papers, Box 101, Anglo-American Oil Treaty Folder.

24. On the disenchantment of the Interior Department, see Gardner to Oscar Chap- man, March 1, 1946, NA, RG 48, File 1–188: Petroleum Reserves Corporation, Folder 2845; Gardner to Chapman, April 12, 1946, NA, RG 48, File 1–188: Petroleum Re- serves Corporation, Folder 2845. On the disaffection of the State Department, see Wil- cox to Clayton, February 19, 1946, NA, RG 59, 800.6363/2–1946.

embraced. It lacked the urgency that once had made it a prize worth the fight. Middle Eastern oil production had increased since the end of the war, and despite trouble over Palestine, Anglo-American relations throughout the region had never been warmer. Even so, oil remained, in the words of one officer, "at the heart of some of the most explosive situations in our international relations." The oil agreement might still serve to defuse some of that explosiveness. As such, it merited endorsement but not deadly combat.[25]

Harry Truman felt the same way. Already embroiled in a dispute over offshore oil rights, he could not afford to embitter independent oil men. He faced another election in 1948, and predictions of defeat made every vote precious. When the Foreign Relations Committee conferred near-unanimous approval on the pact (Connally alone dissented), Truman made no attempt to press the matter. Without active support from the White House, the controversial agreement stood little chance of ever coming to the floor of the Senate, where Connally and fellow Texan W. Lee O'Daniel promised a bitter fight. Five years later, in 1952, the president recalled it, at Connally's request. The Anglo-American Oil Agreement had become, in Truman's phrase, "obsolete."[26]

The agreement had indeed become outworn, though much earlier than Truman chose to recognize. Even before it came to Senate review it had lost its salience. By the end of 1946 American and British companies had largely worked out, as Basil Jackson put it years before, their own salvation in the Middle East. Their transactions restored

25. Wilcox to Clayton, February 19, 1946, NA, RG 59, 800.6363/2-1946.

26. On the offshore oil fight, see Nash, *U. S. Oil Policy,* pp. 190-94. On Senate action, see U. S., Congress, Senate, Foreign Relations Committee, *Anglo-American Oil Agreement. Report to Accompany Executive H,* 80th Cong., 1st Sess. (Washington, 1947); *NYT,* July 2, 1947, July 8, 1947. Connally's dissent came even after the committee had attempted to accommodate his criticisms by adding two amendments that protected domestic operators further. For the text of Connally's amendments, see "Reservation intended to be proposed by Mr. Connally . . .," n.d., LC, Connally Papers, Box 101, Anglo-American Oil Treaty Folder. For O'Daniel's views of the agreement, see U. S., Congress, Senate, *Congressional Record,* 80th Cong., 1st Sess. (Washington, 1947), vol. 93, pt. 7, 8669-70. For return of the agreement to the president, see U. S., Congress, Senate, *Congressional Record,* 82nd Cong., 2nd Sess. (Washington, 1952), vol. 98, pt. 7, 9182, 8502-503.

order and harmony to an unstable situation and, in the process, transformed the Anglo-American Oil Agreement into just another incident in the expansion of American oil interests in the Middle East.

The Early Postwar Oil Deals

The great Middle Eastern oil deals of the past had mostly involved the acquisition of concessions. Sometimes companies traded into existing operations, but most of the time they acquired promising properties. In the first two years after the war another kind of deal came into use. No new concessions were opened; instead, old ones became more and more entwined as the great multinational firms began to place their own interests in order. An enormous consolidation of enterprise occurred. Through long-term supply contracts and outright mergers, American-controlled companies expanded their access to Middle Eastern oil and thus set the system that came to govern the price of world oil. As they did so, they undercut government efforts to carry out a coherent foreign oil policy. That result was not the product of design but rather an unintended consequence of what were primarily commercial maneuvers.

The postwar oil deals grew out of the threat posed by Saudi Arabia's abundant reserves to the existing market positions of major international companies. Aramco, which still monopolized the Arabian concession, had always had trouble finding outlets for its oil. The company had brought in Texaco in 1936 largely to obtain the latter's marketing facilities. By combining with a firm that held a recognized market position east of Suez, Aramco had fit its venture neatly into the world oil trade.

Pressure from Ibn Saud for more money and the wartime demand for petroleum soon brought about an enormous increase in Arabian production. By 1946 Aramco wells were lifting over 100 times the amount of crude they had produced before the war. That expansion yielded more oil than Aramco markets could possibly absorb. Since Ibn Saud's demands for larger royalties made continued development necessary, Aramco managers faced two alternatives if they wanted to keep their concession secure and profitable: either force their way into markets closed to them by cartel arrangements or sell a proprietary interest in their company to others with established outlets. Barging into closed markets brought on the risk of large-scale price wars and offered no guarantee of success, but cooperating with older companies would assure peace within the industry and would furnish the capital needed to expand Aramco operations and to satisfy Ibn Saud.[27]

Aramco elected cooperation. In September 1946 Texaco president Harry T. Klein, responding to overtures made by Jersey Standard and Socony-Vacuum, offered to share the oil of Arabia. Both companies welcomed the approach. As always, they were short of crude for their far-flung markets, a condition aggravated by the recent loss of Jersey's oil fields in Rumania. Even membership in the Iraq Petroleum Company offered the two giants no relief. The reserves of Iraq were meager compared to those of Saudi Arabia, and as the American companies knew, their British partners had consistently kept production in Iraq low in order to avoid undercutting oil from Iran.

Of equal concern to Jersey and Socony were the losses they stood to sustain should Aramco embark on a competitive course west of Suez, where they occupied key market positions. Oil from Latin America or from the United States, sources used by the two companies to supply prewar markets in Western Europe, stood no chance against Arabian crude, which in 1946 undersold the cheapest Western oil by almost forty cents a barrel. A marriage of the four companies—Jersey Standard, Socony-Vacuum, and Aramco parents Texaco and Socal—was, as one executive commented, "a natural."[28]

27. Through 1938 Aramco wells had produced a total of 580,000 barrels. By 1946 oil production averaged 165,000 barrels/day or 59,944,000 barrels/year, Shwadran, *MEOGP*, p. 349. On Ibn Saud's demands for greater royalties, see Memorandum of meeting between Harry T. Klein and representatives of Jersey Standard and Socony-Vacuum, September 4, 1946, reprinted in *International Petroleum Cartel*, p. 121.

28. Memorandum of meeting between Harry T. Klein and representatives of Jersey Standard and Socony-Vacuum, September 4, 1946, reprinted in *International Petroleum Cartel*, p. 121; Jersey Standard had been interested in participating in the Aramco concession at least since 1943, Merriam memorandum conversation with Bohanon, October 4, 1943, NA, RG 59, 890F.6363/64. See also "Standard Oil Company (New Jersey) and Middle Eastern Oil Production: A Background Memorandum on Company Policies and Actions," March 1947, NA, RG 48, File 1–322: Oil and Gas Division. In

What appeared natural to some executives seemed unnecessary to others. A powerful faction within Socal, led by director R. C. Stoner, opposed the merger from the start. Early in June 1946 Stoner had told his superiors that he believed Caltex, the marketing arm of Aramco, could challenge Jersey all over the world "not because we have the markets, but because we have a cheap oil available right now." By dealing with independent American companies such as Phillips, Atlantic Refining, and Sinclair, Stoner reasoned, Caltex could even break into the United States domestic market.

The advantages of the plan were clear to him. Not only would Aramco profit in the long run, but advances on supply contracts could provide the company immediately with capital necessary to expand Arabian development. Those same contracts would also, in his words, "give a number of American companies an interest in Arabian oil, which would be political protection for us in the future . . . since there has been criticism in the United States that this [the Arabian] concession is too big for one company and also there had been strong thought in the world of petroleum that all countries and more companies should have access to foreign petroleum."[29]

Socony-Vacuum's chief counsel, C. V. Holton, also had doubts. The antitrust aspects of the deal worried him. The arrangements, he told Socony president B. Brewster Jennings in October 1946, "would place practical control of crude reserves in the hands of seven companies." "I can not believe," he continued, "that a comparatively

---

1946 the lowest price quoted on the United States Gulf coast for oil was $1.28/barrel. Aramco was selling oil of comparable quality for $.90/barrel. Had a price war erupted, Aramco could have cut its price even further, since Socal and Texaco admitted that the cost of producing Arabian oil was only $.33/barrel. U. S., Congress, Senate, Foreign Relations Committee, Subcommittee on Multinational Corporations and Foreign Policy, *Hearings, Multinational Petroleum Corporations and Foreign Policy,* 93rd Cong., 2nd Sess. (Washington, 1974), hereafter cited as *Multinational Hearings,* pt. 7, 81. Childs to Secretary of State, January 3, 1947, NA, RG 59, 890.6363/1–347.

29. U. S., Congress, Senate, Foreign Relations Committee, Subcommittee on Multinational Corporations and Foreign Policy, *Report on Multinational Petroleum Corporations and Foreign Policy,* 93rd Cong., 2nd Sess. (Washington, 1975), hereafter cited as *Multinationals Report,* p. 48.

few companies for any great length of time are going to be permitted to control world oil resources without some sort of regulation.'' Those observations, though prescient, had little effect on company thinking. In desperate need of crude, Socony moved ahead with negotiations.[30]

By December 1946 the companies had reached an agreement in principle. For the sum of $102 million, Jersey and Socony would receive a 40 percent interest in Aramco. Originally the two were to split that share down the middle, but Socony managers thought the price too high and took only 10 of the 40 percent offered. Jersey eagerly accepted the remaining 30. For their part, Texaco and Socal promised to reduce their holdings to 30 percent each. Further agreements gave Jersey and Socony an interest in the Trans-Arabian Pipeline Company, organized in 1945 by Aramco's parents to construct on a private basis the government's abortive pipeline across the Arabian peninsula. Those agreements furnished Jersey and Socony with the same share in Tapline that they held in Aramco. The cost, $125 million, was again financed through guaranteed loans pending conclusion of the deal.[31]

What delayed the purchase were the obligations Jersey and Socony owed their partners in the Iraq Petroleum Company. The American companies were still bound by the Red Line agreement, which obliged them to acquire oil in the region only through IPC. They had tried to free themselves of the restrictions before the war, but French interests and Calouste Gulbenkian, the Armenian entrepreneur who put together the original Turkish syndicate, had blocked the move. Unless some way of modifying or discarding the agreement could be found, Jersey and Socony would be unable to conclude the Aramco purchase.[32]

30. C. V. Holton to B. Brewster Jennings, October 28, 1946, in *Multinational Hearings*, pt. 8, 116–17.

31. For their part, Texaco and Socal promised to reduce their holdings to 30 percent each. Until the deal was completed, Jersey and Socony also were to guarantee a bank loan of $102 million to Aramco. George M. McGhee memorandum conversation with Orville Harden, December 3, 1946, NA, RG 59, 890G.6363/12-346; *International Petroleum Cartel*, p. 120, 122–28; *O. and G. Journal*, April 19, 1947; Shwadran, *MEOGP*, p. 353.

32. Sampson, *Seven Sisters*, p. 102.

The war furnished Jersey and Socony with a way out. During hostilities the British government had sequestered the French share of IPC (along with Gulbenkian's 5 percent) under its Trading with the Enemy Act. At the end of the war the British returned the confiscated property. When the Compagnie Française des Pétroles and Gulbenkian tried to reaffirm the restrictive features of the Red Line agreement, Jersey and Socony balked. The confiscation, they claimed, had rendered Red Line inoperative. Further, as Jersey president Eugene Holman informed CFP on January 29, 1946, "there had been a substantial change in the attitude of the American public and Government toward restrictive agreements and under current conditions, reaffirmation of the agreement seemed inadvisable." In October 1946 Jersey and Socony, citing their need for more Middle Eastern crude to satisfy market requirements, declared the Red Line agreement void.[33]

Anglo-Iranian, the most influential British company involved in IPC, entered no objections. In itself, an abrogation of the Red Line agreement would do no damage to the British company. With holdings in Iraq, Kuwait, and Iran, Anglo-Iranian already had more crude oil than its markets could consume. But a merger between its American partners and Aramco did threaten its concession in Iran, which competed directly with Saudi Arabia. Jersey and Socony anticipated the conflict. In December 1946, the same month in which the Aramco purchase became public, the two American companies announced an agreement in principle to buy from Anglo-Iranian 134 million tons of crude over a twenty-year period. The three companies also agreed to investigate the possibility of constructing a mutually owned pipeline from the Persian Gulf to the eastern Mediterranean.[34]

33. "Near East Group Agreement: Certain War Time Developments," n.d., enclosed in Stuart-Morgan to Henderson, July 2, 1945, NA, RG 59, 890G.6363/7-245. Holman quoted in Shwadran, *MEOGP*, p. 243, 244. See also Winant to Stettinius, December 5, 1945, *FRUS* (1945), vol. 8, pp. 62-63; McGhee memorandum conversation with Harden and Sheets, August 27, 1946, *FRUS* (1946), vol. 7, pp. 31-32. Will Clayton also attended the meeting.

34. Byrnes to Tehran, January 8, 1947, NA, RG 59, 891.6363/12-3146; George Kirk, *Survey of International Affairs. The Middle East, 1945-50* (London, 1954), p. 84. The French saw immediately the connection between the supply contract and the Aramco merger. When they reported their conclusions to the State Department, officials

The arrangement testified to the commercial finesse of which Jersey and Socony were capable. In one stroke they calmed the fears of the British company, moved closer to ensuring its support for abrogation of the Red Line agreement, and obtained the additional oil they sorely needed. The supply contract insulated Anglo-Iranian against the effects of the impending merger by guaranteeing outlets for surplus oil for the next twenty years. The transaction also held promise of capital and material for a pipeline that Anglo-Iranian had been planning since before the war, and it furnished the British company with an opportunity to exploit the concession shared with Gulf in Kuwait. According to the terms of the contract, Anglo-Iranian could use oil from Iran or Kuwait to meet its obligations.[35]

As it turned out, that option carried an unexpected dividend for Jersey and Socony in their effort to nullify the Red Line agreement. Any increase in Kuwaiti production would naturally be shared by Gulf, which for years had been pressing Anglo-Iranian to remove restrictions on developing the concession. Soon after Gulf managers learned about Anglo-Iranian's supply contract, they negotiated one of their own with Shell. For the next ten years Gulf agreed to provide from Kuwait 30 percent of Shell's crude oil requirements in the Eastern Hemisphere. Access to a new and rich source of oil gave Shell, another participant in IPC, less reason to resist the dissolution of the Red Line agreement. So did promises from Socony-Vacuum of similar supply contracts.[36]

The Compagnie Française des Pétroles and Calouste Gulbenkian were mortified. With the aid of the French government, which owned a substantial share of CFP, they fought the action. All three stood to lose heavily should Red Line be dropped from IPC. Not only would

---

there replied that they understood the transactions to be "entirely separate." Eakens memorandum conversation with Bonnet, January 10, 1947, *FRUS* (1947), vol. 5, pp. 632–33. For the basic documents describing the purchases, see "Heads of Terms . . . ," December 12, 1946, NA, RG 59, 800.6363/1–2847.

35. Byrnes to Tehran, January 8, 1947, NA, RG 59, 891.6363/12–3146.

36. Eakens memorandum meeting with J. F. Drake, February 3, 1947, NA, RG 59, 811.6363/2–347; Sampson, *Seven Sisters,* p. 102. Shell had originally opposed the nullification, Calder to Secretary of State, December 31, 1946, NA, RG 59, 841.6363/12–3146.

they be denied a proportionate interest in Aramco, but they might well lose production and profits from Iraq. The French feared that after Jersey and Socony closed their deal with Aramco, the American companies would have no incentive for increasing production in Iraq, since its oil competed with Arabian crude. Without pressure from the Americans, CFP and Gulbenkian could not possibly persuade their other partners to step up liftings.[37]

For the French government, retarded development in Iraq meant more than lost profits from its share in CFP. France had staked its plans for establishing an independent petroleum industry on oil from Iraq, the only source of franc oil in the Middle East. Deprived of increased production, the French would remain dependent on dollar oil at a time when they, like the British, suffered from exchange problems. That dependence, they believed, would jeopardize postwar recovery.[38]

Those prospects drove French ambassador Henri Bonnet to the State Department in January 1947. He protested the abrogation of the Red Line agreement and asked the department to withdraw any support it might have given the companies in their effort. The department offered Bonnet no help. Instead, Under Secretary of State Will Clayton told him that "the contract which the French Government considered to be abrogated by the actions of Jersey and Socony is between private parties, and . . . it would seem that unless they are able to come to some agreement there would be no other recourse but to the courts."[39]

In a clumsy effort to avoid a rift with the French government, Clayton had obscured the position and activities of the department. By claiming that the United States government had no standing in the matter, he sought to dissociate American officials from the companies involved and to free Washington from responsibility for their actions.

37. Winant to Secretary of State, December 5, 1945, *FRUS* (1945), vol. 8, pp. 62–63.

38. R. Funkhouser to Secretary of State, January 20, 1947, NA, RG 59, 800.6363/ 1–2047.

39. Bonnet to Secretary of State, January 4, 1947, *FRUS* (1947), vol. 5, pp. 628–29; Eakens memorandum meeting with Bonnet, January 10, 1947, *FRUS* (1947), vol. 5, p. 632.

Yet the department had a keen interest in canceling the Red Line agreement and had already begun to press for its repeal. Long a target of government petroleum planners, the Red Line agreement violated their conception of the Open Door by forcing key American companies to accept foreign firms as partners. It also allowed the British to hold down Middle Eastern production through IPC. At a time when national oil policy demanded the conservation of Western Hemisphere reserves, any limitation on production in the Middle East seemed to threaten the safety of the nation.

The Anglo-American Oil Agreement laid the groundwork for ending Red Line, but Jersey and Socony had taken matters into their own hands before the understanding came into force. Even so, the department invoked the oil pact to support the abrogation. A department telegram sent late in November 1946 to the American embassy in London justified that support on the basis of traditional commercial policy and the oil pact: "The Red Line agreement in so far as it restricts the commercial liberties of the parties to it is a kind of private commercial understanding incompatible with the United States views on restrictive business practices. Paragraph three of Article II of the Anglo-American Oil Agreement is clearly directed against such arrangements and the Red Line Agreement was explicitly mentioned at the Anglo-American oil talks as being one of the arrangements under . . . indictment." Three months later, in January 1947, Robert Loftus of the department's Petroleum Division supplemented diplomatic activities by lending official encouragement to the companies. He advised executives from Jersey and Socony that, although they should take French protests seriously and accommodate them as best they could, they should refuse to reaffirm the Red Line agreement.[40]

40. Secretary of State to Gallman, November 29, 1946, *FRUS* (1946), vol. 7, p. 39. The department learned of Jersey Standard's and Socony-Vacuum's plans to press for nullification of Red Line in August 1946. At the time, the department agreed to support the companies with respect to the preservation of the basic conception of the consortium, McGhee memorandum conversation with representatives of Jersey Standard and Socony-Vacuum, August 27, 1946, NA, RG 59, 890G.6363/8-2746. From November 19, 1946 to November 30, 1946, the United States and Great Britain held informal talks in London concerning a variety of oil questions. During those discussions, the American representatives again pointed out that the Red Line agreement contravened the spirit of

Department officials raised no formal objections to the other transactions, despite misgivings about possible violations of the very principles they had cited in supporting revocation of the Red Line agreement. Loftus and Paul Nitze, the investment banker turned diplomat and now deputy director of the Office of International Trade Policy, both complained early in 1947 about the arrangements. As they saw it, the mergers and supply contracts promoted consolidation among the seven major international oil companies—a tendency, they rightly argued, that restricted competition abroad and might deprive smaller companies of a share in Middle Eastern oil. One of those companies, Atlantic Refining, had already lodged a protest with the department. Even worse, Loftus pointed out, the United States government risked the charges of condoning supply, marketing, and pricing practices that ran against official policy on cartels and of cooperating with Great Britain to ''[solidify] the near monopolies enjoyed by the large oil companies.'' Still, neither Nitze nor Loftus was willing to have the department disapprove of the arrangements. The transactions, as Loftus noted, were simply too valuable because they promoted the strategic goal of national oil policy, namely, reducing the drain on Western Hemisphere oil by developing Persian Gulf sources. That goal seemed within reach in view of Jersey's recent disclosures to department officials. The company planned to use its new Middle Eastern acquisitions to supply Europe and the Eastern Hemisphere, while it retained Western Hemisphere reserves exclusively for western markets.[41]

---

the Anglo-American Oil Agreement and that they were advising the American participants in IPC to press for reconsideration of the restrictive aspects of their understanding. The British refused to commit themselves, ''Record of Informal Anglo-American Oil Talks, November 1946,'' n.d., *FRUS* (1946), vol. 7, pp. 44–45. Loftus memorandum conversation with Orville Harden, Harold Sheets, and Brewster Jennings, January 9, 1947, *FRUS* (1947), vol. 5, pp. 630–31.

41. Loftus memorandum for the Secretary's Staff Committee, ''Projected intercompany arrangements affecting Middle East oil,'' February 14, 1947, NA, RG 59, 890F.6363/2-1447; Nitze to Clayton, February 21, 1947, NA, RG 59, 800.6363/2-2147; McGhee memorandum conversation with Orville Harden, December 3, 1946, *FRUS* (1946), vol. 7, pp. 40–43. See also Caltex to Aramco, June 17, 1947, Jersey Standard to Aramco, June 17, 1947, Socony-Vacuum to Aramco, June 17, 1947, found in NA, RG 59, 890F.6363/6-1747.

However, Loftus counseled against blanket endorsement of the merger and supply contracts. Such approval, he cautioned, might leave the impression that the transactions were wholly in accord with official trade policy. Instead he recommended that without recording any formal objections, the department make frank admission of its reservations to the participating American companies. The warning would leave emerging cartel policy unprejudiced and would give the companies a clear indication that they might run afoul of antitrust laws in the future. At the same time, the companies could complete their arrangements without losing the support of their government.[42]

Nitze prescribed a more competitive solution. Late in February 1947 he suggested that Socony-Vacuum buy Jersey's share in IPC and withdraw from the Aramco purchase. He further advised having Socony leave to Jersey alone the supply contract with Anglo-Iranian. Among other things, Nitze maintained, the realignment would "simplify and perhaps arrest the trend toward multiplication of interlocking arrangements between and among oil companies engaged in the international oil trade . . . [and] would retard the growing consolidation outside the United States of the interests of the two largest American oil companies, Jersey and Socony." It would also, he contended, help to reassure smaller American companies, which were worried that Middle Eastern oil was "being preempted by various combinations of large American and British companies." With smaller companies in mind, he presented an alternative plan that involved Jersey selling its interest in IPC to a consortium of American companies. Nitze admitted that such a course would be less attractive to Jersey and Socony and would require "more positive action" on the part of the department.[43]

In an effort to make the transactions more compatible with commercial policy, Loftus and Nitze met early in March 1947 with executives from Jersey and Socony. They discussed Nitze's original proposal,

42. Loftus memorandum for Secretary's Staff Committee, "Projected inter-company arrangements . . . ," February 14, 1947, NA, RG 59, 890F.6363/2-1447.

43. Nitze to Clayton, February 21, 1947, NA, RG 59, 800.6363/2-2147. For development of Nitze's proposal, see Eakens to McGhee, March 4, 1947, NA, RG 59, 800.6363/3-447.

along with two variations that would open the Persian Gulf to smaller companies. One called for IPC to refrain from bidding on new concessions; the other required that either IPC or Aramco sell off portions of its holdings to American companies without property in the Middle East.[44]

Though somewhat shaken by the discussion, the executives rejected the schemes. "They felt," recorded a department official after a follow-up call from Socony, "that any companies not already in the Middle East could get in the same way they are getting in, by buying an interest in an existing concession." That course, Socony failed to mention, had been made more difficult by the oil deals just negotiated. Even so, the response seemed to satisfy department officials, who dropped efforts to reshuffle the arrangements.[45]

Meanwhile the French had turned to the courts in an attempt to block the abrogation and subsequent merger. In February 1947 CFP brought suit in the British High Court of Justice against the American companies and the other partners in IPC. Jersey and Socony replied four months later with a countersuit denying French claims about the validity of the Red Line agreement. Despite the acrimony, the companies were set against airing their affairs in public. By May 1947 they had arrived at a tentative agreement acceptable to all but Calouste Gulbenkian. Stubborn and cagey, Gulbenkian recognized the leverage given him by the pending suit and raised the price for his acquiescence.[46]

At first the American companies tried to enlist the State Department in persuading the obstinate Armenian. When department officials declined to intervene, the companies again moved on their own. In November 1948, on the day before the lawsuit was to come to court, representatives from Socony, Jersey, Anglo-Iranian, and CFP gathered at the Aviz Hotel in Lisbon, where Gulbenkian now lived. In a marathon session that lasted through the night, the negotiators reached a settlement. According to the new Heads of Agreement, as

---

44. Memorandum meeting between Nitze, Loftus, Robertson and Eakens and Orville Harden and B. Brewster Jennings, March 7, 1947, *FRUS* (1947), vol. 5, pp. 651–54.
45. *Ibid.*
46. *International Petroleum Cartel,* pp. 96–105; Shwadran, *MEOGP,* p. 244.

the understanding was called, IPC remained intact. Each party retained its original share of the company. The Red Line agreement was canceled, and the participants waived all claims arising out of it. In what was known as the "Aramco Release," CFP withdrew its suit and the American companies their counteraction, which allowed Jersey and Socony to complete their acquisition of Aramco. CFP, in turn, obtained assurances of increased production in Iraq, where new pipelines would be constructed to meet a development program based on the aggregate requirements of all the partners. As for Gulbenkian, he received a handsome payoff in the form of an additional allocation of free oil.[47]

The oil deals had far-reaching consequences that would ultimately help to establish the Persian Gulf as the base of the world price structure for petroleum. They allowed the large international companies, especially those controlled by Americans, to tighten their hold in the Middle East through a series of interconnected agreements. As far as they could at the time, the companies had entwined their interests to consolidate their control, to restrict competition, and to maintain prices.[48] The oil deals had opened the way for increased development by removing restraints on production and by setting ambitious construction projects that would furnish additional facilities for transporting oil from the region. Just as important, they had ensured that exploitation of the area would proceed according to the planned programs of cooperating companies. No waste would accompany development. Programmed too were the paths along which

47. Nitze memorandum conversation with Orville Harden and Harold Sheets, June 11, 1947, NA, RG 59, 890G.6363/6-1147; Nubar Gulbenkian, *Pantaraxia* (London, 1965), p. 227; *O. and G. Journal,* March 22, 1947.

48. The oil deals did not close the Middle East to newcomers. In 1948 and 1949, the American Independent Oil Company and J. Paul Getty's Pacific Western Oil Company obtained concessions from Kuwait and from Saudi Arabia respectively the half-interests those countries owned of the Saudi Arabia-Kuwait neutral zone. Wilkins, *Maturing Multinational,* p. 321. As it also happened, the large companies failed to maintain prices in the first few years after their oil deals. Lowering them in 1948 and 1949 turned out to be a successful gambit to undercut the price of Western Hemisphere oil in Europe and to challenge American oil in the United States. The ploy helped to enable the companies to raise posted prices twice in the 1950s. Neil Jacoby, *Multinational Oil: A Study in Industrial Dynamics* (New York, 1974), p. 220.

oil from the Persian Gulf was to flow to consumers. Those paths guaranteed that existing marketing positions would remain uninjured, at least for the immediate future. In the first few years after the war, that future—and beyond—looked most promising.

Together the oil deals realized many of the goals that the United States government had endeavored in vain to reach during the war. Oil development in the Middle East had been rationalized and restrictions on production and concession hunting significantly reduced. American-controlled companies had expanded their access to Persian Gulf reserves, which now were destined to relieve the strain on Western Hemisphere sources. The safety of the nation's oil supplies at last seemed assured.

That security came at a high cost. It had been achieved through unregulated arrangements among private companies. The opportunity to shape a coherent national policy for foreign oil was lost. Through the Petroleum Reserves Corporation and more widely through the Anglo-American Oil Agreement, government planners had attempted to institutionalize public responsibility over oil in order to influence its development and distribution for the good of the nation, as those planners saw it. In small but vital ways they were tampering with the structure of the international oil industry. Essentially, they had sought to bend the oil industry to the will of the nation through the use of public instrumentalities that would provide continuous and consistent guidance.

The effort failed. In the course of the early postwar years, government officials abandoned their attempt to assure safety and prosperity through devices other than the oil companies alone. Their inability to sustain the undertaking derived from many circumstances, no one of them deadly but in combination fatal. Partly it was a matter of political feasibility. Domestic oil men and congressional conservatives found a common cause in opposing the expansion of federal authority. Partly it was a weakening of will at the highest levels of government. The president and the State Department simply lost interest as the cold war deepened. Mostly, though, the failure was a result of the enterprise of the large international companies. In effect, those held by Americans became the agents of national policy because they could get the job done without the strains that attended public initiatives. That resolution was as dangerous as it was alluring. The interests of those companies and of the United States government coincided in the first years after the war, as they had during it. But there was no guarantee that they would continue to do so. In the long run, private companies might find profit in commercial arrangements that worked against what public representatives determined as national interests.

The danger was lost on most government officials. Although some bemoaned the anticompetitive tendencies of private cooperation, none was willing to do much about them. It was safer and less complicated in those crucial few years after the war to free oil companies from restraints imposed by their government and so allow them to settle their own households. Antitrust might later be applied to make the requisite adjustments. For now, security and order by private arrangement seemed worth the price.

Epilogue

In the early postwar era, those in government who wanted to invest the oil industry with public responsibility lost the chance. Their undertaking fell victim to the demands of national security, as they were shaped by the war. The war demonstrated an axiom of modern combat: without secure and accessible reserves of oil, the safety of the nation was in jeopardy. It was an old and obvious precept, first established during the First World War but overlooked in the oil-abundant years of the 1930s. The Second World War impressed it again upon the American people and upon their leaders. From Pearl Harbor until the defeat of Japan in August 1945, nearly seven billion barrels of petroleum were produced for Allied use. Six billion barrels came from the United States.[1]

That sacrifice carried fearful consequences for those who made it. Wartime planners worried that in pursuit of victory they might surrender national advantage. At least as early as 1943, officials in several executive departments and in the armed services sought ways to reduce the impact of the war on the oil reserves of the nation. Their search brought them to the Middle East. War made the region prominent; oil made it vital. Through rationalized development, planners hoped to transform the Persian Gulf basin into a wellhead for Europe after the war. The savings thereby afforded Western Hemisphere sources would preserve the independence of the country.

Oil companies exploited those anxieties, mainly out of concern for the uncertain future of their concessions in the Middle East. Haunted by the memory of expropriations in Bolivia and Mexico, unnerved by

1. Jacoby, *Multinational Oil,* p. 37.

209

the specter of British encroachment, and frustrated by concrete restrictions on their operations, American companies enlisted the support of their government. That support, conditioned as it was by alarm over the effects of depletion and by the experience of the New Deal, came to reflect the public functions of earlier New Deal agencies. In the Petroleum Reserves Corporation the government essentially became its own instrument for assuring security. Only through public participation, many wartime planners believed, could national interests truly be served. In time, as the corporation stirred controversy, planners turned to an international agreement to achieve their purposes. That idea proved just as controversial, owing to the demands of antagonistic segments of the oil industry.

Throughout the war, deep divisions within the industry had impeded government efforts to formulate and to carry out a coherent foreign oil policy. Companies confined to the United States would accept no arrangement that bestowed undue advantage on those operating abroad. Fear of competition from foreign oil accounted for their attitude. So did long-standing hostility toward the large international companies and toward the federal government. That apprehension and animosity came to bear on the Anglo-American Oil Agreement.

It was not that domestic oil men, majors and independents alike, were against an international pact. They were agreed on the need to rationalize every facet of the industry, as they had been in 1933. In this instance they were all in favor of a pact that would frame general rules of behavior for oil companies and governments and would reduce restrictions on operating overseas. Their aim was to commit the government to lending diplomatic assistance whenever the companies requested it. That was what they had in mind when they recommended an international accord along the lines of the Interstate Oil Compact. The question remained, as in 1933, who would control the program. Implicit in the oil men's plan was a restricted role for government, which, as the oil companies saw it, would be limited to its proper function of supporting private policy.

Almost obsessively domestic oil men feared the emergence of a pattern of relationships, first visible in the Petroleum Reserves Corporation and later in the oil agreement, that would enhance the role of the state in shaping national policy for foreign oil. The oil pact appeared to be a particularly insidious device. As a treaty, it might be used to extend federal regulation of domestic activities. Even worse, its international oil commission might realize a dangerous potential. Long experience with the Interstate Oil Compact, whose own advisory powers had been given force by local and federal laws, made majors and independents aware that the international commission, if bolstered by similar legislation, might also come to exert control over the industry. In their view the Interstate Oil Compact was an acceptable agency, indeed an essential one. By invoking the sacred notion of conservation it blended local administration and federal controls to obtain government services in support of private price fixing that would be unlawful if furnished by trade associations. The Interstate Oil Compact was a safe device because it served the industry and remained under its control.

No such guarantees attended the international commission, no matter how severely its operation was qualified. Independents, traditionally isolationist and accustomed to working through state legislatures, looked with distaste and mistrust on any international body. Majors were more particular in their concern. Even though their channels of influence ran to executive and administrative agencies, they were uncomfortable with the possibility of a commission filled with government representatives like Harold Ickes, who might not always see the consonance of public and private interests. Even if the companies succeeded in placing friends on the commission, they would still have to contend with the delegates of foreign governments, not nearly as accessible as Washington officials or local politicians.

For their part, the international companies had achieved by 1947 the purposes for which they had intended the oil agreement. Their Middle Eastern properties were now secure, production and marketing now rationalized, and restraints on development and concession hunting curtailed. Cooperation among private companies was accepted as standard procedure by government officials, who lent willing assistance when needed. The international firms still endorsed the agreement because it offered useful statistical services and furnished a set of principles that braced their operations. But their endorsement grew more and more faint as they slowly brought order to the Middle East.

The oil industry alone did not account for the shift in government policy from public to private instruments. Government officials themselves concluded that national interests could be served more expediently by traditional diplomatic mechanisms that supported private companies than by ambitious projects that entailed more direct government involvement. To some extent, that conclusion was forced on them by the unwillingness of domestic oil men to accept government schemes. It followed with greater compulsion from expanding conceptions of national security, conceptions that encompassed the reconstruction of western Europe and the maintenance of stability in the Middle East.

Wartime oil policy had been predicated on the importance of foreign oil to the war effort and to postwar defense. Government planners conceived of the safety of the nation in terms of hemispheric self-sufficiency. They aimed at ensuring enough reserves in the Western Hemisphere to sustain the country in wartime or, if need be, during a troubled peace. Toward that end the development of Middle Eastern oil became essential. Those goals remained at the core of postwar policy, which never disregarded the necessity of conservation at home and exploitation abroad.[2] In the early postwar years, the demands of wider American participation in international affairs gave oil companies added value in the pursuit of national interests overseas. Government officials found that if they simply supported American companies in their everyday operations, the United States could realize important objectives of foreign policy and still satisfy key requirements of national policy for foreign oil, as they had emerged from the war effort.

The official response to Aramco requests for steel in 1947 exemplified the strategy. Because Aramco needed the material to construct its pipeline across the Arabian peninsula, it applied to the Commerce Department for the necessary export licenses. Furnishing

2. See, for example, State Department Technical Committee on Petroleum, ''United States Petroleum Policy,'' November 10, 1947, LC, Papers of Julius A. Krug, Box 66.

Aramco with such releases was bound to raise objections from domestic operators then clamoring for the scarce metal in order to develop reserves at home. Even so, in September 1947 the Commerce Department granted Aramco an export license for 20,000 tons of steel on the grounds that the "strategical, political and economic interests of the United States made such action desirable."[3]

The precise nature of those interests had been clarified in interdepartmental discussions that had preceded the decision. More than a dozen agencies and departments had considered the request. The State Department, with its broad view of affairs, emerged as the strongest proponent. It had endorsed the pipeline project from the start and already had assisted the company in difficult negotiations over transit rights through several Middle Eastern countries. When asked their opinion of the company's application, department officers gave strong support. The United States, they pointed out, had become a net importer of petroleum and had to look abroad to supplement its growing needs. The pipeline—and the steel for constructing it—would assist in developing a rich source of oil that could be used to meet the requirements of the United States and other oil-consuming nations.[4]

It was a simple rationale, direct and persuasive in its connection to the petroleum needs of the nation. But the State Department went further, and therein revealed its aspirations for the salutary effects of private enterprise. The pipeline, department officers argued, would also promote the goals of American foreign policy in the Middle East and in Europe as well. The influx of American capital brought by the

3. *FRUS* (1947), vol. 5, p. 666n; Nitze to Marshall, September 24, 1947, NA, RG 59, 890.6363/8-2447; *O. and G. Journal,* October 4, 1947; Shwadran, *MEOGP,* p. 339. The export license was suspended in June 1948. Pressure from the Senate Small Business Committee, itself under pressure from domestic producers in need of steel, accounted for the suspension. Steel shipments to Saudi Arabia were resumed in February 1949. The pipeline was finally completed in September 1950, *ibid.,* pp. 339-40. For views of domestic producers, see *O. and G. Journal,* March 10, 1949, March 17, 1949.

4. For State Department assistance with transit negotiations, see Byrnes to Gallman, March 16, 1946, Acheson to Gallman, March 25, 1946, *FRUS* (1946), vol. 7, pp. 23, 26. Lovett to Harriman, September 8, 1947, *FRUS* (1947), vol. 5, pp. 665-66. For similar points of view in the Navy and Interior departments, see Walter Millis, ed., *The Forrestal Diaries* (New York, 1951), pp. 323-24; Max Ball to Krug, September 17, 1947, NA, RG 48, File 1-322: Administration, Folder 3178.

project would help to relieve the shortage of dollars along the eastern shore of the Mediterranean and so deflect requests for direct aid from the United States government. As department officers knew, such aid might be difficult to obtain in view of congressional support for a Jewish homeland in Palestine. The large amounts of oil and oil revenue made available through the pipeline would also encourage industrialization and would help to strengthen local economies. Oil and the riches it brought promised stability in the Middle East. Western Europe, too, would profit. Increased petroleum supplies would fuel the Marshall Plan as it endeavored to reconstruct European nations. In short, as department officers envisioned it, the trans-Arabian pipeline would serve as an all-purpose weapon for protecting the Middle East and Europe from political instability and economic failure.[5]

As national interests thus became more and more interwoven with the interests of private enterprise, the wartime effort to define and to carry out a coherent foreign oil policy fell to pieces. Even so, by the early postwar era that effort had produced a record of impressive accomplishment in the Middle East: the all-American character of oil investment in Saudi Arabia had been maintained; construction of a refinery and pipeline in that country was near completion; and, as it worked out, Middle Eastern oil was being used to fuel European recovery. Most important of all, the basis for a sizable Middle Eastern oil industry with strong American participation had been established. By 1947 that commercial system in large measure was set. As government officials saw it, some tinkering might be necessary, perhaps to diversify holdings for the sake of competitive ideals, but nothing more. The structure was basically sound. It had achieved the primary aims of security and order.

So it seemed in 1947. Three decades later the irony of those decisions can be fully appreciated. The security achieved in the early postwar years brought only ephemeral safety. Never more than now have the American people and their European allies been dependent on foreign oil, especially from the Middle East. Wartime planners could not have altered that eventuality. In part it resulted from the accidents

5. Henderson to Gordon Mattison, August 28, 1947, NA, RG 59, 890.6363/8-2847.

of geography, which determine the size and location of oil deposits. It also stemmed from the forces of the marketplace, which guided the activities of private companies, however much they tried to insulate themselves.

All the same, government officials might have reduced the vulnerability that derived from such dependence. In the early postwar years they abandoned the devices that had come to reflect the public vectors of wartime oil policy. They chose instead the more familiar path of pursuing national advantage through private corporations. Their decision rested for the most part on the assumption that commercial and national interests were identical. That premise made such public instruments as the Anglo-American Oil Agreement unnecessary, and as a result, public responsibility over oil was never exerted in continuous and consistent fashion.

Even with all its vague phraseology, even with its potential for seduction by private interests, the oil pact still presented possibilities for constant and responsible planning by both governments and oil companies. It provided a forum where producing and consuming countries might have joined to resolve differences and to explore common ground. Its statistical services could have furnished valuable information about world supply and demand. Its research facilities might have begun early to consider ways of conserving dwindling reserves and of finding new ones. Those possibilities, like the precious fluid itself, vanished too soon, and in the end the men who sought security promoted its collapse.

Essay on Sources

Archival sources provided the bulk of research material for this study. A useful starting point for American records is the *Guide to the Records of the National Archives* (Washington, 1948). Researchers in the Second World War period should also consult the *Federal Records of World War II* (2 volumes; Washington, 1950). Together the guides are an indispensable source for leading scholars through the maze of available information.

A large body of material is located at the National Archives in Washington, D.C. For examining the roots and development of American foreign oil policy, the General Records of the Department of State (RG 59) are vital. They provide a sense of continuity for the whole period of Franklin D. Roosevelt's administration, together with the early postwar years. They also serve as a valuable source of information about American-owned oil companies, since oil executives made frequent trips to the State Department and corresponded with several department officials. The State Department records should be used in conjunction with the Records of the Office of the Secretary of the Interior (RG 48). As Secretary of the Interior and as Petroleum Administrator for War, Harold L. Ickes played a key role in formulating national policy for foreign oil developments during the war years. His various positions are well detailed in those records and in the Records of the Petroleum Administration for War (RG 253), which also hold information about oil reserve prospects at home and abroad as well as the minutes of important meetings of the Petroleum Industry War Council. Both record groups contain copies of the original drafts of the Anglo-American Oil Agreement, minutes from several of the meetings of the Petroleum Reserves Corporation, and from sessions of the preliminary and cabinet-level conferences held in 1944. The minutes of other meetings of the Petroleum Reserves Corporation are located in the Records of Interservice Agencies (RG 334), under files covering the Army-Navy Petroleum Board. The Army-Navy Petroleum Board, under the command of Commodore Andrew F. Carter during most of the war, served as a liaison committee between the army and navy. As a result, and also because of Carter's special interest in foreign oil policy, the attitudes of the military services are well chronicled there. Together with the General Records of the Department of the Navy (RG 80), the Records of the Joint Chiefs of Staff (RG 218), and the Records of the Office of the Secretary of War (RG.107), they furnish a complete picture of the contributions of the military. The Records of the Office of Strategic Services (RG 226) contain some documents about Middle Eastern governments and predictions about postwar oil developments but generally are of little use.

Another rich source of archival material is the Public Record Office in London. Recently that office published an excellent handbook for students of the Second World War, *The Second World War: A Guide to Documents in the Public Record Office* (London, 1972). Not only does it list all the relevant collections for the period, but it supplements them with superb essays about the organization and functioning of the wartime government in London. A superior record-keeping system, along with highly literate civil servants, give the British records a coherence unmatched in American collections. Particularly useful for examining British reactions to American foreign oil policy is the British Foreign Office Political Correspondence (Class F. O. 371). A look at those documents also explodes the myth that the British were seriously interested in undercutting and obtaining the American oil concession in Saudi Arabia. On the contrary, Foreign Office officials were generally pleased with the presence of American oil companies in the Middle East and hoped that the United States would take an active hand in Middle Eastern affairs after the war. Less enthusiastic about American oil companies in the Middle East was the Petroleum Division of the Ministry of Fuel and Power, whose view of matters is contained in F. O. 371 and in War Cabinet Memoranda (CAB 66), War Cabinet Minutes (CAB 65), and Operational Papers of the Office of the Prime Minister (Premier 3). Those records also serve as an overview of British oil policy and diplomacy during the war and furnish an account of British oil company attitudes, particularly of the Anglo-Iranian Oil Company and the Royal Dutch/Shell Group.

Collections of personal papers in the United States and in Great Britain fill in the gaps left by archival sources. The papers of Franklin D. Roosevelt at the Franklin D. Roosevelt Library in Hyde Park, New York, are essential, even though several documents in that collection also appear in federal records at the National Archives. At Hyde Park, material from the Official File (OF), the President's Secretary's File (PSF), the President's Personal File (PPF), and the Map Room collection (MR) is important. Those records are particularly useful in reconstructing emerging petroleum policy in the early years of the war. The diaries of Henry Morgenthau, Jr., also at the Roosevelt Library, provide a few important pieces of information about the fight over the Foreign Petroleum Policy Committee in 1942. Collections of personal papers at the Library of Congress in Washington, D. C., supply important details here and there. The papers of Harold Ickes, recently opened for the war years, are vital. His diary is full of information and gossip, and essential for examining oil affairs. The papers of Herbert Feis contain surprisingly little information about wartime foreign oil policy but do have some material about a few of the oil men in government. The papers of Tom Connally are even more disappointing, although they do contain copies of petitions circulated by his Texas constituents against the Anglo-American Oil Agreement. The papers of Breckinridge Long are of greater assistance. As the State Department's congressional liaison, Long played an important role in efforts to guide the oil agreement through Congress. Those efforts are detailed in his papers. The papers of Edward R. Stettinius, Jr., at the University of Virginia in Charlottesville have nothing new to offer. The Henry L. Stimson papers at Yale University in New Haven, Connecticut, are useful. In particular, Stimson's diary communicates a sense of the cabinet's position on foreign oil policy and especially on Saudi Arabian oil matters. In Great Britain the papers of William Maxwell Aitken (Lord Beaverbrook) at the Beaverbrook Library in London explain Beaverbrook's criticisms of the oil agreement. His dictaphone notes, dictated from memory, give a detailed assessment of what he believed was an American assault on Britain's commercial position and help to put oil matters into perspective by comparing them to civil aviation and monetary policy.

Published government documents furnish another important source of material. The carefully indexed *Foreign Relations* volumes for the period contain a small amount of representative documents, usually an accurate reflection of the more extensive records at the National Archives. Most important for anyone working on oil policy are several congressional hearings and reports. The Subcommittee on Multinational Corporations and Foreign Policy of the Senate Committee on Foreign Relations, *A Documentary History of the Petroleum Reserves Corporation,* 93rd Cong., 2nd Sess. (Washington, 1974), is an indispensable source of government memoranda and reports, which took me months to track down. I had completed my research on the Petroleum Reserves Corporation by the time the collection was published, so it was of little use to me. I was able to piece together a relatively thorough account of corporate activities from the documents contained in those hearings and from the sources previously discussed. Among the most helpful is the Senate Special Committee Investigating the National Defense Program, *Hearings, Part 41, Petroleum Arrangements with Saudi Arabia,* 80th Cong., 1st Sess. (Washington, 1948). Those hearings offer a wealth of information about oil company attempts to entangle the United States government in Saudi affairs during the early part of the war. The testimony of oil executives, together with company telegrams, memoranda, and notes supply firsthand accounts of company activities and strategy. So do the documents in the Subcommittee on Multinational Corporations and Foreign Policy of the Senate Committee on Foreign Relations, *Hearings, Multinational Petroleum Corporations and Foreign Policy,* 93rd Cong., 2nd Sess. (Washington, 1974). Parts 7 and 8 of those hearings are particularly valuable in examining corporate motives for abrogating the Red Line agreement, since many company documents are reprinted there. The Senate Committee on Foreign Relations, *Hearings, Petroleum Agreement with Great Britain and Northern Ireland,* 80th Cong., 1st Sess. (Washington, 1947) and its *Anglo-*

American Oil Agreement. Report to Accompany Executive H, 80th Cong., 1st Sess. (Washington, 1947) offer little new information but do help to sort out opposition and support for the agreement. A sense of the hostility Americans felt toward the British can be obtained from the Subcommittee Concerning Investigations Overseas of the Senate Special Committee Investigating the National Defense Program, *Additional Report of the Subcommittee Concerning Investigations Overseas. Section I—Petroleum Matters,* 78th Cong., 2nd Sess. (Washington, 1944). Important for background on the corporate structure of the international oil industry is the Federal Trade Commission's *The International Petroleum Cartel,* FTC Staff Report Submitted to the Subcommittee on Monopoly of the Select Senate Committee on Small Business, 82nd Cong., 2nd Sess. (Washington, 1952).

Few memoir sources deal specifically with foreign oil policy or the Anglo-American Oil Agreement. Of those that do, Herbert Feis's *Three International Episodes Seen from E. A.* (1946; reprint ed., New York, 1966) offers the fullest account. Feis, economic adviser to the State Department until late 1943, was instrumental in bringing about the agreement, although he left the department before the oil conference. Cordell Hull's *The Memoirs of Cordell Hull* (2 volumes; New York, 1948) records his reasons for resisting the stock-buying effort of the Petroleum Reserves Corporation and for wanting the corporation under State Department control. Most of the other memoirs, autobiographies, and published personal papers are useful in building up background for character sketches and for affording a view of other wartime concerns that touched oil. Helpful here are Harold L. Ickes's *Autobiography of a Curmudgeon* (1943; reprint ed., Chicago, 1969), Dean Acheson's *Present at the Creation: My Years in the State Department* (New York, 1969), Fred L. Israel's edited *The War Diary of Breckinridge Long: Selections from the Years 1939-1944* (Lincoln, 1966), C. L. Sulzberger's *A Long Row of Candles: Memoirs and Diaries, 1934-1954* (New York, 1969), and John Morton Blum's edited *The Price of Vision: The Diary of Henry A. Wallace, 1942-1946* (Boston, 1973). Blum's annotations, in some cases brief character sketches, furnish an excellent introduction to many officials important during the war. Harold L. Ickes's *The Secret Diary of Harold L.*

Ickes (3 volumes; New York, 1953–54) ends in 1941, but for the earlier years the volumes furnish insights into Ickes's views of the oil industry. The volumes should be read in conjunction with archival material, since many passages are elliptical. Tom Connally's *My Name Is Tom Connally* (New York, 1954) is as bare as are his personal papers. Walter Millis's edited *The Forrestal Diaries* (New York, 1951) reveals Forrestal's concern about Middle Eastern oil development after the war.

Trade organizations, along with the Petroleum Industry War Council, published several important pamphlets during the war, which clarify the position of the oil industry on foreign oil policy matters. Those critical of administration policy include the Independent Petroleum Association of America, *The Anglo-American Petroleum Agreement* (Washington, 1944), *The Proposed Arabian Pipe Line—A Threat to Our National Security* (n.p., n.d.), and the Petroleum Industry War Council's *U. S. Foreign Oil Policy and Petroleum Reserves Corporation: An Analysis of the Effect of the Proposed Saudi Arabian Pipe Line* (Washington, 1944). The Petroleum Industry War Council had its National Oil Policy Committee draw up its own prescriptions for public oil policy, *A National Oil Policy for the United States* (Washington, 1944), while the Foreign Operations Committee of the Petroleum Administration for War offered its solutions in *A Foreign Oil Policy for the United States* (n.p., n.d.). Among the most helpful trade journals that recorded the views of individual oil men and companies are the *Oil and Gas Journal,* the *National Petroleum News,* and for the British oil industry, the *Petroleum Times.* Editorials and articles from two corporate publications, the Standard Oil Company of New Jersey's *The Lamp* and the Texas Company's *The Texaco Star,* indicate where those companies stood with regard to the agreement and to oil policy in general.

Scholarly studies of the oil industry, domestic and international, provide a backdrop against which to assess emerging foreign oil policy. Gerald D. Nash's *United States Oil Policy, 1890–1964: Business and Government in Twentieth Century America* (Pittsburgh, 1968) remains the best single historical study of public policy for oil at home and abroad. Nash devotes an entire chapter to wartime oil policy. His study is valuable because it helps to place that policy in a larger context. Joan Hoff Wilson's *American Business and Foreign Policy, 1920-1933* (Lexington, 1971) and Joseph Tulchin's *Aftermath of War: World War I and U. S. Policy toward Latin America* (New York, 1971) contain useful chapters on the intertwining of public and private oil interests abroad immediately after the First World War and during the 1920s. So does Michael Hogan's excellent and interesting *Informal Entente: The Private Structure of Cooperation in Anglo-American Economic Diplomacy, 1918-1928* (Columbia, 1977). Robert Engler's *The Politics of Oil: A Study of Private Power and Democratic Directions* (New York, 1961) complements those studies with an examination of the formal and informal relationships between government and the oil industry. Ellis W. Hawley looks at how the oil industry, among others, fared during the New Deal in his superb book, *The New Deal and the Problem of Monopoly* (Princeton, 1966). He explains clearly New Deal oil policy as well as the problems oil men faced in trying to stabilize their industry during the depression. As the official history financed partly by the oil industry, John W. Frey and H. Chandler Ide's *A History of the Petroleum Administration for War, 1941-1945* (Washington, 1946) has much information about government-industry cooperation during the war but avoids critical analysis. It contains reprints of important documents and lists of oil men who worked for the agency. D. J. Payton-Smith's *Oil: A Study of War-time Policy and Administration* (London, 1971) offers an incisive account of the British wartime experience with oil. Eugene Rostow's sophisticated *A National Policy for the Oil Industry* (New Haven, 1948), written during the controversy over the oil agreement, presents an intelligent critique of the industry's monopolistic tendencies. Rostow discusses the potential impact of the oil agreement on the international and domestic industry and remains undecided about its usefulness.

The international industry has recently come under close scrutiny. An older study, J. E. Hartshorn's *Oil Companies and Governments: An Account of the International Oil Industry in Its Political Environment* (London, 1962), continues to be a solid introduction to the more technical aspects of the industry. Anthony Sampson's *The Seven Sisters: The Great Oil Companies and the World They Shaped* (New

York, 1975) investigates the major international companies. Sampson, a journalist, relies heavily on recent congressional hearings together with interviews for much of his information. His informal and engaging style makes the book readable and allows him to sprinkle his narrative with excellent character sketches of both the companies and their executives. Neil Jacoby's *Multinational Oil: A Study in Industrial Dynamics* (New York, 1974) contains an abundance of useful facts and figures about the international oil industry and argues that during the 1950s and 1960s competition among private companies increased. More important is John M. Blair's *The Control of Oil* (New York, 1976). Blair worked for almost a decade as assistant chief economist for the Federal Trade Commission and for fourteen years as chief economist of the Senate Subcommittee on Antitrust and Monopoly. His book is a scholarly study indispensable to anyone interested in the oil industry. He makes no mention of the Anglo-American Oil Agreement, but he offers a penetrating analysis of the ways in which the large international companies have come to control the supply and marketing of oil throughout the world. Irvine Anderson's *The Standard-Vacuum Oil Company and United States East Asian Policy, 1933–1941* (Princeton, 1975) supplies insights into the complexities of public and private policy in the Far East through the 1930s and on the eve of war. For the activities of American oil companies in Latin America in the late 1930s and early 1940s and for the policies they developed in response to nationalization and confiscation in Mexico and Bolivia, Bryce Wood's *The Making of the Good Neighbor Policy* (New York, 1967) remains the best single study. Wood is especially helpful in describing the evolution of official American policy toward the companies and governments in question. For discussions of how oil developments compare with other corporate investments in raw materials, both Mira Wilkin's encyclopedic *The Maturing of Multinational Enterprise: American Business Abroad from 1914 to 1970* (Cambridge, 1974) and Stephen D. Krasner's *Defending the National Interest: Raw Materials Investments and U. S. Foreign Policy* (Princeton, 1978) are indispensable. Wilkins offers the fullest account yet of the wide range of international corporate activities and of government responses. Krasner provides a more interpretive view, which relies on a statist model for understanding government policy and action.

Middle Eastern oil developments are covered in detail in Benjamin Shwadran's *The Middle East, Oil and the Great Powers* (3rd ed., rev.; Jerusalem, 1973). He gives considerable attention to the oil agreement as it developed from American policy toward Saudi Arabia. Stephen Longrigg's *Oil in the Middle East: Its Discovery and Development* (London, 1954) is another overview but should be read with care in light of Longrigg's close association with the Anglo-Iranian Oil Company. George Lenczowski, *Oil and State in the Middle East* (Ithaca, 1960), and James Terry Duce, *Middle East Oil Developments* (New York, 1952), also cover the subject on a regional basis. Duce, a vice-president of the Arabian-American Oil Company, was head of the Foreign Division of the Petroleum Administration for War for a few years. His book is helpful because it contains graphs, maps, and illustrations of the entire region. Charles W. Hamilton's *Americans and Oil in the Middle East* (Houston, 1962), Leonard Fanning's *American Oil Operations Abroad* (New York, 1947), and Raymond R. Mikesell and Hollis B. Chenery's *Arabian Oil: America's Stake in the Middle East* (Chapel Hill, 1949) adequately deal with American oil company movements in the Middle East, as does Leonard Mosley's *Power Play: Oil in the Middle East* (New York, 1973). Fanning also surveys American oil operations outside the Middle East, while Mosley, a journalist, looks at the reactions of Middle Eastern governments to oil companies. Writing in the midst of the battle over the petroleum pact, Mikesell and Chenery devote a large portion of their book to defending the agreement. George Lenczowski, *Russia and the West in Iran, 1918–1948: A Study in Big Power Rivalry* (Ithaca, 1949), and Mark Lytle, "American-Iranian Relations 1941–1947 and the Redefinition of National Security" (Ph.D. dissertation, Yale University, 1973), serve as reliable guides through the troubled history of oil in Iran. Lytle presents two chapters of thoughtful analysis of the role played by Iranian oil in wartime and postwar diplomacy. Less interpretive but rich in information is Joseph William Walt's "Saudi Arabia and the Americans, 1923–1951" (Ph.D. dissertation, Northwestern University, 1960). Walt gives a lengthy narrative that centers around Aramco operations in Saudi Arabia but offers little in the way of critical commentary and completely ignores British activities. Saudi Arabian oil developments are also covered in H. St. J. B. Philby, *Arabian Jubilee* (London, 1952), Karl S. Twitchell, *Saudi Arabia: An Account of the Development of Its Natural Resources* (New York, 1958), and Roy Lebkicher et al. *The Arabia of Ibn Saud* (New York, 1952). The three are less than disinterested accounts. During the 1930s Philby worked for the Standard Oil Company of California, and Twitchell represented the Arabian government. Lebkicher was employed by Aramco.

For fitting foreign oil policy into the larger wartime picture, Richard Polenberg's *War and Society: The United States, 1941–1945* (New York, 1972) is most helpful. Also of use on the domestic side is John Morton Blum's *V Was for Victory: Politics and American Culture During World War II* (New York, 1976), which does not deal specifically with oil but contains excellent chapters on wartime cooperation between government and industry and on congressional politics. Blum gives careful attention to economic policy during the war in his *From the Morgenthau Diaries: Years of War, 1941–1945* (Boston, 1967). The book helps to place Anglo-American oil policy in a larger framework by explaining the complexities of monetary policy, Lend-Lease arrangements, and other issues of importance to the wartime alliance. So does Richard N. Gardner's *Sterling-Dollar Diplomacy: Anglo-American Collaboration in the Reconstruction of Multilateral Trade* (Oxford, 1956). Other balanced studies of wartime diplomacy that broadened my sense of the period are Herbert Feis's *Churchill, Roosevelt, Stalin: The War They Waged and the Peace They Sought* (Princeton, 1957), William Hardy McNeill's *America, Britain, and Russia: Their Co-operation and Conflict, 1941–1946* (1953; reprint ed., New York, 1970), Gaddis Smith's *American Diplomacy during the Second World War, 1941–1945* (New York, 1965), and John Lewis Gaddis's *The United States and the Origins of the Cold War, 1941–1947* (New York, 1972). Lloyd Gardner presents the best revisionist account of the period in *Economic Aspects of New Deal Diplomacy* (Madison, 1964). Gabriel Kolko's *The Politics of War: The World and United States Foreign Policy, 1943–1945* (New York, 1968), a provocative, if somewhat distorted view of events in the late war years, is also of assistance, although Kolko ignores the extent to which British oil companies were interested in having their government negotiate an oil agreement with the United States. He continues along similar lines in his and Joyce Kolko's *The Limits of Power: The World and United States Foreign Policy, 1945–1954* (New York, 1972). A less strident revisionist account of postwar economic policy, Thomas G. Paterson's *Soviet-American Confrontation: Postwar Reconstruction and the Origins of the Cold War* (Baltimore, 1973) is of greater help to those interested in grasping the essence of postwar economic policy. Specific wartime developments in the Middle East are traced in George Kirk's *The Middle East in the War, 1939–1946* (London, 1952), which takes a critical view of American policy. John A. DeNovo's *American Interests and Policies in the Middle East 1900–1939* (Minneapolis, 1963) is a valuable though unprovocative supplement to Kirk's book. DeNovo traces the growth of American involvement in the Middle East from the turn of the century to the outbreak of the Second World War.

Scholarly and other types of articles contribute a small amount to this study. Herbert Feis, in his "The Anglo-American Oil Agreement," *Yale Law Journal* (August 1946), raises serious questions about the vague wording and purposes of the agreement but comes out generally in favor of it. Two articles by John A. DeNovo, "Petroleum and the United States Navy before World War I" in the *Mississippi Valley Historical Review* (March 1955) and "The Movement for an Aggressive Oil Policy Abroad, 1918–1920" in the *American Historical Review* (July 1956) supply useful information about American oil policy before and after the First World War. More incisive is Michael J. Hogan's "Informal Entente: Public Policy and Private Management in Anglo-American Petroleum Affairs, 1918-1924," *Business History Review* (Summer 1974). John A. Loftus's "Middle East Oil: The Pattern of Control," *Middle East Journal* (January 1948), is also helpful for its cogent description of local laws governing concession contracts in the region. So is Mira Wilkin's "Multinational Oil Companies in South America in the 1920s: Argentina, Bolivia, Chile, Ecuador, and Peru," *Business History Review* (Autumn 1974). Wilkins, with her incomparable eye for detail, underscores the complexity of relationships among international companies, their own governments, and the governments of host countries.

Other materials, some of them of considerable intrinsic value, are listed in the bibliography that follows but proved to be of less importance for this study.

Bibliography

Collections of Personal Papers

Aitken, William Maxwell (Lord Beaverbrook). Papers, Beaverbrook Library, London, England.

Berle, Adolf A. Papers, Franklin D. Roosevelt Library, Hyde Park, New York.

Connally, Thomas, Papers, Library of Congress, Washington, D.C.

Cox, Oscar. Papers, Franklin D. Roosevelt Library, Hyde Park, New York.

Feis, Herbert. Papers, Library of Congress, Washington, D.C.

Hopkins, Harry. Papers, Franklin D. Roosevelt Library, Hyde Park, New York.

Hull, Cordell. Papers, Library of Congress, Washington, D.C.

Ickes, Harold L. Papers, Library of Congress, Washington, D.C.

Jones, Jesse H. Papers. Library of Congress, Washington, D.C.

Knox, Frank. Papers, Library of Congress, Washington, D.C.

Krug, Julius A. Papers, Library of Congress, Washington, D.C.

Landis, James M. Papers, Library of Congress, Washington, D.C.

Leahy, William D. Papers, Library of Congress, Washington, D.C.

Long, Breckinridge. Papers, Library of Congress, Washington, D.C.

Morgenthau, Henry, Jr. Papers, Franklin D. Roosevelt Library, Hyde Park, New York.

Patterson, Robert P. Papers, Library of Congress, Washington, D.C.

Roosevelt, Franklin D. Papers, Franklin D. Roosevelt Library, Hyde Park, New York.

Stettinius, Edward R., Jr. Papers, University of Virginia, Charlottesville, Virginia.

Stimson, Henry L. Papers, Yale University, New Haven, Connecticut.

Truman, Harry S. Papers, Harry S Truman Library, Independence, Missouri.

Watson, Edward M. Papers, University of Virginia, Charlottesville, Virginia.

229

Records at the United States National Archives, Washington, D.C.

Record Group 48. Records of the Office of the Secretary of the Interior.
Record Group 59. General Records of the Department of State.
Record Group 80. General Records of the Department of the Navy.
Record Group 107. Records of the Office of the Secretary of War.
Record Group 165. Records of the War Department General Staff.
Record Group 169. Records of the Foreign Economic Administration (housed in Federal Records Center, Suitland, Maryland).
Record Group 218. Records of the Joint Chiefs of Staff.
Record Group 226. Records of the Office of Strategic Services, Research and Analysis Branch.
Record Group 232. Records of the Petroleum Administrative Board.
Record Group 234. Records of the Reconstruction Finance Corporation.
Record Group 250. Records of the Office of War Mobilization and Reconversion.
Record Group 253. Records of the Petroleum Administration for War.
Record Group 334. Records of Interservice Agencies.

Records at the Public Record Office, London, England

British Foreign Office Political Correspondence, Class F. O. 371.
Confidential Papers of the Office of the Prime Minister, Premier 4.
Operational Papers of the Office of the Prime Minister, Premier 3.
War Cabinet Memoranda (WP and CP Series), CAB 66.
War Cabinet Minutes, CAB 65.

Public Documents

Great Britain. Parliament. *Parliamentary Debates House of Commons.* Volumes 396, 399.
U.S. Congress. *Congressional Record.* 78th Cong., 2nd Sess. 79th Cong., 1st Sess. 80th Cong., 1st and 2nd Sess. 82nd Cong., 2nd Sess.
U.S. Congress. House. Anti-Trust Subcommittee of the Committee on the Judiciary. *Hearings, Part 4, WOC's and Government Advisory Groups.* 84th Cong., 2nd Sess., 1956.
U.S. Congress. Senate. Committee on Foreign Relations. *Hearings, Petroleum Agreement with Great Britain and Northern Ireland.* 80th Cong., 1st Sess., 1947.

————. Committee on Foreign Relations. *Anglo-American Oil Agreement. Report to Accompany Executive H.* 80th Cong., 1st Sess., 1947.

————. Special Committee Investigating Petroleum Resources. *American Petroleum Interests in Foreign Countries. Hearings, Petroleum Resources United States.* 79th Cong., 1st Sess., 1945.

————. Special Committee Investigating Petroleum Resources. *Hearings, American Petroleum Interests in Foreign Countries.* 79th Cong., 1st Sess., 1946.

————. Special Committee Investigating Petroleum Resources. *Hearings, Petroleum Requirements—Postwar.* 79th Cong., 1st Sess., 1946.

————. Special Committee Investigating the National Defense Program. *Hearings, Part 41, Petroleum Arrangements with Saudi Arabia.* 80th Cong., 1st Sess., 1948.

————. Subcommittee Concerning Investigations Overseas of the Special Committee Investigating the National Defense Program. *Additional Report of the Subcommittee Concerning Investigations Overseas. Section 1—Petroleum Matters.* S. Rept. 10, Part 15. 78th Cong., 2nd Sess., 1944.

————. Subcommittee on Multinational Corporations and Foreign Policy of the Committee on Foreign Relations. *A Documentary History of the Petroleum Reserves Corporation.* 93rd Cong., 2nd Sess., 1974.

————. Subcommittee on Multinational Corporations and Foreign Policy of the Committee on Foreign Relations. *Hearings, Multinational Petroleum Corporations and Foreign Policy.* 93rd Cong., 2nd Sess., 1974.

————. Subcommittee on Multinational Corporations and Foreign Policy of the Committee on Foreign Relations. *Report on Multinational Petroleum Corporations and Foreign Policy,* 93rd Cong., 2nd Sess., 1975.

U. S. Department of State. *Papers Relating to the Foreign Relations of the United States,* 1931. Volume 2. Washington, 1946.

————. *Foreign Relations of the United States: Diplomatic Papers, 1933.* Volume 2—*The British Commonwealth, Europe, Near East and Africa.* Washington, 1949.

————. *Foreign Relations . . . 1939.* Volume 4—*The Far East, The Near East and Africa.* Washington, 1955.

————. *Foreign Relations . . . 1941.* Volume 2—*Europe.* Washington, 1959.

————. *Foreign Relations . . . 1942.* Volume 4—*The Near East and Africa.* Washington, 1963.

————. *Foreign Relations . . . 1943.* Volume 4—*The Near East and Africa.* Washington, 1964.

————. *Foreign Relations . . . 1943*. Volume 5—*The American Republics*. Washington, 1965.

————. *Foreign Relations . . . 1944*. Volume 3—*The British Commonwealth and Europe*. Washington, 1965.

————. *Foreign Relations . . . 1944*. Volume 5—*The Near East, South Asia and Africa. The Far East*. Washington, 1965.

————. *Foreign Relations . . . 1945*. Volume 8—*The Near East and Africa*. Washington, 1969.

————. *Foreign Relations of the United States, 1946*. Volume 7—*The Near East and Africa*. Washington, 1969.

————. *Foreign Relations . . . 1947*. Volume 5—*The Near East and Africa*. Washington, 1971.

U. S. *Federal Register*. Volume 8. 1943.

U. S. Federal Trade Commission. *The International Petroleum Cartel*. FTC Staff Report Submitted to the Subcommittee on Monopoly of the Select Senate Committee on Small Business. 82nd Cong., 2nd Sess., 1952.

Newspapers and Periodicals

Chicago Sun
Collier's
Columbia Record
Department of State Bulletin
The Economist
Fortune
Houston Post
LaFayette (Indiana) *Journal*
Los Angeles Examiner
The Manchester Guardian
Memphis Press Scimitar
Nation
New York Herald Tribune
New York Sun

Newsweek
New York Times
Philadelphia Inquirer
PM
San Francisco Chronicle
Saturday Evening Post
Texas State House Reporter
The Times (London)
Tulsa Tribune
Wall Street Journal
Washington Evening Star
Washington Post
Washington Times-Herald

Trade Journals and Corporate Publications

The Lamp
National Petroleum News
Oil and Gas Journal

Oil Forum (known as *International Oilman* before 1947)
Oil News

Petroleum Press Service
Petroleum Times
The Texaco Star
The Texas Oil Journal

World Oil (known as The Oil Weekly
before 1947)
World Petroleum

Memoirs, Diaries, and Published Collections of Personal Papers

Acheson, Dean. *Present at the Creation: My Years in the State Department.* New York, 1969.

Berle, Beatrice Bishop, and Travis Beal Jacobs, eds. *Navigating the Rapids, 1918–1971: From the Papers of Adolf A. Berle.* New York, 1971.

Blum, John Morton, ed. *The Price of Vision: The Diary of Henry A. Wallace, 1942–1946.* Boston, 1973.

Byrnes, James F. *Speaking Frankly.* New York, 1947.

————. *All in One Lifetime.* New York, 1958.

Churchill, Winston S. *The Grand Alliance.* Boston, 1950.

————. *The Hinge of Fate.* Boston, 1950.

————. *Closing the Ring.* Boston, 1951.

————. *Triumph and Tragedy.* Boston, 1953.

Connally, Tom, with Alfred Steinberg. *My Name Is Tom Connally.* New York, 1954.

Eden, Anthony. *The Reckoning: The Memoirs of Anthony Eden, Earl of Avon.* Boston, 1965.

Feis, Herbert. *Three International Episodes Seen from E. A.* 1946; reprint ed., New York, 1966.

Hooker, Nancy Harvison, ed. *The Moffat Papers: Selections from the Diplomatic Journals of Jay Pierrepont Moffat, 1919–1943.* Cambridge, 1956.

Hull, Cordell, *The Memoirs of Cordell Hull.* 2 volumes. New York, 1948.

Ickes, Harold L. *The Autobiography of a Curmudgeon.* 1943; reprint ed., Chicago, 1969.

————. *The Secret Diary of Harold L. Ickes.* 3 volumes. New York, 1953–54.

Israel, Fred L., ed. *The War Diary of Breckinridge Long: Selections from the Years 1939–1944.* Lincoln, 1966.

Jones, Jesse. *Fifty Billion Dollars: My Thirteen Years with the RFC, 1932–1945.* New York, 1951.

Kennan, George F. *Memoirs: 1925–1950.* Boston, 1967.

Leahy, William D. *I Was There.* New York, 1950.

Macmillan, Harold. *The Blast of War: 1939–1945.* New York, 1967.

Millis, Walter, ed. *The Forrestal Diaries*. New York, 1951.

Roosevelt, Elliott. *As He Saw It*. New York, 1946.

Stimson, Henry L., and McGeorge Bundy. *On Active Service in Peace and War*. New York, 1947.

Sulzberger, C. L. *A Long Row of Candles: Memoirs and Diaries, 1934–1954*. New York, 1969.

Truman, Harry S. *Memoirs: Year of Decisions*. Garden City, 1955.

———. *Memoirs: Years of Trial and Hope, 1946–1952*. New York, 1956.

Vandenberg, Arthur H., Jr., ed. *The Private Papers of Senator Vandenberg*. Boston, 1952.

Pamphlets

American Gas Association Committee on Natural Gas Reserves. *Reports on Proved Reserves of Crude Oil, Natural Gas Liquids and Natural Gas*. New York, 1946.

American Petroleum Institute. *Anglo-American Oil Agreement*. New York, 1945.

Carmical, J. H. *The Anglo-American Petroleum Pact*. New York, 1945.

Hill, George A., Jr. *Trends in the Oil Industry in 1944*. Washington, 1944.

Hoskins, Halford L. *Middle East Oil in United States Foreign Policy*. Washington, 1950.

Independent Petroleum Association of America. *The Anglo-American Petroleum Agreement*. Washington, 1944.

———. *The Proposed Arabian Pipe Line—A Threat to Our National Security*. n.p., n.d.

———. *Petroleum in the Western Hemisphere*. Washington, 1952.

Loeb, Carl. *Middle East Aspects of American Oil Companies*. New York, 1949.

Petroleum Administration for War, Foreign Operations Committee. *A Foreign Oil Policy for the United States*. n.p., n.d.

Petroleum Industry War Council. *Action by PIWC on Anglo-American Oil Agreement*. Washington, 1944.

———. *A National Oil Policy for the United States*. Washington, 1944.

———. *U.S. Foreign Oil Policy and Petroleum Reserves Corporation: An Analysis of the Effect of the Proposed Saudi Arabian Pipe Line*. Washington, 1944.

General Studies

Adelman, M. A. *The World Petroleum Market*. Baltimore, 1972.

Anderson, Irvine, Jr. *The Standard-Vacuum Oil Company and United States East Asian Policy, 1933–1941*. Princeton, 1975.

Aramco. *Arabian Oil and Its Relation to World Oil Needs*. n.p., 1948.

———. *Summary of Middle East Oil Developments*. n.p., 1948.

———. *Aramco Handbook: Oil and the Middle East*. n.p., 1950.

Beaton, Kendell. *Enterprise in Oil: A History of Shell in the United States*. New York, 1957.

Berle, Adolf A. *The Twentieth Century Capitalist Revolution*. New York, 1954.

Blair, John M. *The Control of Oil*. New York, 1976.

Blum, John Morton. *From the Morgenthau Diaries: Years of Crisis, 1928–1938*. Boston, 1965.

———. *From the Morgenthau Diaries: Years of Urgency, 1938–1941*. Boston, 1965.

———. *From the Morgenthau Diaries: Years of War, 1941–1945*. Boston, 1967.

———. *V Was for Victory: Politics and American Culture during World War II*. New York, 1976.

Brodie, Bernard. *Foreign Oil and American Security*. New Haven, 1947.

Brooks, Benjamin. *Peace, Plenty and Petroleum*. Lancaster, 1944.

Brooks, Michael. *Oil and Foreign Policy*. London, 1949.

Buhite, Russel. *Patrick Hurley and American Foreign Policy*. Ithaca, 1973.

Burns, James MacGregor. *Roosevelt: The Lion and the Fox*. New York, 1956.

———. *Roosevelt: Soldier of Freedom*. New York, 1970.

Catton, Bruce. *War Lords of Washington*. New York, 1948.

Chandler, Alfred D., Jr. *Strategy and Structure: Chapters in the History of American Industrial Enterprise*. Garden City, 1966.

Davenport, E. H., and S. R. Cooke. *The Oil Trusts and Anglo-American Relations*. London, 1923.

Davies, Vincent. *Postwar Defense Policy and the U. S. Navy, 1943–1946*. Chapel Hill, 1966.

DeNovo, John A. *American Interests and Policies in the Middle East, 1900–1939*. Minneapolis, 1963.

Divine, Robert A. *The Reluctant Belligerent: American Entry into World War II*. New York, 1965.

―――. *Second Chance: The Triumph of Internationalism in America during World War II*. New York, 1971.

Duce, James Terry. *Middle East Oil Developments*. New York, 1952.

Engler, Robert. *The Politics of Oil: A Study of Private Power and Democratic Directions*. New York, 1961.

Fanning, Leonard M. *American Oil Operations Abroad*. New York, 1947.

―――. *The Rise of American Oil*. New York, 1948.

―――. *Our Oil Resources*. New York, 1950.

―――. *Foreign Oil and the World*. New York, 1954.

Feis, Herbert. *Petroleum and American Foreign Policy*. Stanford, 1944.

―――. *The Road to Pearl Harbor: The Coming of the War between the United States and Japan*. Princeton, 1950.

―――. *Churchill, Roosevelt, Stalin: The War They Waged and the Peace They Sought*. Princeton, 1957.

―――. *Between War and Peace: The Potsdam Conference*. Princeton, 1960.

Fitzsimmons, Matthew A. *Empire by Treaty: Britain and the Middle East in the Twentieth Century*. London, 1965.

Frankel, Paul. *Essentials of Petroleum: A Key to Oil Economics*. London, 1969.

Freidel, Frank. *Franklin D. Roosevelt: The Apprenticeship*. Boston, 1952.

―――. *Franklin D. Roosevelt: The Ordeal*. Boston, 1954.

―――. *Launching the New Deal*. Boston, 1973.

Frey, John W., and H. Chandler Ide. *A History of the Petroleum Administration for War, 1941–1945*. Washington, 1946.

Gaddis, John Lewis. *The United States and the Origins of the Cold War, 1941–1947*. New York, 1972.

Gardner, Lloyd C. *Economic Aspects of New Deal Diplomacy*. Madison, 1964.

Gardner, Richard N. *Sterling-Dollar Diplomacy: Anglo-American Collaboration in the Reconstruction of Multilateral Trade*. Oxford, 1956.

Gibb, George S., and Evelyn H. Knowlton. *The Resurgent Years, 1911–1927*. Volume 2 in *History of Standard Oil Company* (New Jersey). New York, 1956.

Gulbenkian, Nubar. *Pantaraxia*. London, 1965.

Hamilton, Charles W. *Americans and Oil in the Middle East*. Houston, 1962.

Hartshorn, J. E. *Oil Companies and Governments: An Account of the International Oil Industry in Its Political Environment*. London, 1962.

Hawley, Ellis W. *The New Deal and the Problem of Monopoly*. Princeton, 1966.

Hewins, Ralph. *Mr. Five Per Cent: The Story of Calouste Gulbenkian*. New York, 1958.

Hidy, Ralph W., and Muriel E. Hidy. *Pioneering in Big Business*. Volume 1 in *History of Standard Oil Company (New Jersey)*. New York, 1955.

Hipple, Peter. *The Petroleum Industry in the United Kingdom*. London, 1966.

Hogan, Michael J. *Informal Entente: The Private Structure of Cooperation in Anglo-American Economic Diplomacy, 1918-1928*. Columbia, 1977.

Hoskins, Halford L. *The Middle East: Problem Area in World Politics*. New York, 1954.

Hurewitz, Jacob C. *Middle East Dilemmas: The Background of United States Policy*. New York, 1953.

Ickes, Harold L. *Fightin' Oil*. New York, 1943.

Jacoby, Neil. *Multinational Oil: A Study in Industrial Dynamics*. New York, 1974.

Kirk, George. *The Middle East in the War, 1939-1946*. London, 1952.

————. *Survey of International Affairs. The Middle East, 1945-1950*. London, 1954.

Kolko, Gabriel. *The Politics of War: The World and United States Foreign Policy, 1943-1945*. New York, 1968.

Kolko, Gabriel, and Joyce Kolko. *The Limits of Power: The World and United States Foreign Policy, 1945-1954*. New York, 1972.

Krasner, Stephen D. *Defending the National Interest: Raw Materials Investments and U.S. Foreign Policy*. Princeton, 1978.

LaFeber, Walter. *America, Russia, and the Cold War, 1945-1967*. New York, 1967.

Larson, Henrietta M., Evelyn H. Knowlton, and Charles S. Popple. *New Horizons, 1927-1950*. Volume 3 in *History of Standard Oil Company (New Jersey)*. New York, 1971.

Lebkicher, Roy. *Aramco and World Oil*. New York, 1952.

Lebkicher, Roy, George Rentz, and Max Stiencke. *The Arabia of Ibn Saud*. New York, 1952.

Lenczowski, George. *Russia and the West in Iran, 1918-1948: A Study in Big Power Rivalry*. Ithaca, 1949.

————. *Oil and State in the Middle East*. Ithaca, 1960.

Leopold, Richard W. *The Growth of American Foreign Policy: A History*. New York, 1962.

Leuchtenburg, William E. *Franklin D. Roosevelt and the New Deal, 1932-1940*. New York, 1963.

Lingeman, Richard R. *Don't You Know There's A War On? The American Homefront, 1941-1945*. New York, 1970.

Longhurst, Henry. *Adventure in Oil: The Story of British Petroleum*. London, 1959.

Longrigg, Stephen H. *Oil in the Middle East: Its Discovery and Development*. London, 1954.

McNeill, William Hardy. *America, Britain, and Russia: Their Co-operation and Conflict, 1941–1946*. 1953; reprint ed., New York, 1970.

Mikesell, Raymond F., and Hollis B. Chenery. *Arabian Oil: America's Stake in the Middle East*. Chapel Hill, 1949.

Millspaugh, Arthur C. *Americans in Persia*. Washington, 1946.

Morison, Elting E. *Turmoil and Tradition: A Study of the Life and Times of Henry L. Stimson*. Boston, 1960.

Mosley, Leonard. *Power Play: Oil in the Middle East*. New York, 1973.

Nash, Gerald D. *United States Oil Policy, 1890–1964: Business and Government in Twentieth Century America*. Pittsburgh, 1968.

Nevins, Allan. *Study in Power: John D. Rockefeller, Industrialist and Philanthropist*. 2 volumes. New York, 1953.

Notter, Harley. *Postwar Foreign Policy Preparation, 1939–1945*. Washington, 1949.

O'Connor, Harvey. *The Empire of Oil*. New York, 1962.

Paterson, Thomas G. *Soviet-American Confrontation: Postwar Reconstruction and the Origins of the Cold War*. Baltimore, 1973.

Payton-Smith, D. J. *Oil: A Study of War-time Policy and Administration*. London, 1971.

Penrose, Edith T. *The Large International Firm in Developing Countries: The International Petroleum Industry*. London, 1968.

Philby, H. St. J. B. *Arabian Jubilee*. London, 1952.
———. *Arabian Oil Ventures*. Washington, 1964.

Polenberg, Richard. *War and Society: The United States, 1941–1945*. New York, 1972.

Popple, Charles S. *Standard Oil Company (New Jersey) in World War II*. New York, 1952.

Pratt, Julius W. *Cordell Hull, 1933–1944*. Volumes 12 and 13 of Robert Ferrel and Samuel Flagg Bemis, eds. *The American Secretaries of State and Their Diplomacy*. New York, 1964.

Public Record Office. *The Second World War: A Guide to Documents in the Public Record Office*. London, 1972.

Rihani, Ameen. *Maker of Modern Arabia* (Ibn Sa'oud of Arabia). New York, 1928.

Roosevelt, Kermit. *Arabs, Oil and History: The Story of the Middle East*. New York, 1949.

Rostow, Eugene V. *A National Policy for the Oil Industry.* New Haven, 1948.

Sampson, Anthony. *The Seven Sisters: The Great Oil Companies and the World They Shaped.* New York, 1975.

Sanger, Richard H. *The Arabian Peninsula.* Ithaca, 1954.

Schlesinger, Arthur M., Jr. *The Age of Roosevelt: The Crisis of the Old Order.* Boston, 1957.

———. *The Age of Roosevelt: The Coming of the New Deal.* Boston, 1958.

———. *Robert Kennedy and His Times.* Boston, 1978.

Sherwood, Robert S. *Roosevelt and Hopkins: An Intimate History.* New York, 1950.

Shwadran, Benjamin. *The Middle East, Oil and the Great Powers.* 3rd. ed., rev.; Jerusalem, 1973.

Smith, Gaddis. *American Diplomacy During the Second World War, 1941–1945.* New York, 1965.

Speiser, E. A. *The United States and the Near East.* Cambridge, 1950.

Stuart, Graham H. *The Department of State.* New York, 1949.

Tanzer, Michael. *The Political Economy of International Oil and the Underdeveloped Countries.* Boston, 1969.

Taylor, A. J. P. *Beaverbrook.* London, 1972.

Thornburg, Max W. *People and Policy in the Middle East: A Study of Social and Political Change as Basis for United States Policy.* New York, 1964.

Tinkle, Lon. *Mr. Dee: A Biography of Everett Lee DeGolyer.* New York, 1970.

Tulchin, Joseph. *The Aftermath of War: World War I and U. S. Policy toward Latin America.* New York, 1971.

Twitchell, Karl S. *Saudi Arabia: An Account of the Development of Its Natural Resources.* New York, 1958.

Vernon, Raymond. *Storm Over the Multinationals: The Real Issues.* Cambridge, 1977.

Walker, Richard L. *E. R. Stettinius, Jr.* Volume 14 of Robert Ferrel and Samuel Flagg Bemis, eds. *The American Secretaries of State and Their Diplomacy.* New York, 1965.

Wilkins, Mira. *The Emergence of Multinational Enterprise: American Business Abroad from the Colonial Era to 1914.* Cambridge, 1970.

———. *The Maturing of Multinational Enterprise: American Business Abroad from 1914 to 1970.* Cambridge, 1974.

Williamson, Harold F., et al. *The American Petroleum Industry.* 2 volumes. Evanston, 1959–1963.

Wilson, Joan Hoff. *American Business and Foreign Policy, 1920–1933.* Lexington, 1971.

Wood, Bryce. *The Making of the Good Neighbor Policy.* New York, 1967.

Woodward, Llewellyn. *British Foreign Policy in the Second World War.* London, 1962.

Articles

Bolles, Blair. "Oil: An Economic Key to Peace." *Foreign Policy Reports,* July 1, 1944, pp. 86–95.

Brewster, R. Owen. "Don't Blame the British—Blame Us!" *Collier's,* December 25, 1943, p. 21, 68, 70.

Cooke, Hedley V. "Foreign Investment in the Middle Eastern Region, 1944–1953." *Middle Eastern Affairs* (April 1954), pp. 109–15.

DeNovo, John A. "Petroleum and the United States Navy before World War I." *Mississippi Valley Historical Review* (March 1955), pp. 641–56.

———. "The Movement for an Aggressive American Oil Policy Abroad, 1918–1920." *American Historical Review* (July 1956), pp. 854–76.

Drummond, Donald F. "Cordell Hull, 1933–1944." In *An Uncertain Tradition: American Secretaries of State in the Twentieth Century,* ed. Norman A. Graebner. New York, 1961.

Feis, Herbert. "The Anglo-American Oil Agreement." *Yale Law Journal* (August 1946), pp. 1174–87.

———. "Oil for Peace or War." *Foreign Affairs* (April 1954), pp. 416–29.

Harmon, Mont J. "Some Contributions of Harold L. Ickes." *Western Political Quarterly* (June 1954), pp. 238–52.

Hogan, Michael J. "Informal Entente: Public Policy and Private Management in Anglo-American Petroleum Affairs, 1918–1924." *Business History Review* (Summer 1974), pp. 187–205.

Hoskins, Halford L. "Background of the British Position in Arabia." *The Middle East Journal* (April 1947), pp. 137–47.

Ickes, Harold. "Oil from Coal: A Must for America," *Collier's,* December 4, 1943, pp. 18–19, 28.

———. "We're Running Out of Oil." *American Magazine,* January 1944, pp. 26–27.

———. "Persian Gulf Oil Furnishes Great Backlog for U.S. Reserves." *The Oil Weekly,* March 6, 1944, pp. 13–15.

———. "Oil and Peace." *Collier's,* December 2, 1944, p. 21.

———. "My Twelve Years with F. D. R." *Saturday Evening Post,* June 5, 12, 19, 26, 1948, pp. 15–17, 34–35, 30–31, 36–37, July 3, 10, 17, 24, 1948, pp. 30–31, 32–33, 28, 28.

"Ickes' Arabian Nights." *Fortune,* June 1944, pp. 123–28, 273–74, 277–78, 280.

Klein, Herbert S. "American Oil Companies in Latin America: The Bolivian Experience." *Inter-American Affairs* (Autumn 1964), pp. 47–72.

Loftus, John A. "Middle East Oil: The Pattern of Control." *The Middle East Journal* (January 1948), pp. 17–32.

"Oil: The First Agreement." *Fortune,* October 1944, pp. 113–14.

Padover, Saul K. "Ickes: Memoir of a Man Without Fear." *Reporter,* March 4, 1952, pp. 36–38.

Pogue, Joseph E. "Must an Oil War follow this War?" *The Atlantic Monthly,* March 1944, pp. 41–47.

Rayner, Charles. "Anglo-American Oil Policy: Basis of Multilateral Trade." Department of State *Bulletin,* November 10, 1946, pp. 867–70.

Sanger, Richard H. "Ibn Saud's Program for Saudi Arabia." *The Middle East Journal* (April 1947), pp. 180–90.

Stone, I. F. "Ickes and the Oilmen: Dual Salaries." *Nation,* January 1, 1944, pp. 6–7.

"Storm over the Anglo-U.S. Oil Agreement." *Petroleum Press Service,* December 1946, pp. 224–26.

"The Great Oil Deals." *Fortune,* May 1947, pp. 138–43.

Trani, Eugene. "Conflict and Compromise: Harold L. Ickes and Franklin D. Roosevelt." *North Dakota Quarterly* (Winter 1968), pp. 20–29.

Wilkins, Mira. "Multinational Oil Companies in South America in the 1920s: Argentina, Bolivia, Chile, Ecuador, and Peru," *Business History Review* (Autumn 1974), pp. 414–46.

———. "The Oil Companies in Perspective," *Daedalus* (Fall 1975), pp. 159–78.

Unpublished Dissertations

Lytle, Mark H. "American-Iranian Relations 1941–1947 and the Redefinition of National Security." Ph.D. dissertation, Yale University, 1973.

Miller, John A. "Air Diplomacy: The Chicago Civil Aviation Conference of 1944 in Anglo-American Relations and Post-War Planning." Ph.D. dissertation, Yale University, 1971.

Nordhauser, Norman E. "The Quest for Stability: Domestic Oil Policy, 1919–1935." Ph.D. dissertation, Stanford University, 1970.

Walt, Joseph William, "Saudi Arabia and the Americans, 1923–1951." Ph.D. dissertation, Northwestern University, 1960.

Index

248